RACE
RELATIONS

RACE RELATIONS

Elements and Social Dynamics

by
Oliver C. Cox

WAYNE STATE UNIVERSITY PRESS   DETROIT 1976

Library of Congress Cataloging in Publication Data
Cox, Oliver Cromwell, 1901–1974.
  Race relations.

  Bibliography: p.
  Includes index.
  1. United States—Race question. 2. Negroes—Social conditions—1964– 3. Negroes—Economic conditions.
  I. Title.
E185.615.C693 1975   301.45'19'6073   75-38572
ISBN 0-8143-1539-9

Publisher's Note

Oliver Cromwell Cox died September 4, 1974, while his manuscript was being prepared for publication. With the permission of the administrator of his estate, the Press undertook the final revision and editing of the work which is now before the reader, something less than Professor Cox had intended, yet a valuable last document from his distinguished pen.

CONTENTS

vii

Contents

Chapter 4   **Significance of Rural Culture for Race Relations**   *53*

Chapter 5   **A Place in the Sun**   *60*

Chapter 6   **Place of Business and Black Capitalism**   *76*

Chapter 7   **Structure of Negro Labor**   *94*

ix

Contents

Contents

CHARTS

TABLES

Contents

INTRODUCTION

Although there is an avalanche of material on race relations, it is surprising how little there is of general works on the subject. My motive in writing stems partly from a desire to fill the gap that causes a problem to concerned teachers. The unsystematized data are very extensive. The present definition of the subject, however, suggests their limits and scope. I do not approach the work merely to gather the most recent information, but rather to present a distinct theory of race relations. Previously, in other places, I have nibbled at contrary theories: the caste theory, pluralism, the Marxist theory, the black bourgeoisie theory, the biological superiority theories, and their derivatives. I propose here, however, to present a more comprehensive analysis. This purpose mostly determines the direction. A valid theory of race relations must necessarily be universalist; it attempts to explain and elucidate certain characteristics of a peculiar culture in context. In *Caste, Class, and Race* I was interested in conceptual definition and societal distinction; in this undertaking I am concerned particularly with the universal manifestation of race relations and their functions, especially in the United States.

I regard the economics of race relations as crucial. Economics involve pivotally the differentiating forces in our type of society. I attempt to define and analyze them, and to show their elemental relationship to race relations in the United States. It is in this context that I expect to demonstrate the critical aspects of Negro exploitation

1

and discrimination. It is here that the Negro comes face to face with almost insuperable barriers to job assignments and to adventures in business enterprise. His subjection to social discrimination has been built mainly upon these concrete economic frustrations. The latter blot out, as nothing else, his "place in the sun."

There is an apparently singular social-class problem arising among members of the race—a problem unknown to other American subcultures. It seems to emerge from forces of racial rejection in the larger society and from the relatively static nature of the Negro social-status structure. The relatively larger lower-status base with its tradition of permanence has engendered elements of lower-class cultural idealism which establish their own vicious circle inimical to efforts toward inclusion in the mainstream culture. I have sought to examine the social ramifications of this tendency.

Sometimes the fact that neither capitalist democracy nor communism is centered in lower-class ideals may be overlooked. The major social movements of the world have little if any creative interest in lower-class culture. In no country does social equality mean a leveling of the social status structure of the major society to meet the cultural accommodations and demands of the lower classes,[1] and the Soviet Union would be the most unlikely place to look for such a tendency. The independent nations of Africa are cool toward it. The leadership of the subcultures of other American immigrants has lost respect for it—if indeed that leadership every countenanced it.

The attempt, therefore, by some spokesmen of the Negro lower class to work within the social penumbra of the black middle class to perpetuate lower-class traits and purposes seems doomed to ultimate disillusionment. In the United States it must eventually be a dead-end movement. The lower class, according to American tradition, should be uplifted and become preoccupied with values of the larger society as a birthright, not encouraged to be smug and obstinate in degradation—the latter frequently referred to as "our black culture" to the gratification of the group's most determined white detractors, who exclaim triumphantly to white liberals "I told you so." The advanced nations of the world have become increasingly dedicated to a functional "war on poverty." The social situation of the "hard core" unemployed in the black ghetto has now been recognized as a national scandal.

Rapidly, since 1954 especially, the Negro problem has assumed a dominant place in the thinking of American people. The country has consciously passed the crisis point of no turning back. The problem has "surfaced." Both government and business have now openly admitted their share of responsibilities for the consequences of cultural subordination. They have thus taken the initiative in developing plans for racial betterment. The major civil rights groups have been willing to cooperate with the central powers in organization and execution of these programs. There are, however, *alienated* Negro groups and individuals who are understandably vexed and confused, and who are explicit in their determination to make the society, both black and white, pay or suffer for past wrongs—all the way from fire, looting, and gunshot, to the blackmail of financial "reparations."

I have attempted to show—and the government seems now to realize it—that the years of racial repression and exclusion have severely limited the capacity of Negroes to compete for the newly available opportunities. Compensatory assistance, therefore, in education, job training, and business enterprise becomes an urgent obligation of the state. The programs should include deprived whites as well as blacks. The road has been tortuous and long but it has been dynamic, exciting, and promising. Indeed, the future of race relations is now more visible and encouraging than ever before.

There can hardly be an explanation of race relations unless one is able to understand or at least to identify the culture and the societal system from which these relationships emerged. It is a sociological fact that racial discrimination constitutes collective, not essentially individual, behavior. Thus I accept in principle Emile Durkheim's approach. To understand conclusions about the collective aspects of the beliefs and practices of a group, one must be able to comprehend the social functions which they fulfill. Different social systems are constituted differently; and major social processes, such as contemporary race relations, must be sought in the elementary constitution of the society.

The various constituent elements of a society—economic, political, religious, familial, moral—tend, more or less, to be integrated differently in different social systems. "For the sociologist as for the historian, social facts vary with the social system of which they form a part; they cannot be understood when detached from it. This is why two facts which come from two different societies cannot be profitably compared merely because they seem to resemble each other; it is necessary that the societies resemble each other."[2] The

3

patterns are recognizable by the relative structural significance of their subordinate systems, which constitute a hierarchy of relevance.

Furthermore, we should guard against attributing the importance of component systems to judgments about their dispensability. A given component may be indispensable and still assume a quite subordinate function in the total societal organization. In fact, given certain essential constituents, supplementary systems and institutions may be expected to follow logically. William Graham Sumner's observation that there is a strain toward consistency in the elements of a society emphasizes this salient characteristic. Once the societal pattern becomes established, it also becomes culturally limited. It does not, therefore, assimilate or reject cultural traits indiscriminately. Some traits, compatible to one society, may remain forever alien to another. The meaning of any social system or institution, therefore, tends to be determined by the pattern of society. The ubiquitous religious function, for example, tends to be defined differently among different societal groups, varying from predominance in some to subsidiary in others, and with widespread variations in beliefs, ritual, and theology.

Societies, major social systems, are historical products. The factors determinative of change in them are both internal and external. Simple, relatively isolated societies tend to be static; complex societies, ordinarily in communication with others, tend to be dynamic. But change may involve either growth or decay; it may be gradual or revolutionary. It may be predictable or peculiarly open to the vicissitudes of history. Contemporary Western society is so distinct from all preceding forms of social organization and relatively so recent that it seems necessary not only to indicate the pertinent differences but also to explain European involvement in it. We shall hope in this way to help clarify the mysticism which largely permeates most discussions of race relations.

Chapter 1

Situations of Race Relations

Morality and Economics

Morality is not in itself the independent variable. It is rather a dependent function of the social system. It is not, to put it simply, the game itself but rather derived conditions involving the order in which the game is allowed to operate and evolve. Race relations, like employer-employee relations, are part of the game. In fact it is possible to view race relations as basically a variety of employer-employee relations. That is what slavery essentially was.[1] To be sure, a capitalist society includes very much more than labor relations, but the totality should not be allowed to obscure the elementary force and locus of developing race relations.

Even in the age of thralldom there was confusion on this point. As Tannenbaum observes: "By one of those peculiar tricks which time and experience sometimes play on man, the accident of Negro labor had been converted into a moral and economic philosophy. It seemed to the South that the best of all societies had . . .

5

been achieved, and by divine prescription it was to remain unchanged forever.''[2] The entirety of institutions constituting the society may thus submerge traits of elementary relationships among the social groups. We shall assume that economic relations form the basis of modern race relations. ''Three centuries ago,'' Julius Boeke says tauntingly, ''Europeans did not sail to the Indies to collect butterflies.''[3]

As we take this point of view, we can anticipate an outcry from almost all the traditional students of race relations. In the past they have invited attention to one unmodified word, ''economic,'' and have thus dealt with it in the simplest possible way. They have accused the writer of ''economic determinism,'' ''Marxism,''[4] or of seeking to explain race relations ''solely,'' ''only,'' ''merely,'' ''exclusively'' on the basis of ''economics.'' After addressing themselves in this fashion to the economic aspects of race relations, these scholars usually move on to emphasize certain startling psychological or political incidents implying that these are at least as significant for an analysis of the society. Such approaches may seem to satisfy the requirements of a detached eclecticism, but they can hardly arrive at a conception of race relations as societally determined, that is, if we think of society as a definable pattern of social relations.[5] The economics of all societies are socially defined, but social factors do not limit the operation of the economic order in the same way in all societies.

Origin of the Situations

When, therefore, we say that economics are fundamental, we are not making a haphazard selection among the institutions of society. The word *economics* or *economy* is in itself meaningless; it constitutes a factor common to all societies. It is the peculiar definition which it achieves in the capitalist system, as differentiated from that in all other systems, which determines the nature of its significance. During the rise of the present economy, its leadership, the great merchants of foreign trade, was not unmindful of this. For example, at the dawn of the transformation of England into a capitalist society, Sir Walter Raleigh presented a memorandum on ''trade and commerce'' to James I which read in part:

> May it please YOUR MOST EXCELLENT MAJESTY, according to my duty, I am emboldened to put your majesty in

mind, that about fourteen or fifteen years past, I presented you a book of extraordinary importance for the honour and profit of your majesty and posterity; and doubting that it hath been laid aside, and not considered of, I am encouraged (under your majesty's pardon) to present unto you one more, consisting of five propositions: neither are they grounded upon vain and idle grounds, but upon fruition of those wonderful blessings where-with God hath induced your majesty's sea and land; by which means you may not only enrich and fill your coffers but also increase such might and strength, (as shall appear, if it may stand with your majesty's good liking to put the same in execu-tion in the true and right form) so that there is no doubt but it will make you in short time a price of such power, so great, as shall make all the princes your neighbors as well glad of your friendship, as fearful to offend you.[6]

Raleigh evinces the tremendous enthusiasm and verve which motivated the creativity of the early seventeenth-century English mercantile class and the implicit obstruction of a still feudalistically oriented monarchy. The way was prepared for the peculiar economic dominance we all know following the English Civil War. It is of importance to emphasize that Raleigh was referring not merely to *economics* unconditionally, but to foreign trade in "true and right form." The early English mercantilists were conscious of the fact that the entire society—its religion, politics, status structure—had to be reorganized if the desirable system of production was to achieve its full powers of growth. This is the subtle differentiating societal force which economists and sociologists must seek to grasp before analysis of constituent institutions can be made fruitful.

Individual freedom—*laissez faire*—and the need to exploit la-bor were both worked out empirically in the rise of capitalist soci-ety. The mercantilist individualism inherent to this system will be found in no unrelated society. It was recognized, even in medieval cities, as necessary for business planning and competitive success. In time, however, this economic attribute, individualism, trickled down, against opposition, to white workers in the society. Capitalist freedom thus tended to have opposing effects on the side of the entrepreneur and the worker, a fact which accounts for the apparent anomaly that in the same society *freedom* and *racial oppression* coexist.

Long before the Declaration of Independence, Sir Josiah Child, the great mercantilist head of the East India Company, wrote:

7

> All men by nature are alike; it is only laws, customs, and education that differ men; their nature and disposition, and the disposition of all people of the world, proceed from their laws; the French peasantry are a slavish, cowardly people because the laws of their country have made them slaves; the French gentry, a noble, valiant people because free by law, birth, and education: in England we are all free subjects by our laws [c. 1690] and therefore our people prove generally courageous. . . .[7]

Without the proper form of social organization, "systems of laws," a domesticated and sympathic religion, a parliament dominated by business interests, a status system distributing prestige according to individual achievement with wealth-producing potentials, the typical economic behavior will either not arise or remain overshadowed and enfeebled. Given a breakthrough, however, the circumambient culture develops in response to the powerful dynamics of the economic order. The capitalist economy is based, therefore, essentially on foreign trade. There can be no capitalism without foreign trade, and a continually expanding foreign trade is necessary to its development. It is this characteristic of the system which provides the basis for the unification of the world. The peoples of the world have thus become interdependent.

Nature of the Situations

Colonialism

The fate of the colored peoples has been enmeshed, sometimes almost passively, in the struggle among European nations for their competitive shares of world resources. Let us illustrate. In the following, the historian Edward S. deKlerck describes the situation of natives in Indonesia as Portuguese, Dutch, and English fought for ascendancy over the vast spoils:

> that nation who gained the upperhand would achieve a reputation for power which in itself would be sufficient to make the [native] princes climb down and be content with lower prices than they had been accustomed to demand. With the ousting of the competitors and consequent awe instilled in the native mind the door was open wide to all manners of arrogant and arbitrary action, the more so as the Europeans looked down upon the native. The voice of conscience was stifled in the temptation to exploit the latter, onerous treaties were concluded thereafter, such as allowed the buyer to fix the price himself, and finally compulsion was imposed, at least, when the demands were re-

8

fused. The right of the strongest attained, in this manner, supreme power. . . .[8]

Colonialism was responsible for the depreciation of the colored peoples of the world, not because they were colored but because of their peculiar economic situation. Since we now understand the peculiar mercantile direction and exploitative capacity of capitalism, it seems possible to identify the situations of race and community relations which developed abroad in the epoch of its dramatic expansion.

We may now plot roughly on two axes the destiny of the non-European peoples of the world as they encountered the great mercantile nations. Population density and complexity of native culture affected primarily the pattern of relationships.[9] We are aware of the limitations of this type of paradigmatic formulation; as a premise, however, it avoids modifying details which may lead to obscurity.

Culture and Density of Native Populations

Culture	Population	
	Sparse	*Dense*
Simple	Displaced	Enslaved
Complex	Amalgamated	Subjected to commercial specialization and labor exploitation

Compared to capitalism, all other cultures of the world, even feudalism which tended to remain dominant in parts of Europe up to the seventeenth century, are weak and naive. The inherent magic of the capitalist market disrupted all of them; it subordinated their power structures and reoriented their ethos toward the universal system. No other culture possessed such a capacity.

When Europeans—and we shall now use the terms *European* and *capitalism* interchangeably—came upon a people of simple culture[10] in a thinly populated country of apparently great exploitative potential, the urge to produce rapidly to cover costs and make profits seemed to leave no alternative but to subject these people to forced labor. It was the culturally obvious way to utilize them and their crude geographical resources. The classic case was that of the Indians in certain areas of the Americas. Under this exploitative urge they were exterminated in the West Indies and in the lowlands of South America; in North America they were socially eliminated and pushed back. Natives of Australia were similarly dealt with.[11] In these areas, particularly, Europeans found new homelands.

Where the population was relatively dense and its culture simple, it could hardly be exterminated or pushed aside by the rigors of exploitation. It was thus made to exist under some form of compulsory labor, mainly in mines and on plantations. The enslavement of Africans in Africa and the replenishment of labor particularly in the Americas is an example of this situation.[12] Other forms of coerced labor on the African continent—the Congo, South Africa, Kenya—the Dutch plantations of Indonesia, and the *encomienda* system of labor in South America also fall within this pattern.

Where the population was moderately sparse but its culture relatively complex as in Mexico and Peru, Europeans also sought to establish homelands, but since the native population could not be consistently displaced, a situation for racial mixture developed, thus giving rise to significant mestizo groups. Racial mixture in this situation has also been influenced by the quality of capitalism inherited by the Spaniards and Portuguese. In recounting the circumstances of this early contact between the races in South America, William Miller writes:

> By the 1540's the reign of the *conquistadores* was virtually over.
> . . . Five million aborigines, unlike those of the later British
> colonies, had survived *conquistador* violence and taken the
> *conquistadores'* God. These aborigines made up the labor force,
> with much smaller numbers of Negro slaves. . . . The Spanish
> elite, meanwhile, quickly imposed its culture and institutions on
> the natives. . . . In 1551 the first new-world universities were
> opened in Mexico City and Lima. Soon imposing new cathe-
> drals dominated the landscape of coastal ports, while all over
> the country hundreds of monasteries plied their business of sav-
> ing souls. In time the established Church owned half the prop-
> erty and collected most of the income of the Spanish empire.[13]

The modified situation in South Africa may be partly explained by this difference in type of capitalism available to the Europeans.

In situations where the population was dense and the culture relatively complex, the Europeans had to deal with it as a resident

10

ruling group, not simply as a resident population. In this ruling-class situation, the Europeans were as determined as ever to extract as large an income as possible. Hence they either proceeded to gain control of the relatively ineffective native government and thus to reorient production toward the world market as, for example, in India, Indonesia, and Egypt,[14] or to oppose the power structure and establish mercantile enclaves in the territory, such as Hong Kong and Shanghai in China,[15] the effect of which was essentially similar.

Exploitation and Conflict

Almost always, in their determination to bring different areas of the world into conformity with the purposes of capitalism, the Europeans encountered more or less serious resistance from the natives. The character of this conflict tended to affect ultimate adjustments.

Japan's population and cultural posture, for instance, predisposed her to an exploitative program similar to that of India. During the original maneuvers in the first half of the seventeenth century, however, she was able to expel the Europeans and almost completely to shut her doors to further contact with capitalism. At the second approach of capitalism, in the late 1850s, with guns foremost, she managed successfully to move ahead with the adoption of fundamental elements of the invading system faster than the steps taken for her commercial subjugation; she therefore forestalled and absorbed them.

It was partly also the determined opposition of the Chinese which saved them from European domination as complete as that experienced by India. In 1857 the Indians themselves attempted unsuccessfully to expel the British East India Company which largely governed them.

Factors of Culture and Time

In particular, then, two significant variables seem to affect situations of race relations: the quality of capitalist culture borne by European expansionists and the factor of time. With respect to culture, two principal systems of capitalism emerged from Europe between about 1500 and 1600: the weak, feudalistic capitalism of Spain and Portugal, and the energetic, businessman's capitalism of Holland and England. In the first, the direct interest of feudal princes and the church restrained the exploitative purpose. This led not only to generally more humane treatment of the colored peoples but also to relative amalgamation with them.

Another result of cultural differences was that the capitalistically weaker group was almost entirely displaced, in all the areas of dense population, by the complex cultures: areas where opportunities for settlement were limited and where competition for commercial advantage was keen. Had the Dutch or English colonized Brazil, the racial situation there would most likely have been similar to that of the southern United States or of South Africa. Interference by the church and crown, therefore, circumscribed the operation of pure capitalist interests.

Time has been critically important because it allowed for fundamental changes in the nature of capitalism and consequently in the situations of race relations. Capitalism, it needs hardly be said, is an extremely dynamic form of culture: it has been evolving as a world system frequently with drastic consequences for its local units. Three systematic changes particularly have resulted in the decline of the status of Europeans as masters of all other inhabitants of the earth: (a) progressive exposure and thus weakening of the instruments of local dominance, principally through international strife for control of foreign peoples and their resources; (b) more or less rapid acculturation of native peoples, a process which communicates nationalism and thus systematization of the forces of resistance to European exploitation; and (c) universal distrust of and revolt against capitalism itself as the most desirable form of social organization attainable.

Industrialization and Race Relations

In any discussion of the economics of race relations, the question of the role of industrialization seems inevitably to arise. As we have attempted to show in another work, modern industrialization constitutes a social phenomenon distinct from industrialization in all previous social systems.[16]

Indeed we should expect the "most civilized province" in Europe at any given time to be precisely the leading capitalist city or nation, and thus the most highly developed technologically.[17] In order to trace the development of modern industrialism, it would be necessary to move from Venice to Florence to the Hanseatic cities, the United Provinces, England, and eventually the United States. At Venice, to mention only the prototype, the finest salt and glass were produced, and in the Arsenal, the world's greatest industrial organization in the twelfth century employing thousands of workers, the finest ships and their technological accessories were manufactured. Industrial secrets were guarded as life itself. According to William C. Hazlitt: "At Venice the arts and sciences were assiduously and affectionately cultivated. Those to which the Republic directed its attention with greatest earnestness, perhaps, were astronomy and astrology, mathematics, trigonometry, chemistry, alchemy, physics and metaphysics. Some of these studies were of essential service in the mastery of geography and navigation."[18] So far as we know, science and technology thrive spontaneously only within the capitalist system, and there is an inherent tendency for them to expand at an increasing rate.

And yet the mere use of science and technology in production, i.e., industrialization, need not create social systems. For example, when the industrial revolution materialized in the middle of the eighteenth century, Great Britain had already achieved all the major elements of a national capitalist system: a sovereign parliament, a critical dependence upon foreign commerce, a national determination to maintain leadership in the system, a mercantile and industrial ruling class, a developed exploitative ideology toward labor, an ascendant Protestant religion, scientific orientation, capitalist freedom, and progressive urbanization. This syndrome provided a hospitable milieu for the "revolution." The introduction of power machinery and other technical processes accelerated a complex rate of growth.

It should be emphasized, however, that industrialization does not merely provide substitutes for existing technology. It is also significantly productive and creative in its own right. Science constantly enlarges the perceptive capacity of the human mind, and relevant technology reduces its dependence upon the natural course of the elements and seasons. Perhaps, moreover, one of the most remarkable facts of the capitalist system is that its transformation has become increasingly dependent on the development of science and technology.

Effects of Industrialization

How, then, does industrialization affect race relations? Not so long ago a group of scholars at the behest of UNESCO approached this question directly. At the very outset difficulty seemed to have arisen over the place and significance of industrialization. In the introduction to the symposium on *Industrialization and Race Relations,* Guy Hunter wrote:

It is particularly important to distinguish between industrialization and earlier social and economic relationships in an area such as Brazil where several races were in contact more than a century before the industrial revolution in Europe, or in East Africa, with its records of trading contacts between Arabs, Indians, Chinese and Africans for a long period before even the Portuguese appeared on the coast. . . . Clearly . . . neither the existence of commerce and capitalism, nor the development of early plantations are in themselves a criterion of industrialization. Nor is the mere existence of towns critical; for there were Yoruba towns, Indian towns, English towns long, long before any industrial revolution.[19]

What the industrial revolution did not or could not antedate was the capitalist city and indeed capitalism itself. The industrial revolution added nothing elemental to the system. It became part of a continuing process of societal development. Herbert Blumer, the theorist of the symposium, became involved with this question. Thus he concludes that industrialization is a passive element in race relations situations. ''[Industrialization] will move along with, respond to, and reflect the current of racial transformation in which it happens to be caught.''[20] And again ''. . . the racial lines as drawn in a society are followed . . . inside the industrial structure.''[21] Still, in further emphasis:

available evidence everywhere sustains the thesis that when introduced into a racially ordered society, industrialization conforms to the alignment and code of the racial order. Where the racial order is clear-cut and firm [as in South Africa or the American South], the industrial apparatus will develop a corresponding racial scheme. . . . *Changes* in the racial order in industry are due to pressures . . . that arise in the outside society.[22]

The author cites ''apartheid'' as a ''striking instance'' of the point he is making. This indeed would seem to be a striking example of the adage about the mountain at labor. There need be no theory about the fact that anyone who goes into South Africa must conform to the racist laws of the state. But Blumer is directing the thrust of his argument against an assumption with which he begins his discussion: that industrialization is a form of social organization characterized by traits inimical to racism, traits that ''would undermine such a racial order.'' The false proposition is thus stated: ''The demands which such a system [industrialization] makes and the forces which it releases would combine to attack the racial order at many points.''

The societal traits which the author lists at that point as "innovations of industrialization" are in fact characteristics of capitalist society—all those traits were present before the coming of the industrial revolution. The factory itself is a medieval city product of capitalism. The addition of steam power hastened capitalist development.

Blumer becomes involved with another concept, that of *change* in the racial situation. Since disruption of a racist situation cannot be expected from internal industrialism, it must come from "outside." This approach tends to regard industry as a passive element in the structure of race relations. For example after listing many types of employment that "may cause resentment and provoke trouble" if awarded to Negroes, the author concludes: "they show clearly that *rational* operation of industrial enterprises . . . may call for differential respect for the canons . . . of the racial order." The impalpable "canons" of the people are thus made to bear the blame.

The important point is to recognize that "industry" is by no means passive in the "well-ordered" racial situation. The place of industrialization as a factor contributing to the racial situation should be studied as an abiding, rather than as an isolated factor emerging, for example, in South Africa and finding it necessary to conform racially. The captains of industry in the area consciously maintain the racial status quo. In reviewing the "outside" forces of change in the American South, Blumer almost saw this. He writes: "Political pressures, the strivings of action groups . . . and pressure by national labor unions reflect the general direction of effort to improve the position of Negroes in American industry. Resistance to this movement is formidable, and the movement has scarcely begun to touch the area of managerial employment (that bastion of white industrial privilege). . . ."[23]

"Inside" forces affecting race relations and industrialization in the American South and in South Africa may be thought of as worldwide. Production in those areas is primarily for a universal market. This universality has always been true of modern race relations. There was, for instance, an international commercial interest in American slavery associated with the domestic one. Abolition had its worldwide ramifications. Indeed, labor relations in general may also be thought of as international. Industrialization in England, for example, expanded the slave trade and speeded up the change in status

15

between workers and employers in that country. The cotton gin was clearly a basis for the expansion and intensification of slavery. It helped to produce a situation which called for the latter's territorial aggrandizement; it precipitated the Civil War and consequently emancipated the race. With industrialization and urbanization a favorable milieu for intensified racial discontent and unrest tends to be established. Industrialization, even in South Africa, increases dependence of that country upon its black labor supply and upon the rest of the world. The process inevitably brings internal racial policies into progressive conflict with opposing racial movements abroad. If nothing else, it increases the necessity for racial repression in South Africa.

In major socialist communities, far greater reliance is put upon science and technology in the drive for economic development than upon opportunities for exploitation of foreign resources. Improvement of the status of minority groups in the Soviet Union, for instance, has centered upon their education for technological production—a difference which has had repercussions on the social status situations of such groups in capitalist countries.

Increasing industrialization may widen the status breach between the races. The widespread movement toward technological specialization and the relatively limited opportunities for education and its application have apparently intensified economic problems for Negroes in the United States.

Industrialization, then, does not of itself create social systems; however, it not only contributes to certain race conflict situations but also leads to social problems peculiar to itself. Its effect must be studied, therefore, in a larger context than that which obtains within factory walls. There seems to be hardly any doubt about the influence of the world socialist movement upon situations of race relations. But there can be no enduring socialist state without an inherently viable, expansible industrial base. Accordingly, we may think of the new orientation of capitalist countries toward the different nonwhite races of the world as somewhat indirectly promoted by the agencies of science and technology.

The Economic Position

In discussing the economic incidence of race relations, it should be emphasized again that this factor represents the concrete structural means by which the Negro is more or less assigned to the status of an outsider. All modern race relations ultimately center about the nature of their involvement with critical economic variables inherent to the system. If we could conceive of Negroes moving unimpededly into the avenues of economic initiative, those especially of business entrepreneurship, we can probably also conceive of a society without a "race problem."

The mainstream of capitalist civilization is constituted by a peculiar economic process, which has been designed and directed by businessmen. This apparently banal fact—to which we shall refer in various contexts—nonetheless differentiates the society basically from all preceeding social systems. Private enterprise, including modern farming, is here the characteristic mode of accumulating wealth and thus achieving power and status—all other means are contributory. Other subgroups, Jews especially, have been able to enter the mainstream and thus largely overcome intolerance. Although Negro businessmen still remain very much on its periphery, they have not been unaware of its central importance.

> The hope of the black man [declared a business representative] lies in the development of business. The businessman alone holds the destiny of his race in the hollow of his hand. My business friends, it all depends upon you; if you do your part well, we advance, we win; but on the other hand, if you do not do your part well, we retrograde, we lose. . . . . The preacher has preached and saved souls; the teacher has taught and trained minds; the lawyer has pleaded and won many of your legal battles; the physician has cured and instructed in the law of hygiene, but to win for our race that all important place striven for by all mankind, namely, commercial freedom, with its consequent human freedom. . . . Drop sentiment—go after business; go after the white man's business. When you get his business you get his respect.[24]

There have been many studies showing the extent to which Negroes become businessmen. The record goes back beyond 1865 to enumerations of enterprises developed by "free persons of color" and even to the trading characteristics of certain African tribes and the occasional shops allowed to favorite slaves in the South.

> In almost all the Southern cities Negroes were the barbers, butchers, mechanics and artisans. They made and sold boots, shoes, and clothing on a small scale. They also kept popular restaurants, cafes, and hotels. . . . A Negro in Charleston built up such a profitable business in making sails that he could buy slaves to assist him in the work.[25]

17

Some of these enterprises, even in the North, amassed wealth into hundreds of thousands of dollars.[26] They were, however, mainly of the individual craftsman type, sometimes serving the general public, but having little or no white competition.[27] They were thus not "integrated" into the dominant commercial system. After 1865 Negro business stagnated in the general depression of the South and then only slowly revived in the new climate of segregation.

The Place of Segregation

Since segregation constitutes the limiting and largely determining factor in the status of commercial enterprise among Negroes, it may be well to examine tentatively the nature of its influence. In this racial situation segregation constitutes positive, purposeful behavior. Almost all other instruments of control and oppression depend upon it. In order to perpetuate the status quo in the postbellum South and to a lesser degree in the North, two principal means were relied upon: disenfranchisement and statutory segregation. Perhaps Henry W. Grady puts these conditions as dispassionately as any of the other colorful, white southern leaders during the last quarter of the nineteenth century. Thus, in order to "re-establish" racial amity it became necessary:

> First, that the white shall have clear and unmistakable control of public affairs. They own the property. They have the intelligence. . . . For these reasons they are entitled to control. Beyond these reasons is a racial one. They are the superior race, and will not and cannot submit to the domination of an inferior race. . . . We hear much of the intimidation of the colored vote in the South. There is intimidation, but it is the menace of the compact and solid wealth and intelligence of a great social system.
> Second, that whites and blacks must walk in separate paths in the South. As near as may be, these paths should be made equal—but separate they must be now and always. This means separate schools, separate churches, separate accommodations everywhere. . . . [The Negro] has ten avenues of employment in this section to where he has one in the North. White and black carpenters and masons work together on the same buildings. White and black shoemakers and mechanics in the same shop. . . . White and black farmers work in the same field. Whatever the Negro is fitted to do, he has abundant chance to do. . . . But the white and black carpenters, working together on the same building go to separate homes at night, to separate churches on Sunday. . . . Happily the records show that the

Negro is prospering. In Georgia he has amassed property [c. 1890] taxed at $10,000,000 and worth twice as much. In every Southern State he owns farms and city property. His children have good schools. He has his churches, his societies, and his sports.[28]

It should be observed that this position of political and social exclusion, enunciated in 1890, was accepted almost verbatim by the great Negro contemporary, Booker T. Washington, particularly in his famous Atlanta Exposition Address of 1895. As he wrote later: "The thing that was uppermost in my mind was the desire to say something that would cement the friendship of the races and bring about hearty cooperation between them."[29] The way he chose to do this was to avoid tampering with political subordination, to imply that Negroes will continue to support the white southerners' initiative—"as we have proved our loyalty to you in the past . . . so in the future, in our humble way, we shall stand by you with . . . devotion"[30]—and, in his frequently cited analogy of the palm and fingers, to welcome social segregation.

But what has segregation meant for the Negro businessman? It has created primarily a Negro community penetrable at will—at least traditionally—by white businessmen, but at the same time it has established severe limits to the expansion of Negro enterprise. In his useful analysis of the Negro's economic situation, Andrew F. Brimmer observes that "segregation has served the Negro businessman in the same way a tariff protects an infant industry."[31] In this sense it has given him a closed market not reachable by outside competition; hence, behind the wall, he is able to sell goods and services of poorer quality or at higher prices.

But this view, while partly demonstrable, seems to be a minor consequence of segregation. The essential fact about a tariff is its internal application and self-interested control. Hence Negro businessmen tend to regard segregation like a blockade—its limits having been imposed from without. Moreover, their segregated "infant industries" can hardly ever hope to grow up. As Joseph A. Pierce puts it:

Negro business, like other business, operates mainly in urban areas, but, unlike other business, it is generally restricted to certain sections of the urban community. The forces of segregation and discrimination imposed two distinct limitations on Negro business. The first arises from the fact that Negro business is, for the most part, solely dependent upon Negroes for its patronage and therefore must be located in sections of the country where large Negro populations are found. Consequently Negro businesses do not have the freedom of action of other businesses. . . . [Second] Business enterprises operated by whites find no barriers which prevent them from entering Negro communities. . . .[32]

The Negro businessman must therefore rely on Negro customers, the lowest income group, a condition also affected by segregation and discrimination.[33] The following further observation emphasizes the latter point but goes on to suggest a derived "psychology," a phenomenon frequently indicated by other students on the subject:

Restricted patronage does not permit the enterprises owned and operated by Negroes to capitalize on the recognized advantages of normal commercial expansion. It tends to stifle business ingenuity and imagination, because it limits the variety of needs and demands to those of one racial group . . . . The practice of Negro business in catering almost entirely to Negroes has contributed to the development of an attitude that the Negro customer is obligated, as a matter of racial loyalty, to trade with enterprises owned and operated to the disadvantage of the Negro in business in that too frequently he has relied upon 'race pride' as an incentive for patronage rather than upon such factors as service, quality of merchandise, and competitive prices.[34]

Familiarity, friendship, racial sympathy, and similar relationships between customer and businessman have also been regarded as militating against the effectiveness of Negro business enterprise.

Chapter 2

Theory of Race Prejudice and Racism

We are assuming in this context that theory refers to any system of ideas which serves rationally to explain empirical data and phenomena. What we seek to show is that a certain culture of unparalleled power and sophistication originated and developed in western Europe; and, driven by its unique wealth-producing employment of capital, expanded inexorably over the whole earth, subordinating in its wake all other groups of mankind and more or less supplanting their cultures. Indeed, its first area of societal subordination and reconstruction was the feudal culture of Europe.

A remarkable fact about this process was that, sooner or later, other peoples became convinced that their own way of life was relatively static and impotent. Racial inferiority thus became identified with the relative simplicity of other cultures and, by the time of World War I, most of the nonwhite peoples of the world had become accommodated to such a definition of their status. It was from this process, as part of the transformed cultures of the earth, that race prejudice and racism derived. To impute the existence of race prejudice is to imply some form of identification with modern culture.

Race prejudice had nothing fundamental to do with the establishment of interracial communities all over the world by imperialist European nations. The various patterns of interaction within these communities were not determined primarily by race prejudice and discrimination. The transportation of West Africans to work in the Americas was a clear act of labor recruitment—recognition of this fact need not involve ethical judgments. Within the interracial situations thus established, however, race prejudice and discrimination followed consistently;[1] and variations in race prejudice have been determined by differences in those racial situations.

The Negro freeman in the North was not exploited like a slave but he was identified with the subordination and degradation of slavery and thus faced race prejudice and discrimination. He became desperately conscious of this when he attempted to get an education, to find a job, or to secure desirable housing. The Booker T. Washington-Theodore Roosevelt incident in 1901 illustrates the way in which exploitative interests ordinarily became determinative of race prejudice and racial discrimination. As President of the United States, Roosevelt invited Washington to the White House and, during the interview, dined with him. The white southern oligarchy, which still had vital interests in Negro labor, rose up in unrestrained indignation.

> The Richmond *Dispatch* exclaimed: "That was a deliberate act. . . . With our long-matured views on the subject of social intercourse between blacks and whites the least we can say now is that we deplore the President's taste, and we distrust his wisdom." [But] Negroes all over the country were delighted at this . . . recognition of their leader. The Washington *Bee* asserted, "The Southern Democrats . . . are shocked, boiled, smitten, and exasperated. In one fell swoop Mr. Roosevelt has smashed . . . their fondest idol. They are fuming . . . because he took a meal of victuals with a coloured gentleman who had been entertained by the nobility of England, and the best people of America."[2]

It is here, then, that the *source* of race prejudice is to be found. It emanates from a powerful, élite interest group which also orients the society on all significant questions. It could not exist in opposition to the wishes and ideology of this class. If it can be shown that the prejudice is socially consistent, it does not seem necessary for sociologists to explain the devious attitudes of exceptional individuals especially when they are of no particular moment. Even so, it should still be emphasized that the white recreant is not free to show his lack of prejudice on a southern street.

When the society as a whole is hospitable to the attitude, its consequential members would tend to recognize it as socially advantageous and thus seek to perpetuate it. Citing Bruno Lasker's *Race Prejudice in Children,* Arnold Rose observes:

> Studies of prejudice among children show how parents, older playmates, and the formal institutions of society not only transmit race prejudice to young children, but force them into the social grooves which require that their actions show discrimination. [This] helps to account for the continuation of prejudice when the original cause has disappeared.[3]

The southern dominant class has had a continuing interest in the maintenance and spread of race prejudice and discrimination—not only in the North but also in other parts of the world. The cause of the difference in expressions of race prejudice, say, in England, the United States, and Brazil will not be found in theories on the inherent or individualistic nature of race prejudice.[4] Race prejudice and discrimination poignantly hold the individual in place so that racial attitudes regarding him can be normally effectuated.[5] The prejudiced person may not even recognize the fact. Caste prejudice in India plays a similar role; the two phenomena, however, are not identical. To the extent that the study of race prejudice is individualized to that extent also it must be regarded as idiosyncratic and thus of little if any particular sociological significance.

Let us turn now to another approach. In an article of considerable perspicacity, Herbert Blumer properly emphasizes the collective nature of race prejudice.[6] And yet, because of the structure of his analysis, the individual appears eventually as the dynamic force in race prejudice. "It is the *sense of social position* emerging from this collective process [by which racial groups form images of themselves and others] which provides the basis of race prejudice." The author identifies certain types of "feelings" among members of the dominant group which characterize race prejudice—feelings which no white person can escape because he is a member of the "dominant group."

It is thus the group that feels, not the individual. "It is impor-

23

tant to recognize that this sense of group position transcends the feelings of the individual members of the dominant group, giving such members a common orientation. . . ." Indeed,

> by virtue of [his] sharing this sense of position . . . a [white] individual, despite his low status, feels that members of the subordinate group, however distinguished and accomplished, are somehow inferior, alien, and properly restricted in the area of claims. He forms his conception as a representative of the dominant group; he treats individual members of the subordinate group as representative of that group.

But Blumer identifies four "basic types of feeling" present in race prejudice:

> They are (1) a feeling of superiority, (2) a feeling that the subordinate race is intrinsically different and alien, (3) a feeling of proprietary claim to certain areas of privilege and advantage, and (4) a fear and suspicion that the subordinate race harbors designs on the prerogatives of the dominant race.

The author explains that the first "three [types] of feelings are present . . . in societies showing no race prejudice, as in certain forms of feudalism, in caste relations, in societies of chiefs and commoners, and under many settled relations of conquerors and conquered."[7] It would seem, then, that the critical factor is not the type of feeling but the type of society which causes the addition of the fourth element to result in race prejudice. The type of social system should, no doubt, affect the quality and operation of the first three types of feeling also.[8] And, if the author had considered the type of society productive of race prejudice, he would probably have been able to explain why the composite attitude tends to be modified in different countries and to what extent certain individuals may reject it even in the United States. Moreover, as "the subordinate race" waxes in power to effect its "designs on the prerogatives of the dominant race," race prejudice tends to be modified.[9] At the conclusion of his paper Blumer refers to "interest groups" and the "social order" but these observations constitute no part of the gravamen of his analysis. Thus the discussion inevitably emphasizes individual "feeling" relative to that of a mystical collective.[10] Perhaps our first realization should be that race prejudice is a peculiar socio-political attitude.

If our analysis of the origin and progress of race prejudice is

24

tenable, we may conclude, as a corollary, that white people have scarcely ever been subjected to race prejudice. No doubt, various medieval European peoples—Norwegian, Danes, Russians—among whom the Germanic Hansa established staples, had a taste of race prejudice. But no people of color have been able to develop and maintain such capitalist strength as would overawe and subject whites as a group to that peculiar condition of economic inferiority that spawns race prejudice.

The Japanese probably went farthest in this direction. But the duration of their imperialistic ascendancy over other Asians has been relatively tentative and brief. Moreover, the chances that other colored nations might develop the crucial economy that could bring whites under their control are becoming ever more remote. The period of such a possibility has apparently lapsed.

Since race prejudice tends to be culturally derived, people of different colored races may become prejudiced against each other. Indeed, a people may manifest race prejudice among themselves in terms of the dominant white culture. One aspect of nationalism among peoples of color has been resistance to such a practice.

Racism and Modern Culture

Racism, like race prejudice, is a relatively recent human development; it did not always exist. It assumes theoretically a knowledge of all the races of mankind. Before the sixteenth century, however, the critical world and its inhabitants were not known to any of its people. Racism, as we know it in modern times, is not merely verbal recognition of physical differences, ethnocentric comparisons among peoples, early mythological speculations about the place of various known peoples in the designs of creation, or invidious remarks by ancient conquerors about the physical and cultural traits of the vanquished.[11] On the whole, we find these observations and remarks erratic and inconsistent: they are not functionally related to any particular earlier culture.[12]

To repeat, then, racism is an element of modern culture developing spontaneously with its rise. From the beginnings of the Spanish and Portuguese explorations, it has had an unbroken and consistent history. Long before northern Europeans had any direct use for it, and before its refinement in that area, the Spaniards, in their relentless exploitation of the Indians in the West Indies, demonstrated severe racism. By the middle of the sixteenth century they were able to declare to the world that they enslaved the Indians to work in the tropical mines because, among other things, of their "barbarous natures," "their sins," their need of religious instruction, and because their labor was naturally due to a people of such "elevated natures" as the Spaniards.[13] From a similar point of view, Dante A. Puzzo observes:

> Racism rests on two basic assumptions: that a correlation exists between physical characteristics and moral qualities; that mankind is divisible into superior and inferior stocks. Racism, thus defined, is a modern conception, for prior to the sixteenth century there was virtually nothing in the life and thought of the west that can be described as racist.[14]

Racism, at this stage, explains and justifies racial exploitation and prejudice; it shows why white dominance over peoples of color is proper and inevitable. At any given time, we should expect it to be identified particularly among the leading imperialist nations. It provides "a simple, direct, apparent-to-the eye explanation of the most complex and perplexing phenomenon of modern times, to wit, the rise of a comparatively small, poor, and backward western Europe to undisputed dominion over the world. Racism, too, provides Europeans with a moral rationale for their subjugation and exploitation of 'inferior' peoples."[15]

As nationalism became integrated with the culture of Europe and of other parts of the world, racial superiority became identified with national ascendancy. According to the supreme practitioner of racism: "A state which . . . dedicates itself to the cherishing of its best racial elements must some day be master of the world."[16] Biological superiority and inferiority, the assumed relative limitations in cultural capacity of different peoples, either explained the hierarchy of nations in Europe and the rest of the world or demonstrated error in the existing hierarchy. The latter event ordinarily called for direct remedial action.

We cannot at this place go into a detailed history of that development. It fashioned the ideology for eventual confrontation among the great imperialist powers, and thus put to violent tests its utility as an explanation of the behavior of human groups. Racism, then, is politically functional. It is, for example, such a conviction which led Stanley Feldstein to trace America's internal racism from the early sixteenth century to modern times in close relationship to periods of national development. "The racism which fostered slavery among blacks," he argues at one point, "also functioned to destroy the nation's original inhabitants."[17]

The Philosophy of Racism

By the opening of the nineteenth century it had become universally obvious that Europeans possessed cultural capacities that transcended those of any other people on earth—all of whom were nonwhite and who more or less willingly admitted this ascendancy. Everywhere, moreover, European cultural achievement was identified with their physical difference, and a long anthropometric and historical search for racial characteristics and European origins commenced. "The nineteenth century was a period of exhaustive and, as it turned out, futile search for criteria to define and describe race differences."[18]

Futility, indeed, was by no means readily apparent. The most fateful discovery came by way of philology which then assumed that racial origins might be traced through a study of the history of languages. Research in this area demonstrated that all European languages, except "Finnish, Turkish, Magyar and Basque," belonged to a common family with Sanskrit the nearest surviving ancestor.

> In Sanskrit literature there were legends about a tall, blond, and muscular people who had vanquished the dark-skinned peoples of India and Persia. The name of these people, the Aryans, was translated by some philologists to mean *noble*, by others to mean *pure*. These blond people, so the theory went on, had spread to Europe, where—although in many countries they were a small minority—they introduced civilization and became the political and intellectual leaders. Since the northern Europeans tended to be blonds, the corollary of the theory was that here were the purest descendants of the original Aryans. Thus the cult of Aryanism was born.[19]

The Aryan-Nordic debate among ethnologists and philologists had only begun. Such questions as precisely who were the Aryans, what were their place of origin and the range of their migrations were never settled. So far as racism is concerned, however, Aryanism embodied final proof of the physical and cultural superiority of the European Nordic. The most influential leaders of this ideology were the French aristocrat Count Arthur de Gobineau (1816–1882) as he developed it in his four-volume work, *Essai sur l'inégalité des races humaines* (Paris, 1853–55); and Houston Stewart Chamberlain (1855–1927), an Englishman who went to Germany in his youth, became enthralled with its "Teutonic"[20] people and their culture, and in 1899 published to their honor a two-volume racist work of praise and phenomenal destiny: *Grundlagen des neunzehnten Jahrhunderts*.[21]

As we have indicated, the rise of racism in Europe and America was coeval with the expansion of capitalism abroad. Both Gobineau and Chamberlain were able to identify the physical and cultural characteristics of the peoples of the world as no other such ideologists could before the sixteenth century. What Gobineau accomplished was a convincing systematization of racist ideas already abroad. But his purpose was tied to an alarming hypothesis that all past civilizations have come to their doom through a mixture of the blood of their Aryan founders with that of the people of inferior races:

> I was gradually penetrated by the conviction that the racial question overshadows all other problems of history . . . and that the inequality of the races from whose fusion a people is formed is enough to explain the whole course of its destiny. . . . I convinced myself . . . that everything great, noble, and fruitful in the works of man on this earth, in science, art, and civilization, derives from a single point . . . it belongs to one family alone, the different branches of which have reigned in all the civilized countries of the universe.[22]

Although Gobineau classified mankind into three great races—black, yellow, and white—the blacks having the smallest capacity for cultures and whites the largest, he emphasized that only a relatively small group of whites constituted the seminal creators of "civilizations." "Almost the whole of the Continent of Europe is inhabited at the present time by groups of which the basis is white, *but in which the non-Aryan elements are most numerous*. There is no true civilization, among the European peoples [nor among any other people], where the Aryan branch is not predominant."

Moreover, Gobineau pronounced a fateful thesis: "The Germanic races, which in the fifth century transformed the Western mind—these are Aryans. . . . Where the Germanic element has never penetrated, our special kind of civilization does not exist." This branch of the white race "originally possessed the monopoly of beauty, intelligence, and strength. By its union with other varieties, hybrids were created, which were beautiful without strength, strong without intelligence, or, if intelligent, both weak and ugly." It seems advisable to quote Gobineau's hierarchical classification of the races because all the later leading racists have followed it—even down to his rather hostile attitude toward the black race. In this, he was conscious that he confronted the egalitarianism of the French revolution and of the American Declaration of Independence.[23] Thus he writes:

> Mankind is . . . divided into unlike and unequal parts, or rather into a series of categories, arranged, one above the other, according to differences of intellect. . . . I have been able to distinguish . . . three great and clearly marked types, the black, the yellow, and the white. . . .
> The negroid variety is the lowest, and stands at the foot of the ladder. The animal character, that appears in the shape of the pelvis, is stamped on the negro from birth, and foreshadows his destiny. His intellect will always move within a very narrow circle. He is not however a mere brute, for behind his low receding brow, in the middle of his skull, we can see signs of a powerful energy, however crude its objects. If his mental faculties are dull or even non-existent, he often has an intensity of desire, and so of will, which may be called terrible. Many of his senses, especially taste and smell, are developed to an extent unknown to the other two races.[24]

A word, no doubt, is said for the enslavement and general exploitation of blacks in Gobineau's recognition that "strict despotism is the only way of governing the negro."

The other two races are similarly characterized, and the Negro invidiously compared to them:

> The yellow races are . . . clearly superior to the black. Every founder of a civilization would wish the backbone of his society, his middle class, to consist of such men. But no civilized society could be created by them; they could not supply its nerve-force, or set in motion the springs of beauty and action.[25]

Among the traits of whites, "the principal motive is honour, which . . . has played an enormous part in the ideas of the race from the beginning. I need hardly add that the word honour, together with all the civilizing influences connoted by it, is unknown to both the yellow and the black man." Gobineau concluded: "If the three great types had remained strictly separate [i.e., without race mixture], the supremacy would no doubt have always been in the hands of the *finest of the white races,* and the yellow and black varieties would have crawled for ever at the feet of the lowest of the whites.''[26]

Although Chamberlain took Gobineau's basic conclusions on racial inferiority for granted, he developed his own Germanic-Aryan hypothesis into an immediate nationalistic force. Manifestly, therefore, racism went beyond a spontaneous instrument of black oppression and exploitation and sought to become a means of subordinating certain white peoples of Europe as well. A broad leap was eventually taken directly from Chamberlain to Adolf Hitler; but here, for the first time, racism met its match in superior countervailing power.

"Physically and mentally," said Chamberlain in 1899, "the Aryans are pre-eminent among all peoples; for that reason they are *by right* . . . the lords of the world.'' And who are the Aryans? ''The Germanic races belong to the most highly gifted group, the group usually termed Aryan." In concluding the first volume of his work he wrote: "I . . . must be satisfied if, in fulfilling the purpose of this book, I have succeeded in showing the distinction between the Germanic and the non-Germanic." Then, after discussing the postulated chaotic social situation among other peoples in Europe because of their non-Aryan traits, he declared: "No argument about 'humanity' can alter the fact that this means a struggle. Where the struggle is not waged with cannon-balls, it goes on silently in the hearts of society. . . . But this struggle, silent though it be, is above all others a struggle for life and death.'' In the introduction to the 1968 translation, George L. Mosse asserts:

> Nothing Chamberlain undertook during the rest of his life could rival the influence of his book. He was now accepted as a Germanic prophet and corresponded with the young Emperor William II who . . . was himself attracted to Chamberlain's work. During the First World War he became a busy propagandist for the German cause. . . .[27]

In 1923, furthermore, Chamberlain met and praised the young Adolf Hitler. It was Hitler's mission, of course, to demonstrate the cultural prowess of Aryanism. It is interesting, therefore, to observe how he abandons all scholasticism in the search for Aryan origins and relies directly upon the elementary function of racism. Thus, in *Mein Kampf,* he asserts:

> It is futile to argue which race or races were the original bearers of human culture. . . . It is simpler to put this question to one-

self with regard to the present, and here the answer follows easily and distinctly. What we see before us of human culture today, the results of art, science, and techniques, is almost exclusively the creative product of the Aryan. But just this fact admits of the . . . conclusion that he alone was the founder of higher humanity as a whole. . . . Exclude him and deep darkness will again fall upon the earth . . . human culture would perish and the world would turn into a desert.

If one were to divide mankind into three groups: culture founders, culture-bearers, and culture-destroyers, then, as representative of the first kind, only the Aryan would come in question. . . . If, starting today, all further Aryan influence upon Japan would stop . . . then a further development of Japan's present rise in science and technology could take place for a little while longer; but in the time of a few years the source would dry out, Japanese life would gain, but its culture would stiffen and fall back into the sleep out of which it was startled seven decades ago by the Aryan wave of culture.[28]

Aside from the function of racism, racists are persons or groups who identify cultural achievement with the biological attributes of normal human beings. This is the fundamental fact which all the racists, from those among the early Spanish and Portuguese adventurers to Adolf Hitler, sought to emphasize. If, then, it could be shown that variations in culture are biologically determined, the racists would be naturally inclined to summon relevant constructions of evolutionary theory in support of their superior-inferior distribution of human intellectual capacity. Before 1859, the year of the publication of *The Origin of Species,* some reliance was put upon the inherent nature of the *stages:* savagery, barbarism, and civilization.

With the coming of Charles Darwin and Herbert Spencer, the mystics also brought into play numerous evolutionary clichés. One of them was that the nonwhite peoples of the world were in various stages of evolution toward Nordic perfection. Observe, for example, how Chamberlain suggests this idea:

As is well known, even our nose . . . which, according to certain followers of Darwin, is on the way to even greater monumentalisation by complete ossification—even our nose . . . stands from the cradle to the grave in the center of our countenance as a witness to our race! We must therefore . . . strongly emphasize the fact that these North Europeans . . . were physically different from the other Indo-Europeans.[29]

31

That is to say, from the "Southern Europeans." Racism has by no means come to an end, but many incidents spawned by the necessities of World War II especially have confronted it with glaring and unanswerable questions.

Race in the United States

In the Unites States race relations tend to be defined essentially by Negro-white social interaction. These interactions have been characterized principally by three major social developments: bondage before 1865; social emancipation from about 1865 to 1954; and, since 1954, mass struggle directly for racial status *equality*. The increments of change, of course, have been determined by the variety of movements during these periods. During slavery, for example, the black population was predominantly rural and plantation bound; after 1865, the group moved increasingly into cities, thus taking advantage of urban wages and anonymity; accordingly, by 1954, Negroes had become mainly urban. This fact, together with the racial implications of the postslavery constitutional amendments, eventually produced a situation in which the manifest alternatives became interracial justice or social disaster. There are, consequently, "natural forces" behind current drives for "racial equality" among both Negroes and whites.

(a) Bondage, 1650 to 1860: enforced labor and social status blackout.

(b) Freedmen, blacks of marginal social status to 1865: subjected to labor exploitation, uncertain social status, and some encouragement to emigrate.

(c) Emancipation, 1865 to 1954: severe labor exploitation, potential right to full citizenship, increasing physical mobility leading to urbanization, and increasing opportunities for minimal education.

(d) Emergence of racial equality movements, 1954 onward: principle of political and social equality stipulated by the federal judiciary; drive for educational, occupational and social equality; congressional enactments emphasizing racial equality; massive black urbanization. As the Negro population insists upon visibility, race problems become urgent for the whole society. Anxiety spreads among the white ruling class. In the light of previous racial repression, special concessions demanded to achieve racial equality in employment and education. As part of the accompanying social effluvia, demands made for racial "reparations." Black nationalism spreads.

32

The Negro Slave Personality

A widely discussed explanation of the American slave personality has been derived directly from analogy with the incidence of
mass exploitation and extermination during the World War II period.
It has been frequently observed that the personality of the Negro, as a
socio-psychological group phenomenon, was forged principally from
his experience in bondage on the large southern plantations. This was
the social milieu which supplanted the heritage of his African tribal
cultures. It has been admitted also that the situation was, on the
whole, an extremely degrading one, centered in the exercise of absolute power by masters over the lives and welfare of the slaves. What,
then, are the predictable consequences for the human personality?

Stanley M. Elkins posed this question and sought a theoretical
answer. In his analysis, he relied not only on historical data but also
on social psychology, sociology, anthropology, and psychoanalysis.
The critical effect on personality adjustment in such a "closed system
of power" was "infantilization," or "infantile regression." The author explains:

> From the master's viewpoint, slaves had been defined in law as
> property, and the master's power over his property must be
> absolute. . . . Absolute power for him meant absolute depen-
> dence for the slave—the dependency not of the developing child
> but of the perpetual child. For the master, the role most fitting
> such a relationship would naturally be that of the father . . . .
> He might conceivably have to expect in this child—besides his
> loyalty, docility, humility, cheerfulness, and (under supervi-
> sion) his diligence—such additional qualities as irresponsibility,
> playfulness, silliness, laziness, and (quite possibly) tendencies
> to lying and stealing. Should the entire prediction prove accu-
> rate, the result would be something resembling 'Sambo.'[30]

Professor Elkins conceived of this syndrome as the characteristic slave personality and sought to conceptualize it. He sought to
show specifically that this personality trait is neither an innate attribute of Negroes nor part of their African heritage but rather an acquired pattern of behavior which we should expect wherever "absolute power" is similarly imposed. He then attempts to find other
social systems that manifest comparable "infantilizing tendencies
under absolute power"—but without success. The caste system of
India, for example, is not slavery and the power of Brahmans is not
absolute. Among the tribal peoples of West Africa not even intertribal

bondage entailed such complete subjection. On this point Elkins asserts:

> No true picture, cursory or extended, of African culture seems to throw any light at all on the origins of what would emerge, in the American plantation society, as the stereotyped 'Sambo' personality. The typical West African tribesman was a distinctly warlike individual; he took hard work for granted; and he was accustomed to live by a highly formalized set of rules which he himself often helped to administer. . . .[31]

Neither feudalism in Europe nor slavery in Latin America generated conditions leading to mass infantilization. "In Latin America, the very tension and balance among three kinds of organizational concerns—church, crown, and plantation agriculture— prevented slavery from being carried by the planting class to its ultimate logic."[32] In the absence of any empirical, societal analogue, therefore, Elkins concludes that slavery, in its tendency to infantilize its subjects is an institution peculiar to the social history of the United States. In other words, it is "unique," unknown to any other culture.

Inquiring into the historical question regarding the origin of this particular institution, Elkins wonders: "Why should the status of the 'slave' have been elaborated . . . with such utter logic and completeness as to make American slavery unique among all systems known to civilization?" And his findings show that "with the full development of the plantation there was nothing, so far as [the Negro's] interests were concerned, to prevent unmitigated capitalism from becoming unmitigated slavery." Given this coincidence of capitalism:

> The master must have absolute power over the slave's body, and the law [developed] in such a way as to give it to him at every crucial point. Physical discipline was made virtually unlimited and the slave's status unalterably fixed. It was in such a setting that those rights of personality traditionally regarded between men as private and inherent . . . were left virtually without defense. The integrity of the family was ignored. . . . [And] the condition of a bondsman's soul . . . was very quickly dropped from consideration.

Essentially, then, this constitutes the situation of "absolute power" which, according to Elkins, produced the infantile "Sambo type. . . . It was a plantation type, and a plantation existence embraced well over half the slave population.''[33]

But what are the elements involved in the operation of absolute power as it proceeds to determine infantilization? Since the phenomenon did not occur in any other traditional society, the author suggests that its analogue may be most clearly observed in the Nazi concentration camps. ''The plantation,'' the author points out, ''was not . . . a concentration camp . . . but it should at least be permissible . . . to speak of the concentration camp as a special instance of human slavery. . . . The only mass experience that Western people have had within recorded history comparable . . . with Negro slavery was undergone in the nether world of Nazism.''

This, then, elucidates the author's hypothesis: the exercise of absolute power will result in ''human slavery'' and ''infantilization'' regardless of ''race'';[34] and this is demonstrated by the similarity of results in the concentration camps and on the plantation.

Elkins's theory seems to make very little if any contribution to our understanding of race relations. The existence of the prisoner was determined by the nature of his penalty, a common extremity of which was genocide. The slave's existence, on the other hand, was based upon servitude, an extremely degrading form of labor. The master's greatest achievement was that of convincing the slave that such labor, for him, was a normal way of life.[35]

As Elkins says properly, the unrestricted power of the plantation owner was ''capitalist entrepreneurial power;'' and an essential characteristic of the slave was his personal marketability. He thus became a valuable element among the factors of production. The Nazi camps were prisoner compounds. Strictly speaking, that plight did not transform ''offenders'' into slaves. The categorical difference in social situation distinguishes not only the patterns of behavior but also operation of the universal trait of ''absolute power.'' In other words the exercise of power does not in itself create forms of social organization. Human power always implies capacity to accomplish specific ends.

The term ''Sambo,'' moreover, seems unfortunate. It is inevitably pejorative and thus nonscientific. It would seem consistent with Elkins's analysis to speak of the inmates of the concentration camps as having been ''Samboized.'' Any prisoner suffering from, say, regression or perversion, could thus be meaningfully called Sambo. Such names have been part of the instruments of racial repression and apparently can no more be cleared of their emotional content than, for instance, the term "nigger."[36]

We do not question the author's recognition that the personality of the broken-in, accommodated, plantation slave was more or less seriously debased and even perverted—it remains doubtful, however, whether the slave was "childish" in the Freudian sense of adult regression.[37] We may agree also that at the center of black personality distortion was destruction of the slave's family. But we contend that both the use of the term "Sambo" and the attempt to identify plantation slavery with the metaphorical "slavery" of the concentration camp are misleading.

"Absolute power," we think, has no significant meaning apart from its manifestation in social situations. So far as human personality is concerned, therefore, we should expect the operation of control and punishment in the Nazi camps to be significantly distinguishable from their seeming counterpart even in the "Russian slave labor camps."[38] To repeat, then, the operation of power acquires its significance from the social situation rather than vice-versa. The author is testing the efficacy of "absolute power" in different social situations. We become involved, moreover, with a differentiation of the personality of the plantation slave woman from that of the female concentration camp internee insofar as they were affected by "absolute power."[39]

The Race Relations Cycle and Assimilation

The "race relations cycle" is a concept introduced by Robert E. Park to describe the process by which people of one race or culture, within the same society, become assimilated to the ways of life of the dominant group. This process, sometimes referred to as a "natural history," is assumed to be a cultural universal involving stages of intergroup adjustment toward eventual assimilation. "In the relations of races," says Park, "there is a cycle of events which tends everywhere to repeat itself. . . . [This] race relation cycle . . . takes the form . . . of contacts [symbiosis or conflict], competition, accommodation, and eventual assimilation which is . . . progressive and irreversible."[40]

The race relations cycle was, however, originally conceived of and developed primarily with reference to European immigration into the United States. It may thus be regarded as a sociology of the melting pot. Park says accordingly: "Assimiliation is a process of denationalization and this is, in fact, the form it has taken in Europe. . . . In America the problem has arisen from the voluntary migration to this country of peoples who have abandoned the political allegiance of the old country and are gradually acquiring the culture of the new."[41]

The stages are elaborated as theoretical concepts in Chapters 5 and 8–11 in Park and Burgess, *Introduction to the Science of Sociology*. The idea of assimilation has been oriented particularly to "Western democratic culture," and to the means by which the various European nationalities are integrated in American society. Race problems arise when the "natural history" of group assimilation is obstructed. Implication of universality, of obstruction, and of the rise of race relations may be gleaned from W. O. Brown's statement of the process:

> the natural history of race conflict appears to be as follows: initial contacts of a symbiotic, categoric sort; physical clash and "war" incident to the struggle for land and existence; temporary accommodation in the form of subordination or partial isolation of the weaker race, fusion following if this race [or nationality] is numerically weak and the mores of the dominant race are flexible, in which case *the race-relations cycle ends* [as has been the case of assimilation of Europeans in the United States]; the emergence of [race] conflict as a struggle for status . . . intensified conflict and the mobilization of the races, accompanied by race prejudice, race consciousness, and race movements; partial accommodation, no solution short of assimilation and fusion liquidating race conflict. . . .[42]

Brown, following Park closely, emphasizes the inevitable struggle for social status.

> It is this struggle for status, for place in a social order, that is at the root of race conflict. . . . The European prefers the native to remain native, realizing that a collapsing native culture means Europeanized natives who will inevitably demand status in the European system. . . . Dominant races [therefore] have a vested interest in the perpetuity of the cultures of weaker races. . . .[43]

In the continuing race relations conflict, the process of assimilation becomes a succession of accommodations. In this sense, then, assimilation may be thought of as eventual intergroup accommodation—a social position which may still be unstable but which does not presage social conflict.

American Jews, for example, have apparently reached some such stage of accommodation. In the foreseeable future, however, the French and English in Canada will hardly attain social fusion. Paradoxically, the dynamics of American Negro assimilation seem more insistent than those of either the Jews or Canadians.[44] Skin color is a spurious obstacle to the assimilative forces of the culture. It serves only as a temporary social dike against which this culture accumulates and repeatedly overflows.

There is thus no apparent social logic to indicate that the process will come to a dead end. As Brown properly emphasizes: "In the long run the only permanent solution of race conflict is the complete absorption and assimilation of the races in a common culture and social order. . . . [R]ace will decline in importance as a source of . . . conflict since, intrinsically, it has no functional connection with ability or economic and social divisions."[45] Indeed, a point will manifestly be reached at which further resistance to Negro assimilation would be societally self-defeating.

Park's race relation cycle has been praised, criticized, and amended by sociologists. In a painstaking examination of Park's and other cycle theories, Professor Brewton Berry asserts:

> If it is true that the relations between racial and ethnic groups follow some universal and inevitable pattern, it would be well for us to know it. . . . We should then be able to predict the course of events. . . . At the present stage of our knowledge, however, it hardly seems possible even to sketch the bare outlines of such a race relations cycle. . . . So numerous and so various are the components that enter into race relations that each situation is unique. . . .[46]

All is indeed confusion from the point of view of historically unlimited promiscuous intergroup "contacts." Regarding the assimilation of cultures and peoples, however, certain clarifying assumptions could be made. Different cultures have different capacities for assimilation. Ordinarily, the greater the complexity of the culture, the greater its capacity to assimilate others. Moreover, a preliterate culture will not assimilate a literate one, but the force of an opposite movement may be persistent. Some cultures, especially those of tribal organization, tend to be racially nonassimilating. Before the coming of capitalist culture, there was no predictable pattern of universal racial assimilation. Assimilation, therefore, is peculiarly an attribute of the capitalist system.

With the advent of capitalism in Italy during the fifth and sixth centuries, an inherent movement toward assimilation of all other peoples and cultures began. This process, developing at an increasing rate, has never abated. In relationship to other cultures, therefore, it has never been superseded; it has always been the relatively dominant culture while others have modified their pattern in order to conform and to communicate with it. Major cultural changes have been predictably one-way changes.

Since capitalist culture has been continually developing and thus necessarily in transition, the nature of the impact of intercultural contact has also been changing. From about the time of World War I, the peoples of the world had come under the influence of capitalism; every major race, therefore, had entered a process of assimilation. As the cultures of the world become increasingly oriented toward the single cultural model, we should expect interpersonal relations to increase. No people are allowed to remain outside the domain of capitalism. Tribal vestiges, nationalism, and the ecumenical religions are, however, major forces restraining the assimilation of peoples.

As we should expect, the capitalist city has been the principal ecological milieu of racial assimilation; and the nation constitutes the administrative unit of the global culture. A predictable "race relations cycle" in this context would seem to be the movement of subordinated peoples from "native tribal status" to national status. Native peoples within one nation tend more or less to assimilate not only to each other but mainly to the culture of the previously dominant nation. Historically, nationalistic groups in Europe tend to resist assimilation.

Assimilation of peoples within a nation will depend upon such factors as historical period, relative size of population, relative cultural advancement, racial policy, place of birth, and extent of amenability to the morality of capitalist culture. Syndromes of such factors establish relative positions of the nations in the global hierarchy of powers.

Assimilation to the culture of dominant peoples—such as that of the United States, Great Britain, France, Germany—continues. Within the colored nations, however, race relations cycles, as conceived by Park, become anomalous. These nations are, of course,

39

mainly artifically contrived entities. We can hardly deduce, from the nature of their constitution, generally applicable sociological rules. The contemporary assimilative cultural model remains beyond their borders. Such places, for example, as India, "East" and West Pakistan, Kenya, and South Africa tend to have fundamentally divergent internal problems of racial assimilation.

In a typical European colony such as, for instance, preindependence India or Nigeria, the totality of native subcultures tends to assimilate to the culture of the relatively small group of exotic Europeans. As these white colonizers withdraw, however, none of the native communities can assume the prestige and authority necessary to replace them culturally. Among other similar groups, the tragedy of the Ibo and Yoruba in Nigeria and the Tutsi and Hutus in Rwanda and Burundi illustrates this. Disparity of language and religion are predisposing factors. The natives, therefore, tend to look to their own subcultures nationalistically, or toward the cultural organization left by the colonists. The basis of assimilation and intergroup unity thus becomes perfection of the capitalist culture implanted by the erstwhile colonists and not development of a common allegiance to any of the native subcultures. The lower the nation in the hierarchy of capitalist cultures, the less its inherent capacity to produce cultural uniformity among its subcultures. In principle, the greater the struggle for social status in the society, the less the tenacity of the culture of its subgroups; and the higher the nation in the global hierarchy of powers, the greater the prestige and assimilative capacity of the dominant culture. For example, we should expect the pull and authority exercised by Portuguese culture upon natives in its colonies to be less than that shown by British culture in British colonies.

Chapter 3

The Seedbed of Race Relations

Current race relations can be understood mainly, though not entirely, by an analysis of the Negro's continuing, post-Civil War, economic role in the South. Indeed, that role and its cultural concommitants served basically to determine his social status not only in the South but also in the nation as a whole.

The Civil War was implicated in a social system which had attained a high degree of consistency. Its logic had become internally rational and thus largely conditioned the personalities of its members, both Negro and white. Slavery had become regionally a socially desirable, successful, and apparently viable way of life with no realistic societal alternative.[1] Slaves constituted 32 percent of the population of the entire South and 45 percent of the Deep South. Emancipation therefore created a colossal economic and social disaster: it abolished bondage without eliminating the animus and its essential economic necessities. According to Frederick Douglass, who lived through the great conflict:

41

> The first feeling toward the [freedman] by the old master classes was full of bitterness and wrath. They resented his emancipation as an act of hostility toward them: and, since they could not punish the emancipator, they felt like punishing the object which that act had emancipated. Hence they drove him off the old plantation and told him he was no longer wanted there. They not only hated him because he had been freed as a punishment to them, but because they felt that they had been robbed of his labor. . . . The thought of paying cash for labor that had been formerly extorted by the lash did not in any way improve their disposition to the emancipated slave or improve his own condition.[2]

A modern analyst reaches similar conclusions:

> Emancipation was not related to any change of mind on the part of white people. The reform was thrust upon the South and never got its sanction. It became rather a matter of sectional pride to resist the change to the utmost. When it became apparent that the North could not, or would not, press its demands with force, the white South found a revenge for the defeat in War by undoing as far as possible the national legislation to protect the freedman. This negative direction of the Southern political will is still, three generations after the Civil War, apparent to the observer. The South did not want—and to a great extent still does not want—the Negro to be successful as a freedman.[3]

Traditional Resistance Economically Based: The Tenant

Decisive factors in the economic structure tended to persist. Negroes were freed with virtually no aptitudes save their physical capacity to work on plantations.[4] Cotton was still the dominant market commodity with bright prospects for future expansion; and the white master class was still in possession of the land or driven to reacquire it in order to resume production. Although there was some disruption of the labor supply—some movement to the cities— Negroes remained overwhelmingly in the rural South. They were indispensable to prosperity in the agricultural area and there was relatively little demand for their services in the cities. The stage was thus set for the reorganization of production, along the lines of the prewar pattern.

Three main possibilities of using the emancipated workers were considered: they could be virtually reenslaved in some acceptable manner, they could be hired as free labor for daily wages, or they

The Seedbed of Race Relations

could be taken into partnership as share tenants. All three methods were tried and more or less adopted, but only the latter took root. For the freedmen, and indeed for all concerned, share tenancy with a landowner's lien on the crops seemed the most desirable. As Calvin L. Beale puts it:

> An entirely new system of relations had to be worked out between the freed Negroes and their former owners. With rather rare exceptions, the freedmen were not provided land by the Federal Government and the land ownership of the planters was not broken. At first, efforts were made to hire the former slaves for wages. The result was not very successful. Cash was scarce for the average planter, the freedom-sensitive Negroes did not respond well to the demands of gang work any longer, and hiring made for an unreliable supply of workers. Soon a predominant system of renting developed in which a family was assigned to work a particular piece of land and receive a share of the crop as wages. This proved to be a more stable arrangement for all and guaranteed that a family would remain until the crop was in.[5]

Share-cropping tenancy became so convenient that it spread from the Black Belt all over the South. It did not, however, meet with similar success in other regions. The United States census of Agriculture (1959) finds that, except for southeastern Missouri, "croppers are not of importance outside the 16 Southern States." Moreover, the southern system increasingly attracted poor white farm operators in the area.

Basically, share-cropping, like other types of tenancy, is a form of business. The census enumerates the land worked by each tenant as a farm. He is, in principle, a risk-bearer and a profit-or-loss taker according to the vicissitudes of the market. It is in this sense that Arthur F. Raper defines broadly the position of types of tenantry relative to that of laborer and full ownership:

> the share renter occupies a middle position between the wage hands and the owner; the wage hand takes no risk and gets none of the surplus; the cropper takes some risk and gets half; the share renter takes more risk and gets all above the rent price; and the owner assumes the entire risk and gets the whole benefit accruing from price and weather, and from any application of personal insight, resourcefulness, or industry.[6]

Landlord and tenant thus constitute a kind of economic partnership that may be explicitly referred to as involving bonds of com-

Chart I
Slaves: Number, 1860

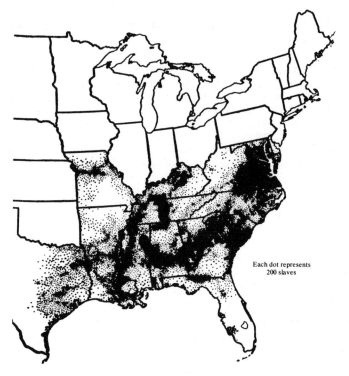

Each dot represents
200 slaves

Source: Lewis C. Gray, *History of Agriculture in the Southern United States to 1860,*
Washington, 1933, vol. 2, p. 655.

mon material interests. Indeed, one can cite instances of growing
sympathy and "solidarity" between tenant and landowner.[7] Their
common enemies would then be the mythical out-group agents who
control the yield and the price of the crop. The system arose from an
interrelated problem. In the bankrupt post-Civil War South, the emancipated masses, who could neither purchase nor rent land, were put
to work by landlords who could hardly pay wages. Both parties were
immediately dependent on income from the crop.

If we could conceive of this situation without the traditions of
slavery, we could probably also envisage a people developing sympa-
thetically together, with advantages accruing to both landowner and

Percent of Farms Operated by Nonwhite Operators (South Only), 1959

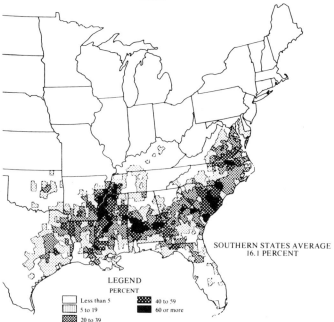

SOUTHERN STATES AVERAGE
16.1 PERCENT

LEGEND
PERCENT

☐ Less than 5   ▨ 40 to 59
▦ 5 to 19   ■ 60 or more
▨ 20 to 39

Source: *U.S. Census of Agriculture, 1959,* Vol. 2, p. 1031.

tenant. "In the absence of land reform and a program of Federal intervention," Beale concludes, "the system was probably the most practical available for getting the agriculture of the South on its feet again."[8] A genuine interest among the old master class in the advancement of the freedmen as well as the white masses to independent proprietorship would have been involved. But traditions tended strongly to persist: "In the eyes of the ruling class, Negroes were fit only for cotton servitude."[9] Thus the ecology of antebellum plantations corresponded closely to the reorganized system of tenancy,[10] as charts I and II indicate;[11] and its abuses proliferated.

Both tobacco and cotton have been dominant labor-intensive crops suitable to plantation organization. Production of cotton, however, has been the principal staple of Negro tenancy. The Black Belt area has been traditionally the center of the plantation system and of the cotton culture with which Negro share-cropping has been iden-

45

tified. In 1929, for example, cotton was produced on 83.5 percent of the farms operated by Negroes, and they accounted for 32.4 percent of all the cotton produced in the South.[12] According to the 1959 Census of Agriculture: "Nonwhite operators in the South were most numerous in the tobacco and older cotton-growing areas. There were very few nonwhite operators in the more northerly states of the South—Delaware, Maryland, West Virginia and Kentucky."[13] William C. Holley and others found that there were on these farms nine Negro families to every white family. As a source of labor, therefore, "the great majority of the plantations were operated entirely by Negro tenants."[14]

Table 1 shows the trend since 1920, when relatively detailed statistics became available, for the number and percentage of farm operators in the South according to race. We include farm laborers also because of their importance, especially in data for Negroes.

Trend and Structure of Tenancy

The major trends indicate a marked decrease in all agricultural workers regardless of color. From 1920 to 1959 the number of farms among whites in the South decreased from about 3.5 million to 1.7 million; and, among Negroes, from 2.1 million to 0.6 million. The 1964 census shows a continuing trend. For example, in 1964, the total of white farm operators was 86 percent of the number for 1959; and the total of Negro farm operators was 64 percent of the figure for 1959. The drop in tenancy during this period was even greater: the number of tenants was 64 percent of the 1959 figure for whites and 60 percent for Negroes. Table 1 also shows the relative structure of Negro and white farm operators in the South.[15]

The structure of tenure distributions is characterized principally by differences in farm ownership, tenantry, and labor. In 1959, for example, full and part owners constituted 66 percent of all farm workers among whites while all tenants, croppers, and laborers came to about 13, 3, and 20 percent respectively. The figures for nonwhites were approximately the reverse of these ratios. Full and part owners constituted only 22.1 percent of the total among nonwhites while all tenants, croppers and laborers were about 24, 13, and 54 percent respectively. Thus Negro farm workers were mainly represented by tenants and laborers.[16] These, however, were the plantation specialists. As Holley and associates observed regarding the way in which plantation crops were produced irrespective of race in 1934 and 1937:

46

"Croppers were the most important type of plantation labor, operating approximately 46 percent of all cropland in both years. Wage laborers were the second most important source of labor and, for all areas combined, operated 41 percent of the cropland in 1937."[17] In 1959 farms operated by croppers produced 51.3 percent of the total cotton production in the South and 35.8 percent of the tobacco.[18]

The designated farm tenant, male or female, ordinarily refers to the head of a family. Landlords prefer families as tenants mainly because of the quantity of labor available. The family, of course, may sometimes be broken up. But the contribution of subordinate members to the labor pool of the family has been frequently recognized and designated as unpaid family workers. The logic of the tenant's inclusion of the women and children in his family in "making the crop" is that he is essentially a farmer, hence the larger the crop, the greater his family income. The income of the labor pool in producing the crop tends thus to be regarded as the economic resource of the entire family. As Allison Davis and his associates see it:

> The strong central authority of the father or mother, reinforced by religious and moral sanctions, organizes all members of the family into a single productive unit, which often includes married sons or daughters and their families (and, in the case of aged tenants, children whom the tenant has adopted to help him on the farm after his own children have left him.) The social authority of the family head, in turn, is the family's productive system.[19]

The system manifestly favors large families; and reciprocally their very size works to intensify dependence upon the system. "Landlords," explains Woofter, "prefer large families to meet the labor demands of the peak seasons, thus encouraging a high birth rate. This high rate of population increase in turn perpetuates the plantation system. . . . [It reduces] the bargaining power of the individual plantation tenant, making it increasingly difficult for him to free himself from the . . . system and become an independent farmer."[20]

Motivation among Tenants

Since the tenant, especially the cropper, is in fact a more or less closely supervised worker, he has relatively little motivation to plan production on the farm in order to utilize slack seasons. At such times the labor of the family becomes an inescapable surplus and a

Table 1

Number and Percent Distribution of Farms by Color and Tenure for the South 1920–1959a

Color and tenure of operator	Number of farms				Percent distribution by tenure			
	1959	1950	1940	1920	1959	1950	1940	1920
Total white	1,729,616	2,777,494	3,269,950	3,481,419	100.0	100.0	100.0	100.0
All owners, mgrs, tenants	1,379,407	2,093,333	2,326,904	2,283,750	79.8	75.4	71.2	65.5
Full owners	856,864	1,269,641	1,185,788	1,227,204	49.5	45.7	36.3	35.3
Part owners	285,418	274,135	185,246	152,432	16.5	9.9	5.7	4.4
Managers	8,906	9,740	13,215	16,548	.6	.4	.4	.5
All tenants	228,219	539,817	942,655	887,566	13.2	19.4	28.8	25.4
Cash	34,376	80,293	189,667	118,913	2.0	3.0	5.8	3.4
Share-cash	15,619	24,367	32,131	14,465	.9	.9	1.0	.4
Crop-share	81,144	202,864	389,561	474,513	4.7	7.3	11.9	13.6
Livestock share	13,198	14,285			.8	.5		
Croppers	47,650	148,708	242,173	227,378	2.8	5.3	7.4	6.5
Other	36,232	69,300	89,123	52,297	2.0	2.3	2.7	1.5
Farm laborers	350,209[1]	684,161[2]	943,046[3]	1,197,669[4]	20.2	24.6	28.8	34.4

Total nonwhite	575,466	1,039,841	1,443,870	2,103,131	100.0	100.0	100.0	100.0
All owners, mgrs, tenants	265,621	559,090	680,266	922,914	46.2	53.8	47.0	43.9
Full owners	89,749	141,482	141,902	178,558	15.6	13.6	10.0	8.5
Part owners	37,534	51,864	31,361	39,031	6.5	5.0	2.1	1.8
Managers	290	239	365	1,770	.1	.1	.1	.1
All tenants	138,048	365,505	506,638	703,555	24.0	35.1	35.0	33.5
Cash	14,855	39,562	64,684	100,275	2.6	3.8	4.4	4.8
Share-cash	2,406	5,656	6,547	8,207	.4	.1	.1	.4
Crop-share	31,714	95,461	89,483	176,711	5.5	9.2	6.9	8.4
Livestock share	946	1,736			.1	.2		
Croppers	73,387	198,057	299,118	333,713	12.8	19.0	20.6	15.9
Other	14,740	25,033	46,806	84,649	2.6	2.4	3.2	4.0
Farm laborers	309,845	480,751	763,604	1,180,217	53.8	46.2	53.0	56.1

aSource except as indicated: *Census of Agriculture, 1959*, vol. 2, chap. 10.

[1] *U. S. Census of Population, 1960*, Characteristics, U.S. Summary, pt. 1., table 257, item "farm laborers and foremen," the South (data for 1960).

[2] *Seventeenth Census of the U.S. 1950*, vol. 2, Characteristics, pt. 1, U.S. Summary, table 159.

[3] *Sixteenth Census of the U.S., 1940*, vol. 3, the Labor Force, pt. 1, table 63.

[4] *Fourteenth Census of the U.S., 1920*, vol. 4, Occupations, chap. 7, table 1, Sixteen Southern States, data for native white parentage and Negro.

burden on its already small annual income. The poor and degraded condition of Negro tenants and agricultural laborers in the South was proverbial. In his detailed study of two Deep South counties Arthur F. Raper explains:

> that the vast majority of [rural families] have but little money; that they buy much of their food, and many of them are dependent upon landlords for subsistence while growing a crop; that they produce only a small proportion of the meat, milk, eggs and cereals which they need for their own tables; that they live in unattractive and uncomfortable dwellings; that they have scant household funishing and but little reading matter; and that they own and work with the crudest kind of agricultural tools—in short they maintain a very low plane of living.[21]

Southern tenancy includes a significant percentage of white farm workers, a fact frequently considered by students of this subject. The physical conditions of life for them tend to be hardly better. They are limited by the prevailing traditions of production, and constitute the mass of illiterate poor whites. Again, as Arthur F. Raper puts it: "Since the plantation system forces white tenants and Negro tenants into competition there is but little possibility of either group rising unless both rise."[22]

There are differences, however. As we have noticed in Table 1, white tenantry constitutes a relatively small percentage of white farmers in the South, and only about 3 percent of white farm workers are croppers, compared to about 13 percent for Negroes—approximately 48,000 to 73,000 in actual numbers. White tenants tend to be concentrated on the smaller plantations which follow the organizational pattern set by the larger systems. The great plantation owners "through their control over large acreages of the best land and of large numbers of tenants and laborer families, dominate the economic, political and cultural life."[23] White tenants, however, probably create greater problems of control for the landlord than Negro tenants. As Allison Davis and associates explain:

> Neither obedience nor deference is demanded of [the white tenant] in those situations in which his behavior is merely that of one white individual to another. [But when he enters the plantation situation] where almost all tenants are colored, he must behave virtually as a colored tenant, and must accept the same treatment. This situation gives rise to strong antagonisms be-

tween the planter and his white tenants, which result in insubordination by the white tenant, in demands which the planter considers excessive, in mutual suspicion, in attempts by the white tenant to cause trouble between the planter and other tenants, and in other violations of the customary relationship. As a result, the planters are generally antagonistic to white tenants and prefer the properly subordinated colored tenants.[24]

Although Woofter found, in his study of plantations in 1934, that 42 percent had both Negro and white tenants,[25] these biracial units were distributed on component farms by race. The two groups did not work together in the same field. Of his plantation sample, only 5 percent were operated entirely by white tenants. There were white and Negro overseers, but Negro overseers supervised only Negro tenants. "The hired white overseer [of colored field workers], usually the twenty-five to thirty-five year old son of a distant tenant, is the direct descendant of the slave driver. . . ."[26] The problem of white tenancy, then, has been one of poverty induced by the peculiar system of farming in the South and of continuing support for the ideology of bondage.[27]

The Negro Farmer

The extent of farm ownership among Negroes in the South has been relatively small. It varies from state to state but is most limited in plantation areas. For the region as a whole, table 1 shows that in 1959, there were 1,142,282 white full and part farm owners, and 127,283 nonwhite full and part owners—or about 11 percent of the former. There has been a downward trend for both groups, but the number of nonwhite farmers has been decreasing at a faster rate. Moreover, there has been a distinct difference between the size and value of these categories of farms. As of 1959:

> Farms of nonwhite operators in the South were small with an average size of 56 acres and 27 acres of cropland harvested as compared with an average size of 382 acres and 93 acres of cropland harvested for white operators. The average value of land and buildings was $7,328 for nonwhite operators as compared with $37,816 for white operators.[28]

Farms owned by Negroes were situated mainly in the old cotton and tobacco belts, and they were relatively restricted to these field crops. There was greater diversification of product among white

51

farmers.[29] Considering his relatively limited means, the Negro farm owner tended nevertheless to become a leader in his rural community. "He is the permanent resident of an otherwise shifting Negro farm population; [hence] he provides . . . much of the support for the local institutions of his race."[30]

The Negro's struggle to own land called for more than mere economic competence. Indeed, his very desire to own land was regarded as a social presumption. "Many white people," observes Raper, "still feel that the Negro should remain a tenant, and that he is getting out of 'his place' when he attempts to become independent through ownership of land. This attitude explains why the Negro seldom buys land on the open market, why he must have the personal assistance of some landed white man to become an owner, why he usually purchases the less desirable land."[31] His very success in purchasing land tends thus to become a mark of leadership; he has been able to make the proper contacts with white men of status and power in the community; hence his "purchase has been the result more largely of a personal equation than of a purely business transaction."[32] He has had, moreover, to overcome the technical pitfalls peculiar to the transfer and holding of title to his farm; and he has probably found that, in many rural zones, ownership of land is off bounds to him.[33] As an agricultural producer and businessman, therefore, he has been able to act positively mainly by submitting to the white rural oligarchy.

Chapter 4

Significance of Rural Culture for Race Relations

We are interested here not so much in the particular study of the Negro American in agriculture as in identifying the focus and social situation which generated the characteristic pattern of race relations in the United States. The significance of relevant data does not change from census to census. The relationship of the Negro farm worker to the white, landlord class on the southern plantation tended to constitute the pivot of the inferiority-superiority definition of the groups for the entire nation. This relationship merits special attention because it became the generative seedbed of the racial tradition which spread not only to other parts of the country but also to Europe and Asia.

The pattern of discrimination can be consistently dealt with only as an inherent function of the major social system. We would dissipate the critical attributes of the relationship were we to generalize about the structurally alien caste system of India, thralldom in the

53

ancient world, feudalism in different parts of the medieval world, or the intense in-group characteristics of African tribalism. As Woofter quite properly remarks: "The plantation system is bound up with the cash-crop system."[1]

Economic compulsions peculiar to the capitalist market drove illiterate, unskilled freedmen into basic productive alliances with dispossessed whites and held them there in spite of the vexations of exploitation and the persistence of master class frustrations.[2] Although the relationship was an interactive one, we should not lose sight of the fact that the way of life of the colored people, and indeed of the South as a whole, remained largely dependent upon the dominant interests and leadership of the great planters:

> plantation customs and ideology set the pattern for relationships in smaller farm units. This is true because of the dominance of the plantation in southern rural life. Large planters persistently emerge as the political and economic leaders of the cotton areas. Even if there are only four or five large plantations in a county. The ownership of these considerable properties and the prestige of success on a large scale make it easy for the planters to assume prominence in community control if their personalities fit them for leadership. Add to this a sentimental attachment to land as a symbol of aristocracy and the consequent family ties to the land, and the plantation stands out as the basis for a hereditary oligarchy in southern community life.[3]

Besides the plantation oligarchy, the Black Belt merchant-financier and the lawyer-politician, "who knew how to make of little or no effect the Thirteenth, Fourteenth, and Fifteenth Amendments,"[4] converged into a structure of conservative authority which gradually enveloped and overwhelmed the freedmen.[5] The persistent influence of this force, plus dependence on the land for daily bread, brought the Negro farm operator close to total submission. Says Raper:

> Man-land relations, landlord-tenant patterns, the white primary, the expenditures for public schools, the location of the churches, the everyday doings of whites and Negroes all foster the sentiments and differentials which define and maintain the Black Belt's way of life. From the local point of view there are few problems: the tenant is improvident, dependent, and childlike and the planter furnishes him food and supervises his labor; mortal violence sometimes overtakes the Negro. . . . Lynching

is resorted to . . . when the implied threat of it appears to be losing its efficacy.[6]

Conditions of Dependence

The social process of production perpetuated and demonstrated these attributes of the tenant. Although there are various types of tenancy, Negro tenancy has been especially characterized by landlord supervision, season subsistence credits, and provision of working capital for the operation of the farm and for housing. The tenant, on the other hand, worked in the field—sometimes under overseer direction—and received his means of subsistence, including shelter and fuel, as a charge against his annual income derived from the sale of his share of the cotton or tobacco produced on the farm. The primary opportunity for control and abuse of the tenant arose from the fact that traditionally the landlord not only kept and verified accounts of advances but also settled all conditions for sale and division of the crop. He was abetted by the subservience, intimidation, and illiteracy of the tenant.

According to the situation, the landlord could present to the tenant terms involving completed transactions regarding the price of provisions advanced to him, the amount of interest charged for the period of the loan, the final quantity and quality of the harvest, his income from its sale, or a face-to-face agreement concerning the size of his share. Ordinarily accounts were settled once a year at harvest time; but variations even in this could rebound to the advantage of the planter. It is also of importance to note that the landlord resisted any attempt by the tenant to hold him to formal written agreements. That would contravene the paternalistic, primary relations which define the tenant as a nonjuristic, dependent juvenile.[7] Thus, according to T. J. Woofter and associates:

> the relations between landlord and tenant are traditionally informal. Detailed agreements are not usually worked out and contracts are practically never written. Such records of advances and repayments as are kept are almost always in the hands of the landlord. This becomes a complicated account when debts from previous years are carried forward and added to current advances. This situation places the absolute control of relationships in the hands of the landlord and the fairness of settlements is largely dependent upon his sense of justice. The tenant's only recourse is to move, which of course does not adjust his past transactions but merely enables him to seek more satisfactory conditions.[8]

After having subsisted on a modicum of provision, however, the tenant could find himself not only in debt but also restricted in his attempt to transfer from farm to farm.[9] In periods of labor shortage especially, the landlord relied upon state legislation to immobilize his workers. Laws were designed to prevent tenant families from moving until the crop was harvested in the fall or until all debts incurred as allowances were repaid. Since the books of the landlord were ordinarily the only record of the tenants' indebtedness, he could present them annually with end-of-year balances, including obligations to liquidate them at the next harvest. This well known situation, called *peonage,* achieved legal sanction in a number of states—Alabama, Florida, Georgia, Mississippi, North Carolina, South Carolina—and constituted traditional practice in others.[10]

Peonage lost favor during the great Depression, and has not resumed its earlier strategic role. During World War II, Gunnar Myrdal and his associates concluded: "We do not know whether the present shortage of farm labor has brought about any new increase in . . . debt-peonage. What we do know is that the whole legal system previously gave the tenants but little protection against such abuses and that, so far, there has been no fundamental change in this legal system . . . . It is certain, anyway, that there is some debt-peonage left."[11] The more recent advances in mechanization of farm production in the region and the Negro's newfound status in the law have doubtless reduced the practice to a minimum.

Intimidation

Nothing, perhaps, indicates so well the continuity of conditions of bondage than the planter's conception of himself as inheriting the prerogative to punish physically the tenant and members of his family, sometimes including females, for breaches of rules and practices. Informal physical punishment constitutes the ultimate source of coercion and intimidation directed against Negroes of the South. The worst manifestations occurred in rural plantation areas. The immediate causes of physical chastisement included charges of disrespect, stealing, refusal to work, and other forms of disobedience. Allison Davis and associates found stealing to be the most common reason for whippings. They explain: "The fact that stealing is the charge upon which most beatings are justified is the result both of the fact that the ownership of property is the basic principle of the society and of the fact that stealing is the most frequent offense of tenants."[12]

The most serious aspect of this form of intimidation, however, was that the formal judicial and police systems of the states condoned it. Colored people inevitably came to feel that, for them, the country was ruled by men, not by laws. The landlord or his agents administered floggings, even lynchings, with no fear of the consequences. "Threats are usually as effective as the use of violence because colored workers realize that the threats of white landlords are supported by the whole caste system. . . ."[13] The practice must be viewed as a basic form of social control in the South. And from there the tradition of assaulting Negroes with impunity spread over the rest of the nation.

Planter aggression has been expressed by such derogatory terms as "nigger," "Sambo," and "boy." In the Black Belt these epithets were commonly used by the sheriff and his deputies, sometimes almost as effectively as the whip. To call the adult person "nigger" was to assume accommodation to the forces of intimidation. Its implied challenge could be used as a test of the efficacy of more concrete racial controls. To address the Negro man as "boy," as the planter ordinarily did, was to strike at the very roots of his manhood, independence, and self-esteem. In the Deep South it was a constant reminder of his inferior status. Childlike personalities and behavior, according to Raper, could be viewed as a direct outcome of plantation organization and practices:

> The improvidence and dependence of the plantation workers rest primarily upon the demands of the plantation: they must be amenable to instructions, must live in the houses provided, must accept the merchant's and landlord's accounting, must remain landless. The very life of the plantation system is threatened when the tenants accumulate property, exhibit independence.[14]

Irresponsibility

Probably the most costly aspect of the system for its colored members has been its tendency to generate irresponsibility among them. Irresponsibility tended to become a trait of the Negro masses. It contributed to the instability of their family life and to the slovenly state of its physical upkeep. It has been doubtless accountable for the disreputable community existence that followed when the group moved into towns and cities, as well as for the relatively weak incentives toward formal education.

Myrdal recognizes this point when he says that the Negro

57

tenant is "given to understand that his racial status provides an excuse for not being able to shift for himself, and that modest acceptance of a low position would rate a reward bigger than that offered for courageous attempts to reach a higher position."[15] Stupidity, as a cultural trait among Negroes, has had its value, particularly among slaves. It was nurtured by masters who looked upon any initiative with suspicion. Slaves, on the other hand, tended to cultivate it as a means of avoiding all undirected or unsupervised work, and as an explanation for idleness. Even though it has now lost much of its original utility, the tendency to appear stupid still tends to persist, especially among the Negro lower classes. In another age, both white and Negro comedians—Bert Williams, Amos and Andy, Stepin Fetchit—simulated and exploited this situation, portraying stupidity as an elementary characteristic of the group.[16]

Manifestly, then, the primary purpose of labor exploitation on the plantation necessarily curtailed and perverted the existence of its black masses; it denied them access to the inherent individualism and competitiveness of the dominant American way of life. There has been, moreover, an abiding interest in maintaining these traditional traits of racial inferiority.

A Word on Migration

The continual movement of both whites and Negroes from the Deep South into other parts of the country tends to keep the nation alive to the culture of racism, the "seedbed" phenomenon already referred to. On the whole, the "push" of the Negro population from the rural South has been greater than the inducements or "pull" of the cities. Both, of course, have operated to determine the extent and direction of the movement.[17] Factors contributing to the push include: relative severity of labor exploitation on southern farms, invasion of the boll weevil reaching disaster proportions from about 1910,[18] soil erosion and depletion, major transfers of cotton farming to western states, labor recruitment in the South during World War I, economic depressions of the early twenties and thirties, New Deal and subsequent limitations of farm acreage, and, most recently, mechanization of cotton and tobacco production.[19] The pull of the cities gained momentum as their colored population expanded and lines of communication between acquaintances multiplied. Contributing factors include: greater freedom from exploitation and social abuse, higher income and public relief, improved opportunities for economic and educational advancement, increased political recognition, and diversification of urban life.[20]

There seems to be nothing to indicate future reversal of the trek of Negroes from agricultural pursuits in the South. Reversal calls for success as a businessman on the farm under increasingly severe competition. The prospects, however, appear to support Beale's conclusion that "if the widespread and long entrenched disadvantages under which Negro farmers operate are not soon corrected, Negro farmers may well disappear as a significant group in American agriculture before the end of the twentieth century."[21]

The problems of race relations will continue to be associated with the American metropolis. The great cities are confronted with the heritage of racial pathologies from the rural South in addition to those inherent in the urban situation. The migrant, as L. V. Kennedy puts it, is involved in "a double adjustment from life in the South to life in the North and from rural conditions to those prevalent in a highly organized urban center."[22] In the urban milieu his immediate and abiding problem remains principally that of opportunity for employment.

Chapter 5

A Place in the Sun

The principal hope for the Negroes' cultural inclusion in American society centers about their success as businessmen. An important secondary avenue is the urban job. If the goal of participation in entrepreneurship is ever to be achieved, it must come largely through training and the possibility of advancement.

Eli Ginzberg points out that Negro employment is a dependent function of white attitudes:

> the key determinants of the growth of minority group employment are noneconomic forces, such as changed attitudes and behavior of the white majority with respect to minorities. The changes in attitudes that have opened up new opportunities for Negroes are reflected in hiring policies, in the educational and training programs available to them, in their eligibility for trade union membership, and in other ways.[1]

60

One is tempted to ask: are attitudes self-generative and self-modifying? Obviously there are two essential variables: the significance of changes in the economic status of Negroes and the forces limiting these changes.[2] Attitudes of the "white majority" do not constitute independent variables and are not self-generative. Moreover, race prejudice cannot be satisfactorily explained as deriving fundamentally from biological data for the facts remain but relevant attitudes change radically. These attitudes may be properly explained as derivatives of economic interests; this does not imply that such attitudes may not be diffused or signify a cultural lag.

Probably few would seriously question the fact that slavery involved both blacks and whites in a "peculiar" economic system of production. Besides their major master-selected employment on plantations,[3] slaves were allowed to compete with white workers, including white craftsmen, in southern cities. In reality, however, "the white mechanic was competing with the slave owner whose cheap slave labor, financial resources, and political power gave him every advantage."[4] Table 2, derived from a census of occupations for Charleston, S.C., in 1848 (with minor corrections from reference to the original by myself), suggests the intensity of that relationship.

It is from this type of structure and tradition that patterns of American racial attitudes and practices derive; and of greatest importance is the realization that it might have been to the interest of the employer—here the master—to employ Negro slaves over the objections of white workers. In a reference to this tradition during Congressional Hearings on the 1964 civil rights bill, Senator Jennings Randolph declared:

> Now . . . gentlemen, the word 'discrimination' does not appear in this legislation. We are today considering more than just discrimination. We have approached, or we are actually at, one of the greater watersheds of history. We are thinking in terms of repairing those ill practices which have been prevalent for a century, and which had their roots in two centuries of slavery.[5]

Soon after the Civil War an accumulation of state laws had a most telling effect on the Negro's economic ambitions and on the planter's correlative interests. For instance, one of those discriminatory laws proclaimed that "no person of color in South Carolina could practice the trade or business of an artisan, mechanic, or shopkeeper or other employments on his own account unless he had purchased a

Table 2

Selected Occupations of Male Workers by Race in Charleston, South Carolina, 1848

Occupations	Male Slaves	Free Negroes	White Males
Apprentices	43	14	56
Bakers	39	1	35
Blacksmiths & Horseshoers	40	4	49
Cabinetmakers	8	0	26
Carpenters	110	27	117
Coachmakers & Wheelwrights	3	1	26
Coopers	61	2	20
Masons & Bricklayers	68	10	60
Millwrights	0	5	4
Painters & Plasterers	25	4	18
Printers	5	0	65
Ship's Carpenters & Joiners	51	6	52
Tailors and Capmakers	36	42	76
Tinners	3	1	10
Upholsterers	1	1	10

Source: Robert Evans, Jr., "The Economics of American Negro Slavery," in Report of the National Bureau of Economic Research, *Aspects of Labor Economics* (Princeton, 1962), p. 189. Derived from J. L. Dawson and J. W. DeSaussure, *Census of the City of Charleston, S.C., 1848,* Charleston, S.C., 1849, pp. 29–35.

license from the judge of the District Court."[6] In this way the black labor supply of the plantations was protected. But the significant fact is that any people who could be thus imposed upon with impunity must expect extreme contempt: generically, therefore, race prejudice followed economic expression.

As Kenneth M. Stampp points out, "the economic degradation of the Negroes strengthened the white man's belief in their innate conviction that for Negroes to possess substantial political power was unnatural, even absurd."[7] Furthermore, it has been observed that those aspects of the Negro's personality and behavior which most seriously impeded his economic progress—improvidence, apathy, self-hatred, family disorganization—are equally the product of slavery and its aftermath.[8]

The Key

In an important sense, then, the job may be considered vital in race relations. According to W. Willard Wirtz, secretary of labor, "President Kennedy . . . made clear in his civil rights message the fact that he considered this whole matter of *fair employment practices* basic to the whole civil rights program."[9] Elementary group frustration tends to center about employment deprivation. (And, let us remark incidentally, this problem does not arise among castes in a caste system.)

Roy Wilkins put it this way before a Congressional committee: "Although the affronts in public accommodation are most abrasive to the spirit, the deeper hurt, the one that ramifies all other areas of living, is economic deprivation and discrimination."[10] Similarly, David J. McDonald, president of the United Steelworkers of America, emphasizes the direct consequences of employment limitations:

> There is no insult like the refusal of a job or a promotion because of color. And there is no sense of frustration which can match the frustration of the unemployed. Until we deal with that problem we will not truly deal with the racial problem in America today.
> I have no way of proving this, of course, but it is my firm belief that if Negroes could obtain true job equality, the other facets of discrimination would quickly disappear. But even if I am wrong, it is self-evident that the Negro will truly achieve the recognition which he seeks, and to which he is entitled, only when he achieves equality in the area of employment.[11]

If functional limitations in our society constitute its primary social frustration, they will also determine the nature and direction of unrest among the group.

Senator Hubert H. Humphrey admonishes: "Anyone familiar with the basic causes of racial unrest and turmoil in the country knows that until we come to grips with the problem of job discrimination and inequality of job opportunities, as well as the inequality of job training and education, we will be considering only partial solutions to the civil rights crisis."[12]

Basis of Responsibility

In a social system such as ours, it is sometimes difficult to assign determinative force to factors affecting social problems. Sometimes indeed it may seem impolitic for the social scientist even to make the attempt. Exclusion of potential employees from legitimate areas of the productive system means discrimination and thus observable behavior: behavior, however, which may not necessarily be purposeful or invidious. The practice may have become an expected way of life and thus difficult to isolate and extirpate. As W. Willard Wirtz points out, it must be realized "that a good deal of [employment] discrimination . . . has become institutionalized." And Henry Spitz, general counsel of the New York Commission on Human Rights, finds "Discrimination . . . so ingrained in our national life that it cuts across the entire board, and it all depends on how intensively you probe in any one particular field [of employment] as against another."[13]

Effects Upon Learning

In short, then, employment discrimination has had pivotal cultural consequences for Negroes. It has generally limited their aspirations, dulled their interest in production, and severely curtailed the range of their skills. It has usually led them into a posture of functional unreadiness. "Many technical and professional jobs are available," says John F. Henning, undersecretary of labor, "and cannot be filled because minorities are not traditionally chosen to fill them. Negroes who are forced to take jobs beneath their capabilities and cannot aspire for advancement do not inspire their children to improve their education to meet a similar blank wall."[14] Consequently, education becomes of less value to Negroes than to whites, and we should expect to find "many Negroes overqualified for the jobs they hold."[15]

But the societal conditions that serve to restrict their access to employment also leave them inadequately educated for normal employment demands. It follows that even if all occupational avenues were instantly made accessible, the present generation would find itself unprepared to take advantage of them. It is to this situation which Whitney Young, late executive director of the National Urban League, refers when he says:

> We have no illusions that a complete absence of employment discrimination will immediately solve the problem of unemployment for many Negro citizens since many failed to secure the skills needed in a modern work world because they felt it was useless and because of economic reasons.[16]

But the question of allocating responsibility for characteristic patterns of Negro employment remains. Although in specific situations the variables may be complicated, there exists a hierarchy of influences consistent with societal trends. Positive employment discrimination seems to rest primarily with employers and their employment agencies, and secondarily with labor organizations. These three interact with and generate negative racial attitudes among the generality of whites. Let us consider them specifically.

Role of the Employer

We have made frequent allusions to the consequences of thralldom in the economic progress of Negroes. No other American minority has had a comparable experience. The masters' control was for all practical purposes absolute, and very much of the subsequent political history of the South revolves around the struggle of the successors of that powerful oligarchy to continue pre-Civil War racial status relations. Reconstruction, we should remember, was not a *direct* accommodation between the freedmen and their former masters but rather between the two great regional interest groups. The newly liberated were too unprepared for significant, direct participation; and the partially subdued oligarchy was not ready to accept them as face-to-face competitors.

Because of this inherent opposition by planters and businessmen, the civil rights conferred upon blacks by the Congress were of relatively little immediate value. Charles and Mary Beard sum up the situation:

> It was an almost insuperable task which the Republican administration encountered in trying to give civil rights to a class that had no economic power or social organization. Seeing the logic of the situation, the radical wing of the party proposed to face it by transferring to the freedmen a part of the soil they had tilled; but, when asked for a bill of particulars, the advocates of this heroic remedy surrendered. The slaves had not been accustomed to any village cooperation akin to that practiced by the servile peasants of old Europe. They did not have historic rights in cottages and plots of land. They knew little or nothing about the managerial side of agrarian economy. If land was given to them outright, there was little reason to believe that they could find the capital with which to develop it or could show the proprietary skill or knowledge necessary to hold it against speculators and sharpers in general. Obviously any effort to establish the ex-slaves on an economic foundation involved im-

65

mense difficulties even if the idea of confiscating the land as well as the master's personal property had been acceptable to the majority in Congress.

In these circumstances the Washington government, apart from attempts to give temporary economic relief through a freedmen's bureau, confined its work on behalf of the Negroes mainly to conferring civil and social rights upon them in paper proclamations.[17]

A remarkable and probably unique tradition currently affecting Negro employment is that, for hundreds of years, their major employers looked upon their education and training, sometimes with good reason, as a portent of social disaster.

Economic Costs of Job Discrimination

Attempts have been made to calculate economic costs to the nation, region, or community of partial and inefficient use of available nonwhite labor. According to the National Alliance of Businessmen: "Every year billions of dollars are lost in income and spent on welfare because of unemployment. But there is a greater cost, a human one."[18] The economic loss incurred or income foregone, through inadequate employment or restricted use of this major factor of production, has been assessed in terms of gross national product.

John F. Henning, undersecretary of labor, reported to a senate committee that "if . . . nonwhites were able to make the same contribution to production, given their present educational attainment, GNP could be increased by about 1.8 percent." If, however, we consider resulting changes in the occupational structure of nonwhites, which would enhance productivity of the self-employed and thus "entrepreneurial income," we should expect the gain in GNP to increase by as much as 2.5 percent (1963), or about $13 billion. Henning reasons, furthermore, that if nonwhites were allowed not only to produce freely on the basis of actual educational skills but also on the assumption that they were as fully educated as whites, they would add *in toto* 3.2 percent to the gross national product: some $17 billion. The author concludes "that we are wasting about one-third of the potential contribution of the nonwhite workers."[19]

Other studies have reached similar conclusions. For instance, James G. Maddox and his colleagues—after taking into consideration the smaller income of Negroes relative to educational attainments, differences in the occupational structure of whites and Negroes due to discrimination, and differences in educational and training pattern—assert that "the total estimated loss in Negro earnings resulting from discriminatory practices in employment and inequalities in educational opportunities was $13 billion. This was approximately 2.7 percent of GNP in 1959."[20] The 1966 *Economic Report of the President* placed the figure for unbiased employment as high as 4 percent of GNP, or a racial deficiency of about $27 billion.[21]

It seems obvious, then, that if equal opportunities to acquire education and skills together with the chance to employ them without racial discrimination were available, nonwhites would be able to make a greater significant economic contribution to the total economic production of the United States. There are also social costs, less easy to measure but hardly less vital to the welfare of the people.

Social Costs

We have attempted to emphasize the central place occupied by our peculiar form of economic organization within the social system. Generally speaking, the hierarchy of influences seems to move from business organization, labor organization, unemployment and employment, and cultural parity indicated by opportunity for education and training. This follows a simple but fundamental principle. C. B. Spaulding puts it thus: "If we look at any society, we are likely to note that the value system and the societal organizations generally give expression to the interests and needs of those who are [its] most dominant and active members."[22]

We may therefore expect the actions of businessmen and the vicissitudes of the society controlled by them to affect significant trends in race relations. President Roosevelt dealt with the economic position of the lower classes in such a way as to give impetus to the current movement for racial integration. As Ginzberg and Eichner point out:

> In seeking to stimulate the economy and alleviate the effects of depression, the federal government during the 1930's did more to assist the Negro than any government, federal, state or local, had done in the entire prior history of the nation. The government had not suddenly become deeply concerned about the Negro, but it was determined to play an active role in directing the economy and in improving the status of vulnerable groups in the society—and the Negro was in the direct path of these efforts.[23]

67

Yet the problem still persists, largely because there remain effective "citadels of conservatism"; and, as might be expected, they are mostly to be found in the South. In a discussion of resistance to change in that region, Marvin Hoffman and John Mudd concluded: "The white community wants no part of a program in which Negroes participate as equal partners, now or in the future. No effort to deal with the root causes of poverty is likely, since the social policy of the white power structure has been to preserve a sufficient supply of cheap unskilled labor and, when this population becomes superfluous, to encourage emigration."[24] The Deep South thus continues to be the reservoir of opposition to economic change. Such groups as the National States Rights Party, financed by businessmen, organize efforts to oppose cultural development of the race throughout our country.

Daniel P. Moynihan puts it as follows:

At a time when most of the people in this country are making more money than ever, we have many people who are property-less in the most personal sense. They possess no education, no position, no connections. Our economic system isn't using them. This is a problem American business must face. If American business doesn't face it, we could become the kind of country that you and I don't want, that nobody wants, but that's the way it might turn out.[25]

Thomas Pettigrew thinks the changes sought in race relations go to the very heart of American social organization; he asserts:

I predict that as the reform movement proceeds through the 1960's, some basic structural changes in American society will have to occur before viable race relation solutions are possible. These changes include wider employment, a different taxation base, an extension of the minimum wage to cover service workers, and massive retraining. Clearly, the problem we are trying to solve transcends the boundaries of civil rights and reaches into the basic structure of American society.[26]

If racial subordination derives from "free competition" and individualistic economic planning by businessmen, then logically the situation could be reformed only by some sort of central economic planning. This seems also to be the view of Nat Hentoff:

The point is that planning need not be synonymous with regimentation. A democratically planned economy, based on the application of resources to the meeting of the genuine needs of all Americans, can provide much more diversity of opportunity for meaningful work and leisure than now exists. Poverty can be eradicated without creating overstuffed homogeneity. On the other hand, a fragmentarily planned economy, such as ours now is, cannot solve the human problems of automation and will not allow most of the poor to escape from their ghettos. . . .

Although the odds at present are heavily against a major re-education of the electorate within this decade, the civil rights actionists may startle us again. The ultimate irony in American race relations may yet be that the bitter insistence of the Negro revolt will have provided the initial impetus for basic social and economic change for all Americans.[27]

This is not the occasion for an analysis of elementary social change in American society. Perhaps the problem of race relations has been moving in the wake of that change rather than serving as its cause. And yet it is difficult to see how Negroes can acquire economic and political freedom and equality, especially in the South, without some major displacement of American conservatism.

The Challenge Accepted: Hard-Core Unemployment Faced

In the sixties, amid the rise of popular sentiment against the hardships of the Negro job seeker, the United States government assumed leadership in a concerted effort to abolish "hard-core" unemployment, particularly in the black ghetto. This was unprecedented in that it sought to change the character of the community by involving white businessmen directly in the process. Instead of relying completely on the support of the chronically unemployed by welfare payments, it was decided to eliminate them through special education, training, and absorption in industry.

There have been many programs concerned with the training and hiring of unemployed workers, especially since the passage by Congress in 1962 of the Manpower Development and Training Act, but it was not until 1967 that action became directed primarily at the hard-core unemployed.[28] In that year the U.S. Department of Commerce estimated that there were 500,000 hard-core unemployed in the major cities of the nation.

President Lyndon B. Johnson sent a special message to Congress in January 1968 requesting 2.1 billion dollars to finance a manpower program, to be developed jointly with business, in an effort to find employment for these disadvantaged workers by June 1971. In an explanation of the plan, a representative of the Department of Commerce said to a conference of business leaders meeting in St. Louis on January 26, 1968: "We [the federal government] will pay the difference between the cost of training a normal job applicant and training a hard-core unemployed applicant. . . .If it costs $500 to train a normal applicant and $2,500 to train a disadvantaged applicant, we will pay the $2,000 difference. If you agree with this basic concept, then we ask you to come up with proposals for your company."[29] Congress did not grant the full financial support requested by the president.

To meet this challenge, however, a National Alliance of Businessmen (NAB) was organized early in 1968, and its program was called "Job Opportunities in the Business Sector (JOBS)." The purpose of the Alliance was to secure jobs for the hard-core unemployed in some 130 cities where the group was set up on a community-wide basis. Contracts involving cost of training and employment of disadvantaged workers were made with a representative of the Department of Labor. "The Alliance team in each city is composed of business executives on loan from their companies, whose function it is to secure job commitments from community business leaders, and a representative of the U.S. Department of Labor, who facilitates the actions required to recruit the disadvantaged and refer them to jobs."[30]

A critical difference between this program and earlier manpower training plans was that businessmen not only assumed responsibility for recruitment of black chronically unemployed workers but also for developing ways and means of training and holding the worker on the job. The programs ranged from advice and counsel about physical appearance, transportation, and attitude on the job to reorientation discussions with the immediate supervisors of the new workers.[31]

It has been recognized that the racial attitudes of fellow employees could be crucial in any attempt to accommodate the disadvantaged worker. To assuage the impact of this relationship the help of labor unions had to be sought. The AFL-CIO established a Human Resources Development Institute to support the JOBS program in various cities. The HRDI—sometimes called the "buddy system"—trained regular rank and file workers to affiliate personally on a one-to-one basis with the new employees to help them through the probationary periods.

Success of Hard-Core Employment Program

Role of the Business Community

The program is complex, still in transition, and therefore constantly being reorganized or modified.[32] Two aspects of the movement seem to point to the future: (1) society seems to be moving into a position where it cannot comfortably allow adult citizens, able to work, to go unemployed and thus to rely for economic support either upon welfare payments or criminal activities; (2) society seems to realize that it cannot continue to allow private industry, which controls some six out of every seven urban jobs, to disregard the training and employment needs of disadvantaged workers. Perhaps it is this apparent determination which introduces an element of finality in the movement: the program cannot and must not be allowed to fail. In other words, a significant group of employers have seemingly come to regard joblessness among the hard-core unemployed as partly their own problem.

In 1969 the National Alliance of Businessmen (NAB) reported that thousands of private firms in some 130 cities had successfully hired and trained hard-core people for work previously performed only by those already educated and trained. And they added: "It has been abundantly clear, in the Alliance's first year, that the American business community can and will rise to this challenge with vigor and determination."[33] The following excerpt from a *Life* magazine editorial titled "Business Zeroes In on Poverty" (Dec. 15, 1967) further suggests the changing temper of this group:

> Like Ford's and others', G. E.'s experience with slum-recruited labor has been discouraging: most applicants cannot meet minimum standards, those hired show record absenteeism and turnover, etc., etc. "There is nothing to be gained, and perhaps something to be lost, by arguments over whose fault it is that many people are so poorly qualified for productive work. It exists as a fact," said [Gerald] Phillippe, [chairman of the General Electric Company, in a speech before NAM's Congress of American Industry.]
>
> So instead of waiting for slum Negroes to shape up, he urges business to change its traditional testing, interviewing and training methods. "Instead of employment practices that screen *out* people, we need ways to screen them *in*." Phillippe added that if government jobs should prove to be the principal solution to this problem, "it would mean a failure by business leadership." Nor is he talking about WPA-type or custodial jobs, but jobs with a

future that would bring slum families into the mainstream of American life.[34]

To meet the problem some businessmen have attempted to move in three principal directions: to employ qualified Negroes in areas previously closed to them (for example, a few companies now regularly recruit white-collar workers in Negro colleges); to provide, at their own expense, apprenticeships and other training to prospective Negro employees; to hire and train hard-core unemployed largely at government expense.

Although many claims of signal success have been made, a number of studies have shown that relatively little has been accomplished in the way of fundamental change in the labor market position of these workers.[35] Significant improvement still depends mainly upon tight labor supply, pressure from Negro militants, and governmental watchfulness.

The Question of Quotas

We have stated that the AFL-CIO has expressed willingness to cooperate in the employment programs for the Negro lower-class worker. It should be recognized, however, that certain important reservations still remain. One of these is the need for preferential treatment of the traditionally disadvantaged worker. "Positive hiring quotas," suggest the editors of *Newsweek,* "may . . . become necessary if Negroes are to be assured real equality of opportunity."[36] Quotas may alter the trend of white workers to reject integrated situations, and may forestall tokenism in black employment. On this point Charles Silberman argues:

> A formal policy of non-discrimination, of employing people "regardless of race, color, or creed," however estimable, usually works out in practice to be a policy of employing whites only. Hence Negroes' demand for quotas represents a necessary tactic: an attempt to fix the responsibility for increasing employment of Negroes on those who do the hiring (or in the case of the trade unions, on those who control access to the job.) As soon as we agree that special measures are necessary to overcome the heritage of past discrimination, the question of numbers—of how many Negroes are to be hired in what job categories—inevitably arises. Not to use numbers as a yardstick for measuring performance is, in effect, to revert to "tokenism." The point is not whether there is some "right" number of Negroes to be employed—obviously there is not—but simply that there is no meaningful measure of change other than numbers.[37]

In this respect, however, leading labor unions have mostly remained adamant. The position George Meany takes in the following statement suggests the general attitude of white organized labor toward assimilation of the disadvantaged black worker:

> Some advocates of equal employment opportunities have urged that, because Negroes have been discriminated against in the past, they should be given special preference in hiring today.
>
> Such superior hiring preference, or superseniority in layoffs, would be designed to give the Negroes a greater, and consequently unequal, priority in hiring and job tenure.
>
> I do not believe such preference is justified. No individual white worker should be penalized for past practices in which he may have had no voice. Furthermore, these demands reject equality of opportunity; they would merely replace one kind of discrimination for another.

As such, Meany concludes, they should be rejected.[38] This systematic unwillingness to relax tradition in order to accommodate the outsider tends to generate militancy among Negroes.

Militancy and the Job

A word should be said about Negro militancy, and the motivation of businessmen. It has probably been conceded that rioting in the ghettos has had some positive residuum. The central cities, no doubt, will continue to be the ecological heart of capitalism, and it has been physically vulnerable. Negroes cannot be permanently locked into their ghettos at sundown as Jews were in many medieval cities. More and more the police are becoming incapable of restricting their mobility.

Most leading businessmen would probably say that provision of more jobs alone will not eliminate violence in the slums; and yet, according to their own estimates, there seems to be no other single remedy. In an appeal to businessmen in an effort to solicit their cooperation in finding employment for ghetto dwellers, Henry Ford II warned: "It is no longer merely a matter of social justice and principles of democracy. Our very national unity and domestic peace are at stake."[39]

We are not suggesting that riots are reasonable or reliable means of achieving equality of opportunity for Negroes—they have been too erratic and socially costly. Their purpose is too generalized and ill-expressed, their leadership scattered. Employers tend to relax as soon as the mass flare-up in the ghetto has been appeased or brought under control. As early as 1970, it was said:

> One or two years ago, the fear of riots in the black ghetto was a major spur to equal employment opportunity programs, especially in retail trades, utilities, and transportation companies which served the ghetto. That fear has now abated considerably. At one time it was possible to make some gains through *moral suasion,* but the power of persuasion appears to have abated as companies have become more aware of the full cost implications of proposed changes in their employment practices.[40]

We are not certain that "moral suasion" has lost its efficacy. This instrument was deliberately abandoned by militant Negroes operating within the nonviolent movement.

Responsibility of Government

In a situation where industry, labor, and even civil rights actionists have become indecisive and relatively remiss in their determination to bring the Negro people into the cultural mainstream, the critical burden of responsibility seems to remain with government. Indeed, even during the period of positive developments among business and labor leaders, politics had become a decisive catalyst.

Government can and does set employment goals, determine hiring quotas, and provide direct financial assistance to those companies which train and employ disadvantaged workers; and appoint special commissions, such as the Equal Employment Opportunity Commission, to oversee and control discrimination in employment and encourage development and execution of programs in private industry. State and local governments also have great power to insist upon the employment of the disadvantaged. There is, however, no substitute for vigilant action by the federal government.

President Lyndon B. Johnson seems to have been fully aware of the importance of this leadership. As part of his plan to play down the federal role in race relations, however, President Richard M. Nixon apparently relaxed this obligation. Such phrases as "benign neglect" cropped up early in his administration. The Johnson program thus fell apart. According to one source: "In a move which promises to have important long-range consequences, the Nixon Administration has undertaken to shift primary responsibility for planning and administering manpower development programs to the states and localities.''[41] We may expect the results of his decision to be similar to those of his plans for neighborhood control in the field of education; the very states and localities where enthusiasm and sympathy for the program are most vitally needed will most likely be uncooperative and resistant. But major laws and court decisions are already on the books; they, more than the political aberration, point the way to the future.

Chapter **6**

Place of Business and Black Capitalism

The matter we take up now goes to the very heart of the Negro problem in the United States. Presidential candidate Richard M. Nixon seemed to have sensed this when, on April 25, 1968, in a political broadcast, he advocated "black capitalism" as a major solution to the racial situation.[1] To the extent that Negroes become conscious of their vital stake in American society, to that extent also we should expect them to be solicitous about its preservation.[2] The way to its realization, however, has been devious and obscured. The organization of most small businesses among Negroes—businesses which mostly fail or necessarily remain small—do not reach the root of capitalist motivation.[3] As one journalist put it: "What blacks need and are entitled to is unrestricted access to the mainstream of economic life, and this is not going to be accomplished, for blacks any more than for whites, by ownership of small businesses in the ghetto."[4]

Attitudes of giants in business tend normally to trickle down to small businessmen. Accordingly, the white small businessman may also become motivated by some creative possibility "no bigger than a man's hand" on the horizon of his enterprise. There have been enough successes of this kind, in the United States especially, to warrant such enthusiasm. We should therefore expect most white small businessmen to assume the characteristic business posture.

What seems even more remarkable is that in certain respects the masses of white people also come to embody traits of the businessman. He has conditioned them to adjust normally to demands of *his society* for punctuality, attention to business, loyalty, rationalism, progress, ambition. Most professional men are thus, in orientation, small businessmen; and, of course, modern farming has become largely part of the business of capitalist production. The culture of the general white population especially tends to be disciplined by and to move in harmony with critical imperatives of the businessman's society. In its sermons, the church, especially the Protestant church, ordinarily emphasizes the morality of the businessman's behavior.

Meaning of Business among Negroes

And yet, for the Negro population, this vital avenue to personality development has been distorted and stymied by segregation and discrimination. It is not that Negro businessmen have been slow to see the way. One can find, even in antebellum literature, references to the emphasis which Negro leaders put upon the primary importance of business and upon elements of the capitalist spirit. Since 1900, the meetings of the National Negro Business League has provided a hospitable environment for applauding the achievements of Negro businessmen. As one advocate expressed it:

> The respect of other Americans for Negro personality depends probably more on the economic and commercial advancement of the Negro than on all other factors put together. This respect cannot be gained unless Negroes become efficient conductors of commercial and industrial enterprises.[5]

Marvin Harris emphasizes the crux of the difficulty: the hostile, distorted economic potential of the available Negro market. Henry A. Hill, President of the Riverside Laboratory, Inc., in Cambridge, Massachusetts, himself a Negro businessman, expresses the same idea when he says:

> For growth potential to materialize . . . Negroes must have not only adequate educational training but also full and free opportunities to move into United States industry. . . . We must . . . be welcome in the whole structure that is so characteristically a part of modern business. We must be welcome in sales, marketing, production, trade associations, and professional societies. We must also be able to travel as first-class citizens, to live in decent neighborhoods, in good houses, to welcome our associates to our dinner table, and to be welcome at theirs.[6]

The Negro businessman, then, should not be socially confined if he is to take advantage of the creative, economic prospects available in the larger capitalist society. He should not have to be preoccupied with his own freedom of movement or with that of his representatives; with the possibilities of a standing boycott against his products by the larger society; with white competitive aggression and laws limiting his access to the labor market; or with the drifting away of his clientele because of developing desegregation. Perhaps it may not be an exaggeration to conclude that American capitalism has thus far largely excluded the Negro from the chance of participating on its most inspiring and creative level. As a businessman, he has been circumscribed and turned back.[7]

Black Business: Rebuilding the Ghetto from Within?

The ghetto was never an area characterized by business enterprise, hence it is not likely to be rebuilt by what is known as *replacement* of lost businesses.[8] The ghetto has been mainly a residential area involving economically supplemental provisions. It has thus been defined by residential ecological processes—an influx of lower-class, black residents in the wake of an exodus of white dwellers, after some resistance. The ghetto has also signified extraordinary decay and collapse, particularly of private homes. The small high grade businesses that serviced the white community usually departed along with the whites and were followed by lower grade businesses of the cultural type that serviced the incoming Negro residents.[9] The flight or decline of the former white enterprises in the face of the different standards of the ghetto has thus been culturally determined.

Negroes do not ordinarily think of the ghetto as the most likely place for finding jobs; and they do not look mainly to neighborhood stores for their major consumption of goods. The ghetto, therefore, has not been conceived of as a place of commercial or industrial expansion. The great majority of Negroes work elsewhere in the metropolitan area.[10] Ghetto income has been largely acquired in white-controlled commercial and industrial enterprises outside the ghetto. The day starts with black (as well as white) workers moving into the normal production areas of the city. Sometimes they go to the suburbs for employment in larger factories or stores.

To say—as some Negro nationalists do—that white consumer-goods merchants take everything out of the black community and return nothing is to assume that the ghetto is productively self-sufficient. Apparently, however, the only reasonable civil right the Negroes might consistently claim, in this situation, is that of nondiscriminatory employment in or out of the ghetto.[11] The larger part of the sum total of income will always be located outside the ghetto. The major businesses of a great city are not ordinarily intended to serve the needs of residents in the city—let alone its ghetto inhabitants. People are drawn to its environs to produce goods for the world. The peculiar problem of the black businessman has been that of competition for as large a share as possible of the black workers' needs; and his approach has been mainly that of securing this business noncompetitively.

The ghetto, however, cannot properly be regarded as an underdeveloped country either by black nationalists or by white political leaders.[12] It cannot be successfully subjected to economic closure; and attempts to industrialize it would be to displace but not to eliminate it, by changing its function. As one writer puts it: "[The Negro] exports the ghetto's only asset, labor, for unlike frontiers, colonies, or underdeveloped nations, the ghetto has no natural resources to attract foreign capital investment."[13]

Rosenbloom and Shank say of black capitalism: "The effect on the income economy is bound to be marginal. In our opinion, manpower training, consumer education, improved public services, and similar strategies have greater immediate impact on the income of the poor than can entrepreneurship."[14]

What seems to be implied, then, is the following: Since we cannot have businesses of mainstream variety in their normal, ecologically defined locus, we shall think of the ghetto as a comparable societal area with potentials for creating its own economic demand and supply. In such a milieu, the small black business with governmental support may be made to thrive. This, however, involves intensified ghettoization, a deceptive movement toward black community self-sufficiency within the larger societal context of social desegregation.[15] Ghettoization facilitates exploitation of the poor by the unscrupulous among both blacks and whites, and it hastens the departure of the Negro middle class. The apparently successful use of black business as a leverage for social control in the ghetto may therefore be only transient.[16]

The Entrepreneur and Social Control

Denial of free access to entrepreneurship constitutes, therefore, the Negro's fundamental economic deprivation and social limitation. It truncates the social pyramid whose upper reaches are necessary to define and give meaning and animation to the base. It deprives the Negro population of its innate leadership and thus of social models for discipline and self-control. The way of life of the successful white businessman—whose every mannerism and social style tend to be observed and copied more or less consciously by the general white population, a phenomenon which gives consistency and substance to social norms—seems to remain relatively circumscribed, foreign, and culturally inaccessible to the Negro masses. At this critical nexus a socio-psychological hiatus apparently takes effect. Major white businessmen hardly serve the Negro as a "reference group." The powerful myth that every American citizen or his progeny is at least a potential member of the exemplary class hardly enlightens the Negro's social vision. The foundations of "Negro society" thus tends to be distorted; and this no doubt accounts for much of Negro behavior that sometimes seems erratic and inexplicable.

A genuine Negro bourgeoisie, like its white counterpart—as Mr. Nixon saw clearly—would self-interestedly direct its influence towards community prosperity and uplift because an orderly, progressive social climate is of elementary value to the businessman.[17] As a group, their control over the economic life of the masses would give them implicit authority to determine those ends. We shall see forthwith, however, that the employment capacity of Negro businessmen is necessarily miniscule and dependent; hence their ability and interest in exerting informal community leadership tends to be commensurably feeble.[18]

The Business Situation in Practice

Given the social situation, the question arises as to the specific achievements of Negro business enterprise. The Negro businessman remains largely outside the major forces of capitalism: foreign trade, international banking, wholesale transactions on commodity exchanges, direction of the money market, major manufacturing in metals, clothing, foods, lumber, and mass transportation. His opportunities have come largely from limited, small-scale, face-to-face distribution of specific consumer goods and services in segregated communities. Thus the larger the size of the Negro community, the wider has been its business prospects, but they remain qualitatively on about the same level. Thus, according to one recent observation: "Black businesses in Buffalo . . . are small, service-oriented businesses not requiring much skill or capital, largely on off-street locations serving small neighborhood markets."[19] Traditionally Negro businesses have been located particularly in the South.[20]

Table 3 shows the number and distribution of minority group firms operating in 1969 and their financial receipts compared to the country's total. Of the 322,000 minority-owned business enterprises, 163,000 were owned by Negroes, and 100,000 and 59,000 by Spanish speaking and all other minorities respectively. In terms of the percentage of all American firms, these "minority" firms came to 2.2, 1.3, and .8 percent respectively. The enterprises were heavily distributed among the retail trade and service industries. These two categories constitute about 100,000 of the Negro-owned establishments. A large number consisted of gasoline filling stations, grocery stores, eating and drinking places, beauty and barber shops, and miscellaneous retail stores.[21]

Total receipts of all Negro businesses, before deductions for costs of operations, were less than one-half of one percent (0.3 percent) of receipts for all American industry. Of the 163,000 Negro-owned firms, 125,000 had no paid employees and of these the average annual receipts, in 1969, were $7,000. The 38,000 firms with paid employees had average annual receipts of $95,000. These employer-firms accounted for 82 percent of the total receipts of all black-owned firms. They employed a total of 152,000 persons, an average of four employees per firm. Table 4 gives comparable figures for Spanish-speaking and other minorities. The Negro population ratio compared to the extent of business participation emphasizes the very limited capacity of the group to provide for its own employment.

As we should expect, Negro business organizations belong mainly to the category of individual enterprise. Accordingly, 148,000 of the 163,000 black-owned firms were registered as sole proprietorships, 11,000 as partnerships, and somewhat less than 4,000 as corpo-

Table 3
Comparison of Number of Firms and Business Receipts of Minority-Owned Firms to Total Business Activity

Industry division	Number of all firms*	Firms (1,000)							
		All minorities		Negro		Spanish speaking		Other minorities	
		Number of firms	Percent of all firms	Number of firms	Percent of all firms	Number of firms	Percent of all firms	Number of firms	Percent of all firms
ALL INDUSTRIES, TOTAL	7,489	322	4.3	163	2.2	100	1.3	59	.8
Contract construction	856	30	3.5	16	1.9	10	1.2	4	.4
Manufactures	401	8	2.0	3	.8	4	1.0	1	.2
Transportation and other public utilities	359	24	6.7	17	4.7	5	1.4	2	.6
Wholesale trade	434	5	1.2	1	.2	2	.5	2	.5
Retail trade	2,046	97	4.7	45	2.2	33	1.6	19	.9
Finance, insurance, and real estate	1,223	22	1.8	8	.6	8	.7	6	.5
Selected services	1,803	101	5.6	56	3.1	29	1.6	16	.9
Other industries and not classified	367	35	9.5	17	4.5	9	2.5	9	2.5

Receipts (million dollars)

Industry division	Receipts of all firms*	All minorities		Negro		Spanish speaking		Other minorities	
		Receipts	Percent of all receipts	Receipts	Percent of all receipts	Receipts	Percent of all receipts	Receipts	Percent of all receipts
ALL INDUSTRIES, TOTAL	1,497,969	10,639	.7	4,474	.3	3,360	.2	2,805	.2
Contract construction	92,291	947	1.0	464	.5	300	.3	183	.2
Manufactures	588,682	650	.1	303	.1	212	(Z)	135	(Z)
Transportation and other public utilities	106,040	395	.4	211	.2	115	.1	69	.1
Wholesale trade	213,196	939	.4	385	.2	275	.1	279	.1
Retail trade	320,751	5,178	1.6	1,932	.6	1,689	.5	1,557	.5
Finance, insurance, and real estate	86,670	539	.6	288	.3	109	.1	142	.2
Selected services	61,858	1,464	2.4	663	1.1	507	.8	294	.5
Other industries and not classified	28,481	527	1.8	228	.8	153	.5	146	.5

(Z) Less than .05 percent

*Based on data from Internal Revenue Service statistics of income for 1967.

Source: U.S. Bureau of the Census, *Minority-Owned Businesses: 1969*, Washington, D.C., 1971, p. 2.

Table 4

Comparison of Average Receipts for Minority-Owned Firms With and Without Paid Employees

Item		*Total*	*Negro*	*Spanish speaking*	*Other minority*
All minority-owned firms:					
Number	1,000	322	163	100	59
Receipts	million dollars	10,639	4,474	3,360	2,805
Firms with paid employees:					
Number	1,000	90	38	33	19
Receipts	million dollars	8,934	3,653	2,814	2,467
Receipts per firm	$1,000	99	95	86	131
Firms with no paid employees:					
Number	1,000	232	125	67	40
Receipts	million dollars	1,705	821	546	338
Receipts per firm	$1,000	7	7	8	8

Source: U.S. Bureau of the Census, *Minority-Owned Businesses: 1969,* Washington, D.C., 1971.

rations.[22] From this it appears that only about 3 percent of Negro business enterprises were incorporated. It was already recognized in 1929 that "more than ninety percent of Negro businesses . . . are individual in form. . . . This means that the businesses will hardly go beyond the life of the men who started them, . . .that [they] can never hope to expand as they should; and the larger syndicates will soon push them out because of their greater buying power and efficiency."[23]

Three categories of business enterprise, wholesale trade, manufacturing, and finance—especially banking—tend to constitute the heart of capitalist productivity; and in both the number of firms and income, as shown in table 3, Negro participation in these constitutes very much less than one percent of the American total. Of the 1,600 black-owned firms engaged in wholesale trade, the largest, numbering 240 with gross receipts of $95 million, as indicated by the 1969 census, dealt in groceries and related products.[24]

In manufacturing, "lumber and wood products," 1,300 firms had gross receipts of $51 million. The total of 3,000 manufacturing enterprises included: apparel and other textile products (162 firms), and chemicals and applied products (fifty-five firms). In 1969, the gross annual receipts of all Negro-owned firms engaged in manufacturing was about one-tenth of one percent of the total receipts of all American firms thus engaged.

Financial Institutions

There were 35 banking enterprises with gross annual receipts of $24 million and 104 insurance carriers with $133 million annual receipts.[25] These institutions presumably represent the center of the financial structure of the Negro business community. However, they constitute but a relatively small percentage of the resources available in this field. Both investments and savings, moreover, are likely to flow into the mainstream competitive market.

Without going into details of the differential operations and management of these financial institutions, certain observations relevant to race relations are in order. Although there are no complete statistics on the distribution of Negro savings and insurance among bank and insurance establishments, it has been estimated that only a small fraction of the total goes to Negro-owned financial institutions. Thus, in addition to the tendency to patronize white-owned banking firms, most Negro communities are not entirely provided with capital by Negro banks. Regarding life insurance, Andrew F. Brimmer observes that "the great bulk of coverage is provided by the leading insurance companies serving the general public. In fact, any one of the largest companies (such as Metropolitan or Prudential) probably has on its books far more coverage on Negro lives than the amount outstanding in all Negro-owned companies combined."[26]

This situation became the object of an extensive boycott in the early thirties among Negroes in Chicago, against the Metropolitan Life Insurance Company in order to induce employment of members of the race as agents. The editors of the *Chicago Whip*, a militant Negro newspaper, compared the number of jobs created by the relatively small Negro-operated insurance companies to the total exclusion of Negroes from employment by Metropolitan. With hardly any success, they asked Negroes to withdraw their patronage.

The insurance movement itself, one of the most settled areas of Negro business, took root at the turn of the last century when many white companies began openly to discriminate in rates (based upon higher mortality tables) and even to turn down Negro business altogether.[27] There are still many types of coverage that the Negro enterprise does not carry: group insurance, insurance against accident liability, fire and other property insurance.[28] Moreover, according to current trends, Negro enterprises encounter increasing competition from leading white risk-bearing corporations in the Negro insurance market.

The tendency of Negro-owned financial institutions to show profits in their service to the black public has been regarded as one of their principal values. Provision of capital to Negro entrepreneurs, who are likely to find general sources particularly stringent, constitutes another important function. Furthermore, Negro banking itself, relatively small though it is, still provides occupational opportunities and administrative involvement which are socially edifying and structurally significant for the group.[29]

Geographical Location

So far as geographic location is concerned, the Old South, the South Atlantic division, as shown in table 5, seems to be holding its own. In 1969 it was the area with the largest number of Negro enterprises, about 47,000, with gross receipts of $1,051 million. The East North Central followed with 30,000 firms and $1,009 million receipts.

Value of Segregation

The Negro businessman's inevitable dependence upon segregation for the expansion of his market has confronted him with obvious predicaments. Students of the subject have been concerned about its consequences. "Running like a theme through these pages," says Pierce of his own study, "is the dilemma of the Negro businessman who, as a Negro, disapproves of segregation but as a businessman has a vested interest in segregation because it creates a convenient market for his goods and services."[30]

One frequently hears nationalistic appeals for patronage, but there has been no concerted drive among Negro businessmen for continuance of segregation *per se*. The feeling seems to be that while segregation exists it should be utilized, but every social effort should be exerted toward its abolition. It is in this sense that Kinzer and Sagarin assert: "It is not the Negro in business that is faced with an ideological dilemma, so much as it is *American business* that is faced

Table 5

**Negro-Owned Firms and Gross Receipts
by Geographic Divisions, 1969***

Division	Number of Firms	Gross Receipts ($1,000)
UNITED STATES	163,073	4,474,191
New England	1,720	59,616
Middle Atlantic	22,672	615,454
East North Central	30,296	1,009,705
West North Central	6,339	178,565
South Atlantic	46,945	1,050,918
East South Central	13,248	404,277
West South Central	23,069	599,290
Mountain	1,801	54,251
Pacific	15,960	421,477
Not specified by area	1,023	80,338

*Source: U.S. Bureau of the Census, *Minority-Owned Businesses: 1969*, Washington, D.C., table 2.

with this dilemma."[31] This was written in 1950, before the modern nationalistic surge in race relations.

The Prospects

We have attempted to depict the potential role of the Negro businessman in race relations. What then are his prospects? One can cite many isolated instances of remarkable success.[32] Since, however, his record as a whole has been anything but impressive, the question of direction has been constantly raised. There seems to be three principal avenues more or less regarded as legitimate directions for the Negro businessman: (1) racial separatism and nationalism in order to monopolize the Negro community market, by force if necessary; (2) direct competition for an unlimited share in the mainstream economy—the way of the Jews; and (3) reliance mainly upon economic aid from government and from white private enterprise to gain a larger competitive share of the ghetto market.

The first of these movements has been both organized and spontaneous. White businesses in the ghetto have recently suffered

87

picketing and vandalism by both organized and unorganized groups. Members of such organizations as the revamped CORE and the Black Muslims have confronted white businessmen with conditions under which they could establish enterprises or continue to operate in the Negro community. This has contributed to the outflow of white small businesses, especially those engaged in services and other direct relations. The campaign, however, has obviously heightened concern for employment of Negroes in managerial positions by large corporations operating local outlets. It has also given certain Negro small businessmen a monopolistic chance in the ghetto. And yet, the process has not been a simple one. In 1968, for example, the Small Business Administration (SBA) observed:

> The extent of penetration of Negro ownership of business [in Washington, D.C.] appears to show no appreciable difference over the last decade. Most businesses were acquired by Negroes ten or more years ago. During these past ten years about the same number of businesses were acquired by whites from Negroes as were businesses acquired by Negroes from whites.[33]

Among the negative consequences are increasing isolation of the ghetto and out-migration of some of the most highly motivated and ambitious Negroes. Moreover, as already suggested, there has been no clear assurance that all the places of former white businesses, especially those involving technical skills, would be taken by Negroes. At least some of the traditional demands of residents would be transferred to businesses in other communities. Thus attempts to drive out the white businessman do not of themselves create situations leading to reciprocal growth of Negro business.

The second idea of working toward unlimited access to the larger market is clearly a legitimate ideal. It represents a perennial drive stimulated by economic forces in the mainstream. This, in fact, remains a traditional desideratum among Negro businessmen. We find it constantly expressed and advocated with approbation in their periodic conventions. It has been hindered, however, mainly by the devious obstructions of white racism and segregation. Even Negro professionals—lawyers, physicians, teachers—tend to be thus limited.[34] From this point of view the black businessman's concern about economic expansion into the open market becomes yet another aspect of the racial movement. It remains as yet an unrealized ideal. The government still conceives of the Negroes' aspiration in the world of business as directed toward and even restricted to the "Negro community."

Implementation of President Nixon's Approach

Just as President Johnson gave primary attention to problems of unemployment in the ghetto, so President Nixon, originally at least, viewed the situation as one requiring Negro businesses to achieve a self-sustained momentum. Civic-mindedness could be indirectly stimulated by creating black vested interest in it. It would serve business interests to keep alienated Negro citizens in line.[35] The President therefore urged development through such agencies as the Department of Commerce, the Small Business Administration, and the Office of Minority Business Enterprise. White corporations could lend their assistance voluntarily by means of private projects or as agents of the government. George Eckstein notes:

> Among the private agencies, there are the Urban Coalition, national and local; Coalition Venture Corporation, and Capital Formation, Inc., both working with the Coalition in New York; the Interracial Council for Business Opportunities (NAACP); the National Urban League, and some CORE units. In addition, some of the large banks, notably Chase Manhattan and First National City, have put special officers in charge of minority business loans.[36]

These are but a few of many national organizations and independent businesses that have shown some interest in supporting Negro business in the ghetto.

We are not concerned here with retracing the details of this development. No magic has been introduced. Business still has to make profits to remain active and the ghetto continues to be an especially limited environment.[37] In March 1969 President Nixon created a separate agency, the Office of Minority Business Enterprise (OMBE) to coordinate all efforts by the government to bring blacks and other minorities into the nation's economic mainstream.[38] In November of the same year this office in the Department of Commerce devised a program which seemed attractive to corporations; it was called Minority Enterprise Small Business Investment Companies (MESBICs).[39] Each MESBIC is sponsored by an established corporation which has to put up at least $150,000 of its own funds. The SBA agrees to add twice as much. Thus a MESBIC is primarily a lending institution with control of at least $450,000 capital.

The borrower, the Negro or other minority small businessman, would be obligated to both the lending corporation and the government. It is assumed that the corporation's equity in the MESBIC would not only give it concern for the security of the loan to the minority business but also a direct interest in the success of its client's enterprise. The minority businessman has to repay the loan with interest in about fifteen to twenty years. It is thus anticipated that MESBICs would even make money. Moreover, as Rosenbloom and Shank point out: "If high returns . . . happen to accrue, the presumption is that they will be plowed back into the minority communities and not flow out to further enrich the already affluent white community."[40]

The program has had considerable criticism mainly on grounds that if non-MESBIC, small businesses among Negroes are already subject to relatively high rates of failure, clients of the MESBICs would be even more so. "There is no incentive for substantial equity capital to move toward minority enterprise . . . and it is not realistic to expect new businesses to be successful if they use debt capital alone."[41]

By June 1970, only nine white companies had established MESBICs and perhaps only one, still not standing independently from the parent, could claim plausible success.[42] Secretary of Commerce Maurice H. Stans answered critics by saying in part: "The point is that now there are corporations investing in minority business; there are more minority Government contractors. There is more Federal money in minority banks. These changes will accelerate as time goes on."[43] The first and only black MESBIC was organized in 1973.[44]

Contributions of White Private Business

The projects of banks and private businesses supported by the government are myriad, and plans vary almost as extensively as the projects themselves.[45] The following illustrates the factors that could be involved in the promotion of a single black business. After considerable negotiation, Xerox Corporation of Rochester, New York, decided to establish a subsidiary among Negroes. It planned to employ about 100 blacks and to produce about $1,000,000 worth of transformers which the corporation promised to purchase. The project was housed in an abandoned clothing factory situated a few blocks from the site of Rochester's 1964 riots. Xerox trained the workers. A militant Negro minister headed the business. Financing included "a United States Department of Labor training grant of $445,677 as well as a mixture of federally backed loans and 'seed money,' totaling around $350,000, contributed by Rochester businesses."[46]

This business was started before the establishment of MES-BICs in 1969. The estimate of a Xerox representative is revealing. "The task," he said, "of starting this new business was difficult because we were responding to a social need rather than a business necessity in the form of a marketable product."[47] Although Negro managers of the firm praised it as an important advance in open market operations, it manifestly lacked the essential elements of commercial and industrial motivation. It had to be supported and patronized as a moral obligation; and there were no apparent prospects of its achieving independent, competitive existence. But it indicates the kind of business which Negroes should have been able to enter normally as businessmen.[48]

The basic illusion, as we have already intimated, seems to suggest that the ghetto constitutes an incipient nation—a black colony—which is destined to achieve independence and thus to be an economic and political duplicate of the United States. In October 1968, to illustrate, Howard Samuels, National Director of the SBA under President Johnson, told a gathering of Negro businessmen in Chicago that "*Project Own* is designed to treat the inner cities [the ghettoes] as underdeveloped nations by providing capital and talent to assist the residents in building their own businesses."[49] As we have indicated, this conception may harbor treacherous consequences. Apparently it has been responsible for more utopian thinking by and for American Negroes than has arisen among any legitimately national people during the last century.[50]

The Solution

Many reasons have been advanced for the insignificant role of Negroes in business: low income of the slums, lack of capital, lack of managerial skill, undisciplined and poorly trained labor, and so on.[51] It seems to us, however, that Negroes mainly do not have a hospitable *cultural milieu* for the growth of business among them. Irresistible hostility, open or implied, comes from both ghetto masses and white leadership. Small businesses in the ghetto, especially groceries and dry goods stores, tend to be looked upon as fair game. Black community rationalization for this attitude is that all business income accumulates through implicit fraud.[52]

Headlines such as the following, "Black Business Hit Hard by Ghetto Thieves,"[53] are common in the Negro press. Another mode of attack has been customer insistence upon credit with no intention of making settlements. The bad check is also common. Moreover, the small businessman is likely to maintain his store in conditions similar to the common deportment of this ghetto customers—disorderly and unclean. The amiable, confident attitude, the "salesman's face," the appearance of willingness and readiness to serve without being familiar—these are characteristics frequently not expected of Negro businessmen. Carolyn S. Bell remarks: "An incompetent repairman, a lackadaisical counterman, or a careless shop worker will waste materials, alienate customers, and cost more than he brings the firm in sales."[54]

Business, even small business, is at the forefront of Western cultural advancement. Its managers are the normal leaders; they tend to be self-assured and possessed of dependable "know-how." Rejection of such an awareness and attitude among Negroes by whites has been one of the critically limiting forces in the Negro's commercial advancement. "Clearly," concludes Alan Andreasen, "it is morally imperative that blacks be given the opportunities to develop the viable business system that white society, through denial and discrimination, has long prevented them from developing."[55] Apparently the most effective way to counteract this traditional white resistance would be nondiscriminatory employment of Negroes in managerial positions and in labor unions. This would also be consistent with the general economic trend away from small business constrictions.[56] Negroes will tend to feel included when they are in fact included. There is here, no doubt, a persistent element of the hen-and-egg situation. However, according to one observer: ". . . minority-group members rarely if ever hold . . . management positions. So the would-be ghetto entrepreneur may lack access to capital because he has been denied access to the employment that would give him the skills to manage capital."[57] Small business, as the Black Muslims seem intent upon showing, may thus rationalize a separate form of race relations.[58]

Progress in desegregation of the culture as a whole constitutes the ultimate force behind inclusion of Negro businessmen. It has been argued that since segregation produced the supportive, isolated market and the specialized business institutions, abolition of the ghetto would not only dissipate that market but also integrate its leadership. From his own study of the subject, Andrew F. Brimmer seems to reach similar conclusions:

> with a change in the aspiration among potential Negro businessmen, better preparation on their part and a genuine commitment to equal opportunity by leaders in the corporate business community, the future could be promising for a number of Negro businessmen. . . . Desegregation of the marketplace is already well underway and will require desegregation in the ownership and management of business enterprises as well.[59]

Complete statistics on this process are not available. Ever since the thirties, however, partly in answer to employment boycotts in Negro communities, an increasing number of local and chain dry goods department stores, groceries, gasoline stations, and similar retail establishments, has been turned over to Negro managers. Just as the first Negro sales employees in certain white business establishments were introduced tentatively into public outlets in Negro communities and then transferred to nonsegregation, personnel on the managerial level may be apprenticed and then integrated into the general economy.[60]

93

Chapter 7

Structure of Negro Labor

Unemployment

In any society, man's work identifies him with his social system; and, in our own, the primary preoccupation of maturing adults is that of finding and holding a job. Unemployment for him thus assumes the aspect of a personal tragedy. For Negroes as a whole, through good times and bad, it has ordinarily been a deprivation twice as severe as for whites. Between 1950 and 1953, for example, the ratio of Negro to white unemployment in the United States was about 1.8; it remained at 2.0 times or more for the long period between 1954 and 1969, had a dip to 1.8 in 1970 but returned to 2.0 in 1972. The generally high rate of unemployment among "teenagers" intensifies the problem still further. In 1970, black youth sixteen to nineteen years of age had an unemployment rate of about 29 percent compared to 14 percent for white.

This quantitative economic difference constitutes the basis for a qualitative difference in the cultural position of Negroes. Variations

94

in unemployment for both groups correlate with the business cycle but the trend for Negroes is more erratic. Rashi Fein observes: "The Negro frequently faces unemployment rates which—if faced by all workers—would be considered a national scandal."[1] It would indeed amount to a national economic calamity. Table 6 and chart III illustrate the relationship.

Table 6

**Unemployment Rates* by Color, Sex, and Age,
1960, 1968, and 1970**

Subject	Negro and Other Races			White		
	1960	1968	1970	1960	1968	1970
Total	10.2	6.7	8.2	4.9	3.2	4.5
Adult Men	9.6	3.9	5.6	4.2	2.0	3.2
Adult Women	8.3	6.3	6.9	4.6	3.4	4.4
Teenagers[1]	24.4	25.0	29.1	13.4	11.0	13.5

*The unemployment rate is the *percent* of the civilian labor force unemployed.

[1]"Teenagers" refer to persons 16 to 19 years of age.

Source: U.S. Department of Commerce, Bureau of the Cenus, *The Social and Economic Status of Negroes in the United States,* 1970, p. 49.

If the trend of the ratio of total nonwhite-white employment, as shown in chart III, were reversed, we might have had an encouraging argument for the future and grounds for belief that current economic policies are leading to the elimination of employment disparities between the races. It seems to point, however, in an opposite direction; and, incidentally, to the plight of Negro urbanization. The slight downward movement of the gap since 1968 is associated with generally higher unemployment.

As we should expect, unemployment tends to center in the slum areas of the great cities—especially areas populated predominantly by Negroes. Table 7 illustrates unemployment rates in these communities.

95

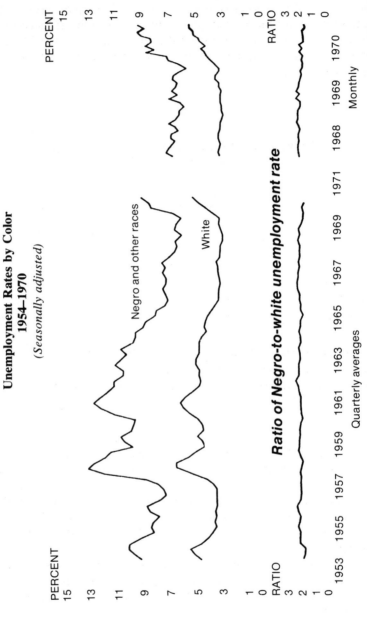

Chart III

Unemployment Rates by Color
1954–1970

(Seasonally adjusted)

Negro and other races

White

Ratio of Negro-to-white unemployment rate

Source: U.S. Department of Labor, Bureau of Labor Statistics, *Employment and Earnings*, Vol. 17, No. 7, January 1971, p. 13.

Table 7

**Unemployment Rates in Nine Slum
Areas, November 1966**

Unemployment rate in the United States	3.5
Unemployment rate in nine slum areas, average	9.3
Subemployment* rate (Unemployment and underemployment)	
Total, nine slum areas	32.7
Boston: Roxbury area	24
New Orleans: several contiguous areas	45
New York City: Central Harlem	29
East Harlem	33
Bedford-Stuyvesant	28
Philadelphia: North Philadelphia	34
Phoenix: Salt River Bed Area	42
St. Louis: North Side	39
San Francisco: Mission-Fillmore	25

*Subemployment includes (1) those actively looking for work, (2) part-time workers wanting full-time employment, and (3) full-time workers earning less than standard weekly wages.

Source: U.S. Department of Labor, *Social and Economic Conditions of Negroes in the United States,* October 1967, p. 97.

Young Negroes about to enter the labor force suffer the highest differential rate of unemployment; the most highly unemployed of this group are Negro female teenagers. In 1970, for example, black women eighteen to nineteen years of age had an unemployment rate of 33 percent compared to 12 percent for whites.[2] There has been a significant tendency, however, for the Negro unemployed teenager (16–19) to remain in school. Between 1963 and 1970, for example, the percentage of this group still in school increased from 22 to 34 percent.

Negroes experience not only disproportionately high rates of unemployment but also relatively long periods when they are out of work. In 1970, average long-term unemployment (fifteen weeks or more) for Negroes and whites was 1.3 and 0.7 percent of the labor force respectively. In other terms, nonwhites constituted 11 percent of the civilian labor force but 19 percent of the long-term unemployed.[3]

The relatively unfavorable unemployment status tends, moreover, to characterize the occupational structure from top to bottom.

97

Table 8 shows concentrations among manual workers and laborers. The 9.1 percent unemployed among white nonfarm laborers are not nearly so significant as the 10.5 percent for Negro and other races because laborers constitute a much larger number of the black labor force than they do the white.

Table 8

Unemployment Rates of Male Civilian Labor Force by Occupation and Color, 1970

Occupation	*Negro and Other Races*[1]	*White*	*Ratio of Negro and Other Races to White*
Total, Civilian labor force	7.3	4.0	1.8
Experienced labor force	6.6	3.6	1.8
Professional and technical	2.0	1.8	1.1
Managers, officials, proprietors	2.0	1.2	1.7
Clerical	5.2	3.2	1.6
Sales	4.0	2.7	1.5
Craftsmen and foremen	5.2	3.7	1.4
Operatives	7.5	5.7	1.3
Nonfarm laborers	10.5	9.1	1.2
Private household workers	(B)*	1.3	(B)*
Other Service workers	6.8	4.7	1.4
Farm workers	4.5	2.1	2.1

[1]Negroes represent over 90 percent of classification, Negro and other races or non-whites.

*Base too small to be shown separately.

Source: U.S. Department of Commerce, Bureau of Census, *The Social and Economic Status of Negroes in the United States,* 1970, table 50.

Unemployment among Negroes tends to stand out even more prominently when compared to that of other minorities. Table 9 shows the relatively high labor force participation rates of Japanese and Chinese and their low unemployment rates. The civilian labor force here is the sum of employed and unemployed persons (i.e., roughly persons who are able and willing to work but who did not have a job at the time of the survey.)

98

Table 9

**Labor-Force Participation Rates and
Unemployment Rates, by Race, 1960**

	Participation Rate	*Unemployment Rate*
	Total labor force as percent of the group's population	*Unemployed as per- cent of civilian labor force*
Negro	57.6	8.8
Japanese	61.3	2.8
Chinese	65.8	3.9
White	65.0	4.9

Source: U.S. Department of Labor, Bureau of Labor Statistics, *The Negroes in the United States,* 1966, p. 98.

Negroes are confronted by double risks of unemployment: the excesses induced by the normal fluctuations of business activity involving prosperity and recession; and by the relatively closed door set up mainly by employers. It is the latter force especially that creates the peculiar problem. The following pronouncement by Senator Joseph S. Clark suggests the sensitivity of Negro employment rates to the first, and the moral question involved in the operations of the latter:

> Our victories, when we win them, will be hollow and meaningless if we turn our backs on the pleas of our minorities, not for favoritism, but for an *equal chance to get a decent job* and thus bring their standard of living more nearly in line with that of other groups in the economy. To be always at the end of the hiring line; always the first to get the pink slip; always the sweeper or washroom attendant and never the machine operator or sales manager—this is the shameful role in which we have cast the 10 percent of our population whose skin is not white.[4]

In a study of the relatively rapid growth rate of manufacturing in the South, Alan Batchelder observes: "Manufacturing's southern migration to new markets and new sources of raw material has distributed American resources more efficiently. It has taken jobs to poor whites but not to poor Negro men. Between 1950 and 1960, the

99

number of jobs in southern manufacturing rose by 944,000. Of these 944,000 jobs, 12,000 went to Negro women (proportionately fewer than to white women); none went to Negro men."[5] The flight of industry from metropolitan centers to suburbs tends to have similar effects upon Negro labor.

Employment

A distinguishing fact of Negro employment is its peculiar structure: it is relatively weighted at its lower reaches. It has been changing slowly, however, toward the goal of equal employment opportunity.[6] In 1910, for instance, white-collar workers constituted 3 percent of the total occupational structure for Negroes but 23 percent of the total for whites. In 1970, as table 10 shows, the figures changed to about 28 and 51 percent respectively. Table 10 also emphasizes the fact that decreases in Negro private household workers, laborers, and farm workers continue to be significant. Outstanding increases for this same period, 1960 to 1970, are registered for professional and technical and for clerical workers.

These data verify similar conclusions by Jaffe and Gordon that there has been "more upward mobility among nonwhites especially in the white-collar occupations.[7] Improvement in job status, they explained, has been due, to a very considerable extent . . . to government action, both government hiring and the enforcement of fair employment practices." Among professionals and managers, for example, these writers point out, government employment accounted for 58 percent of the change (1950–1965) among whites and 70 percent among nonwhites.

Regarding employment by the national government, the U.S. Department of Labor concludes: "Negroes were 15 percent of all Federal Government employees in 1970 compared to 13 percent in 1965. However, Negroes held only 3 percent of the higher grade jobs under the Federal Classification Act, 4 percent of the higher grade Postal Field Service jobs, and less than 10 percent of the Wage Systems jobs paying $8,000 and over in 1970."[8]

The significance of the place of economics in race relations is particularly apparent in the racial employment situation in the South. In that region nonwhite employment is "concentrated much more heavily in low-paid, unskilled occupations than in other regions, whereas white employment is distributed about the same . . . as elsewhere."[9] In both situations, for example, white-collar workers

Table 10

**Employed Persons by Race and Occupation,
1960–1970**

(Annual averages)

Occupation	1960		1970	
	Negro and other races	*White*	*Negro and other races*	*White*
Total number employed thousands	6,927	58,850	8,445	70,182
Percent	100.0	100.0	100.0	100.0
White-collar workers	16.1	46.6	27.9	50.8
Professional and technical workers	4.8	12.1	9.1	14.8
Managers and administrators, except farm	2.6	11.7	3.5	11.4
Sales workers	1.5	7.0	2.1	6.7
Clerical workers	7.3	15.7	13.2	18.0
Blue-collar workers	40.1	36.2	42.2	34.5
Craftsmen and kindred workers Operatives, except transport	6.0	13.8	8.2	13.5
Transport equipment operatives	20.4	17.9	23.7	17.0
Nonfarm laborers	13.7	4.4	10.3	4.1
Service workers	31.7	9.9	26.0	10.7
Private household	14.2	1.7	7.7	1.3
Other	17.5	8.2	18.3	9.4
Farm workers	12.1	7.4	3.9	4.0

Source: U.S. Department of Commerce, *Social and Economic Status of the Black Population in the United States, 1972,* Washington, D.C., 1973, p. 49.

101

among whites constitute about 40 percent of the employment structure, while the same group among Negroes makes up about 17 percent of their employment distribution for the United States as a whole but only 11 percent in the South. We should expect the quality of these jobs to be also differentially affected.

Age and the Structure

Another revealing characteristic of the structure of Negro employment is its relative age distribution. We should expect Negro youths, both male and female, to be in the labor market to a greater extent than white youths. Differences in social status and functional prospects call not only for greater devotion to education but also for longer periods in school for white youths. In 1970, for example, "going to school" was given as a reason for not being in the labor force by 75 percent of white persons aged twenty to twenty-four but by only 59 percent of nonwhite.[10] Other reasons, not including long-term physical and mental illness, kept 35 percent of the Negroes and other races in this age group out of the labor force and 23 percent of the whites. At all ages, there was in 1970 a larger percentage of white males in labor force participation than nonwhite males. This was true only for white females under twenty years of age. Table 11 shows that Negro women under twenty are less likely than whites to be in the labor market. Why is this so?

In a previous study this writer attempted to show that the phenomenon is probably associated with status degradation incident to the type of employment available to Negro girls.[11] Thus, compared to white women, it is the married Negro woman, and not the single, who is most highly employed. The data for 1930, shown in table 12, bring out this point quite clearly.

To generalize, the Negro married woman has been a working woman while the white married woman has been regarded as a "home maker." And this has been true of the marital situation for all age groups. In 1930, the ratio of the percentage of Negro married women to the percentage of employed Negro married women age fifteen to nineteen years of age (21:34) was approximately 0.6; while for white women of the same age the ratio (12:25) was 0.5. At age forty to forty-four, the ratio of the percentages married to employed married women was 1.5 for Negroes to 4.0 for whites.[12] Thus, the tendency of Negro married women to be employed, relative to the tendency of white married women, increased with age.

Table 11

Labor-Force Participation Rates, by Race, Age, and Sex, 1970

(Includes Armed Forces. Annual averages)

Age	Men		Women	
	Negro and other races	*White*	*Negro and other races*	*White*
Total, 16 years and over	78	81	50	43
16 and 17 years	35	49	24	37
18 and 19 years	65	71	45	55
20 to 24 years	86	87	58	58
25 to 34 years	94	97	58	43
35 to 44 years	94	97	60	50
45 to 54 years	88	95	60	54
55 to 64 years	79	83	47	43
65 years and over	27	27	12	10

Source: U.S. Department of Labor, *The Social and Economic Status of Negroes in the United States,* 1970, table 41.

Table 12

Percent of Total Number of Negro, Native White, and Foreign-Born Women 15 Years of Age and Over *Gainfully Employed* in the United States, by Marital Status, 1930

Race and Nativity	*Single and Unknown*	*Married*	*Widowed and Divorced*	*Total*
Negro	28.1	44.7	27.1	100
Native white	60.8	24.8	14.5	100
Foreign born	49.6	31.3	19.1	100

Source: *Fifteenth Census of the United States, Population,* vol. IV, tables 26 and 68, 1930.

Although the data for 1960 still illustrates this fact, it should be observed, as shown in table 13, that there has been a decided tendency, since 1930, for older white married women to be employed.

Table 13

Female Labor Force, by Marital Status, Age,* and Color, for the United States (in percentages), 1960

Age	Single		Married		Widowed and Divorced	
	Nonwhite	White	Nonwhite	White	Nonwhite	White
14–15	92.7	96.8	6.8	2.9	.3	.2
16–17	85.5	92.7	13.9	6.9	.6	.4
18–19	74.9	78.7	24.3	20.3	.7	1.0
20–24	46.7	46.3	50.3	50.4	3.0	3.4
25–29	22.6	24.0	70.2	69.5	7.2	6.6
30–34	12.9	16.0	76.5	75.7	11.0	8.3
50–54	8.0	13.1	63.0	65.0	30.0	22.0

Source: U.S. Census of Population, 1960, vol. 1, table 196.
*By age 54, the point may be observed.

By 1980, according to projections by the U.S. Department of Labor, nonwhites in all age groups will increase their percentage of the total labor force. And this change, as shown in table 14, will be especially evident among younger workers.

The Professions

The professions call for long periods of education of a relatively high order, and are thus distinguished by more than ordinary prestige. The occupational structure of typical professions among Negroes, as shown in table 15, reveals strikingly the effects of monopolistic competition and exclusion. In this employment distribution of Negro professionals, two facts stand out: (1) the small 3 percent of the total, and (2) the relatively greater weight contributed by clergymen and teachers to the category. The latter, especially the ministry, are likely to include large numbers with relatively little formal education and training.

Table 14
Nonwhite as a Percentage of Total Labor Force by Age, 1960 and 1980
(Numbers in thousands)

Age	1960				1980			
	White	Non White	Total	% of Total	White	Non White	Total	% of Total
16 years and over	64,210	7,894	72,104	10.9	87,872	12,072	99,944	12.2
26 to 24	11,239	1,481	12,720	12.0	19,394	3,161	22,555	14.0
25 to 44	28,111	3,767	31,878	11.8	37,902	5,505	43,407	12.7
45 to 64	21,747	2,380	24,127	9.8	27,422	3,124	30,546	10.2
65 and over	3,113	266	3,379	7.0	3,154	282	3,436	8.2

Source: U.S. Department of Labor, *Manpower Report of the President*, January 1966, table.E-5, p. 232.

105

Table 15
Negro and White Employment in Professions, 1950–1960

Occupation	1950 (in thousands)			1960			Negroes as percent of employment*		Percent change 1950–1960	
	Total	Negro	White	Total	Negro	White	1950	1960	Negro	White
Professional workers	2,970	75	2,887	4,479	113	4,324	3	3	49	50
Clergymen	161	18	142	196	14	181	11	7	-23	28
Dentists	73	1	71	81	2	78	2	3	31	10
Lawyers and Judges	174	1	173	205	2	202	1	1	47	17
Musicians and music teachers	76	6	70	82	6	76	7	7	3	9
Physicians and surgeons	180	4	176	213	4	205	2	2	12	17
Teachers	286	19	166	475	31	442	7	6	65	66

*Percent of employment in the category: thus 2 percent of all dentists in 1950.
Source: U.S. Department of Labor, Bureau of Labor Statistics *Negroes in the United States*, 1966, p. 117.

Teachers are about equally divided between elementary and secondary schools. They are semi-professional; and they are essentially government employees. Their role in the subcultures of the nation, however, should not be minimized. In 1960, Negro "college presidents, professors, and instructors," not shown in the table, were about 2.5 percent of the total (U.S.) professional and technical workers. Although lawyers, judges, and dentists had high percentage increases during the decade 1950–60, they still constitute an inordinately small proportion of total employment in these fields.

The first broad observation regarding Negro professionals is that they have been socially restricted to serve Negroes almost exclusively in Negro communities. They tend not to compete for "white trade" in white communities. White professionals, however, have been relatively free to compete for Negro patronage—especially higher status patronage. Because of the relatively small size and the racially circumscribed limits of their market, Negro professionals have been less likely than whites to become specialists. Moreover, discriminatory access to public and semi-public institutions—hospitals, clinics, and laboratories; courts; colleges and universities—has been a factor in transferring potential clients of Negro practitioners to white specialists.[13]

The supply of white professionals relative to the population is not only greater but also more uniformly distributed over rural and urban areas of the country. Of necessity, then, considerable portions of the Negro population—especially in the South—must avail themselves of the limited opportunity to utilize the services of white practitioners or do without. The prospects of Negro recruits to the professions to correct this imbalance are not bright. For the immediate future there will be an increasingly broadening range of employment opportunities open to Negro college graduates and thus a decreasing concentration on the typical professions.[14]

Perhaps the history of the Negro lawyer in the South illustrates as strikingly as any other situation the effects of institutional restraint upon the career of Negro professionals. His problem of gaining admission to the bar after Reconstruction, his almost certain defeat in cases involving whites before southern juries, and his virtual confinement to general practice—instead of assignments as institutional and corporation counsel[15]—tended obviously to restrict him to marginal areas of the profession. There was thus abundant reason for Negro clients to turn to white advocates in times of trouble.

As we should expect, the civil rights movement has affected Negro professionals in various ways. In general, wherever federal government influence extends to the institutional structure of the nation, the services of related Negro professionals tends to be "desegregated." This fact has had far-reaching consequences regarding the transformation of the professional Negroes' attitude toward the "free enterprise" system. When, for example, the Medicare bill was first introduced in Congress early in the sixties, Negro physicians, through their relatively small National Medical Association, went along spontaneously with the giant American Medical Association to oppose it as a step toward socialism. Eventually, however, they arrived at a self-interested resolution in favor of the law, which was opposed to that of the American Medical Association.

Medicare, passed by the Congress in 1965, has tended to equalize racial opportunity in medical practice, to disregard the race of patients, and to end racial discrimination in the use of hospital facilities. Free, voluntary associations of professionals may become, like many of the county AMA affiliates in the South, racially exclusive and monopolistic, hence only some superior force like the federal judiciary or the Congress will be able to restore them. The struggle for equality in the practice of the professions is by no means over.

Chapter 8

Demographic Correlates

Introduction

In the foreseeable future, Negroes will become an increasingly urbanized group. Indeed, with the exception of the Japanese and Chinese, relatively small American minorities, they are already the most highly urbanized group in the United States. The great cities not only provide jobs and welfare relief but also anonymity and density in numbers which facilitates in-group consciousness and cultural reassurance. The latter tends to be of peculiar value for a people that sometimes consider themselves as culturally shut in. And yet, the extreme disadvantages of ghetto life still remain.

Whatever the influence of an African origin on Negroes might have been, it now seems practically unidentifiable.[1] Negroes came, through the initiative of others, mainly from many culturally dissimilar areas of West Africa. As any one who has visited that region knows, the various tribal languages and cultural norms are, even to this day, a source of profound divisiveness. The English, French, and

109

Portuguese languages, in addition to westernized institutions, tend to form the basis of intertribal communication and political cooperation.

In other words, even in Africa, Western culture provides the principal means of developing black solidarity as well as material cultural advancement. What is inevitably growing and expanding on the continent, therefore, is not African culture but mainly Western culture and its societal implants. Moreover, whites are everywhere in this area helping to lead and promote the transition. The sub-Saharan, indigenous cultures, let us recall, are largely pre-literate and static. As Africa continues to move into the dynamic context of universal progress, those cultures will, no doubt, automatically recede. Although the people are understandably sensitive to any attempt by Europeans to treat them as pre-independence "natives," there has been no viable "back-to-Africa" movement—such as that suggested by Garvey or by South Africa—led by black Africans. The alternative of returning voluntarily to the inefficacy of the tribal village—in both the physical and the intellectual sense—seems to be the obvious road to modernization. That is what the rise of such cities as Accra and Lagos means.

We shall assume, then, that the Negro way of life, so far as it is distinguishable, constitutes an American cultural development. The more typically southern its situation, the more specifically it can be identified and characterized. (It may be readily distinguished, for example, from black Jamaican culture—not to mention Haitian, Cuban, or Martiniquan.) The longer the urban residence and the older the middle-class status of the Negro group, the more indistinguishable and typically American is its culture. The identifiable American subculture derives mainly from the social system of the old plantation in the Deep South.

Even so, there is currently a movement to revive "African culture" among Negro Americans. The urge, incidentally, seems to be quite flattering to some inhabitants of that continent. For instance, Dr. Essien-Udom, a native Nigerian scholar educated in the United States and specializing in race relations, affirms:

> I am convinced that the liberation of Afro-Americans in Harlem and elsewhere in America ultimately lies in an understanding, appreciation, and assertion of his Afro-American and African cultural heritage. It is the exploitation and assertion of cultural and spiritual heritage that will help to usher him into freedom-land during the second century of emancipation. In this, he will

be engaging in tasks comparable to those of his African brother. Herein lies the foundation of our freedom and liberation; and such is the meaning of the voices from within the veil represented, though inadequately, by the nationalistic movements of Harlem.[2]

To be consistent, this premise should be applicable to Negroes in all the *Americas*. It is easy to see why nationalists, indeed most Negroes, should be ethnocentric about Africa—a tremendous country with peoples of different, sometimes utterly conflicting, cultures but traditionally slandered in the West as peoples without compassion. The western stereotype of the area has been so persistent and derogatory that, in the past, many Negro Americans have been loath to associate themselves with it.[3] Today, however, when Africa has become an open book and when balance is being restored through objective research, the emotionalism of black nationalism seems anachronistic.

By the time the "seasoning" period was over, the American bondsmen were on the whole effectively de-Africanized—they themselves left hardly any writing descriptive of that process—and slavery set the stage for the inescapable black cultural reformation. Kenneth Stampp indicates some of the elements of repression under which this acculturation took place:

> Most of [the freedmen] had by then lost all but a tiny fragment of their African culture. Though in slavery they had been denied full participation in the white man's culture, their ambition was to become an integral part of American society. They knew how to make a living as freemen, because they had experience as farmers, as skilled craftsmen, as domestic servants, or as unskilled urban laborers. What they still needed were economic opportunities, training in the management of their own affairs, and incentives for diligent toil.
>
> Because the ante-bellum slave codes had prohibited teaching slaves to read and write, only a small minority of Negroes were literate. In this respect, as in most others, slavery had been a poor training school for the responsibilities of citizenship. It gave Negroes few opportunities to develop initiative or to think independently; it discouraged self-reliance; it put a premium on docility and subservience; it indoctrinated Negroes with a sense of their own inferiority; and it instilled in many of them a fear of the white men that they would only slowly overcome.[4]

Even before 1865, however, there was considerable social differentiation among Negroes;[5] and development since then has followed the general pattern of social-class formation. There has been in recent sociological literature considerable reference to Negro middle-class separation from the masses. Although there is nothing to show that there is any less of a continuum of the indices of social status among Negroes than among whites, it appears that there is a unique factor which characterizes their entire social structure. The mere fact of status differentiation seems to be inconsistent with the overwhelming condition of race as an identifying attribute. In other words, differences in wealth, occupation, family, education, and so on, are inevitably socially hierarchical, but racial membership is supposed to reduce all these to their lowest common denominator. Frederick Douglass, the famous champion of Negro rights, who rose from slavery to upper middle-class status, seems to have been perplexed by the inherent contradiction. Consider the following:

> My presence and position [as a United States representative with a commission to Santo Domingo] seemed to trouble them for its incomprehensibility; and they did not know exactly how to deport themselves towards me. Possibly they may have detected in me something of the same sort in respect of themselves; at any rate we seemed awkwardly related to each other during several weeks of the voyage. In their eyes I was Fred Douglass suddenly, and possibly undeservedly, lifted above them. The fact that I was colored and they were colored had so long made us equal, that the contradiction now presented was too much for them.[6]

This fact of racial identity tends to keep the status hierarchy among Negroes psychologically obscure. Although physical manifestations of social distance among whites are much more overt and insistent, their upper classes are seldom characterized as "dissociated from the masses."[7] Had both Douglass, the ambassador of the United States, and the ship servants been white, the normal expressions of deference associated with their respective roles would have been considered natural. Moreover, an important basis of social class differentiation among whites, that between employer and employee, has been relatively nonexistent among Negroes. African societies, it needs hardly be said, have some of the most exacting systems of social differentiation.

With the movement of Negroes into the cities we should expect many more of them to attain middle-class status.

Relative Size of Population

Relative numbers are an important factor in American race relations. The irreversible ratio of blacks to whites in the United States forecloses any chance that Negroes might develop, in the foreseeable future, a successful nationalist movement through democratic means. Negroes never constituted more than about one-fifth of the total population. The high point was reached during the period centering around the revolutionary war; and, from that time on, it has declined to approximately one-tenth of the total.

Obviously, a population grows in two ways: excess of births over deaths, and immigration. The difference in the increasing relative proportion of whites, as shown in table 16, has been due mainly to immigration. The slave trade, abolished by federal law in 1807, gradually cut down African immigration to zero; but European immigration continued unabated. The emergencies in Europe during World War I and progressively stringent immigration laws enacted since that time tended to confine the American population growth mainly to natural increase.

It should be observed, however, that Negro migration from the South and European immigration are phenomena of quite distinct dimensions. "Even during the years from 1960 through 1966," it has been pointed out, "the 1.8 million immigrants from abroad vastly outnumbered the 613,000 Negroes who departed from the South" to live in other regions of the country.[8] As a result of net migration—emigration versus immigration—between 1960 and 1970, which includes movements of the armed forces, the Negro resident population was reduced by 180,000 while that of whites increased by 2,377,000.

Since 1940 there has been a slight upturn in the percentage of Negroes in the United States. There is, however, no expectation that this will move dramatically upward from the approximately 11 percent of total population which they now constitute. Indeed, immigration, though small compared to pre-World War I, is still made up largely of white persons; and there are indications that the Negro birth rate may be now beginning its return to normal. Between 1960 and 1970 Negroes had a natural increase, births over deaths, of 20.6 percent and whites 10.4 percent: about 4 and 16 million respectively.

Regional Distribution

Distribution of the population throughout the United States indicates further the significance of relative numbers. Traditionally,

113

Table 16

Negro Population in the United States, Percent of Total, and Relative Rate of Increase, 1790–1970*

Census Year	Total Population (in thousands)	Negro Population (in thousands)	Percent Negro	Percent Increase Total	Negro
1970	203,185	22,673	11.1	13.8	19.6
1960	178,464	18,860	10.6	18.4	25.4
1950	150,697	15,042	10.0	14.4	17.0
1940	131,669	12,866	9.8	7.2	8.2
1930	122,775	11,891	9.7	16.1	13.6
1920	105,711	10,463	9.9	14.9	6.5
1910	91,972	9,828	10.7	21.0	11.2
1900	75,995	8,834	11.6	20.7	13.8
1890	62,948	7,488	12.3	25.5	17.6
1880	50,155	6,581	13.1	30.1	22.0
1870	38,558	5,392	13.5	22.6	21.4
1860	31,443	4,442	14.1	35.6	22.0
1850	23,192	3,639	15.7	35.9	24.5
1840	17,069	2,874	16.8	32.7	23.4
1830	12,866	2,329	8.1	33.5	30.5
1820	9,638	1,772	18.4	33.1	28.6
1810	7,240	1,378	19.0	36.4	32.9
1800	5,308	1,002	18.9	35.1	31.7
1790	3,929	757	19.3	. . . .	. . . .

*Coterminous United States.
Source: U.S. Department of Commerce, Bureau of the Census.

the Negro population has been identified with the South—and properly so. As late as 1920, 85 percent of the group still lived there. By 1970, however, after its continuous decline, only about half the Negro population remained in that region. Table 17 compares the considerable percentage change since 1940 with the almost stationary percentage, 27 to 28, for whites. Percentages of the general population have been increasing especially in the West, but obviously more significantly for Negroes: from 1 to 8 percent of their number since 1940.

Table 17

Percent Distribution of the Population by Region and Color, 1940 and 1970

Subject	Negro		White	
	1940	*1970*	*1940*	*1970*
United States (millions)	12.9	22.7	118.2	177.6
Percent, total	100	100	100	100
South	77	53	27	28
North	22	39	62	54
Northeast	11	19	29	25
North Central	11	20	33	29
West	1	8	11	18

Source: Unless otherwise indicated, our source for population data is U.S. Department of Commerce, Bureau of the Census, *The Social and Economic Status of Negroes in the United States,* 1970.

In 1970, the approximately 11 percent which Negroes comprised of total United States population made up 19 percent of the people in the South, 8 percent in the North, and 5 percent in the West. We should expect the proportion of blacks in the South to continue to decline—it was 24 percent in 1940—and, with this movement, the urban-rural composition of the Negro population will also continue to change.

Urban-Rural Distribution

Urbanization

There is apparently nothing so consequential in the cultural future of Negro Americans as their urbanization. It has been a development of transcendental importance for the nation as a whole. Capitalist culture is esentially modern city culture, and the great metropolises of the United States are its ultimate expression.

Expansion of the Negro population has been confined almost entirely to the central cities of the metropolitan areas. Of a total increase of 3.8 million in the Negro population between 1960 and 1970, central cities accounted for 3.2 million. For the same period, and for the first time, the census shows an actual decrease of about 1 percent of the white population in the central cities. There was a decrease of 4 percent in the Negro population outside the metropolitan areas. Table 18 presents this distribution by area.

115

Table 18
Population Distribution Inside and Outside Metropolitan Areas, 1970

Area	Negro Population (millions)	Percent	White Population (millions)	Percent
United States	22.7	100	177.6	100
Metropolitan Areas	16.8	74	121.3	68
Central Cities	13.1	58	49.5	28
Outside Central cities	3.7	16	71.8	40
Outside Metropolitan Areas	5.8	26	56.4	32

The tendency of Negroes in the North and West to live in the metropolitan areas is further emphasized in the regional distribution of the population. "In each region, except the South, over 90 percent of the Negro population lives in metropolitan areas." But although only about half the population in the South lives in metropolitan areas, the trend in that region has also been in the same direction.

The Negro population tends thus to be increasingly concentrated in the central cities of the metropolitan areas; and "the larger the metropolitan area, the greater the proportion of Negroes in the central cities," and, since 1960, the greater the percent of Negro population increase. Table 19 shows, moreover, an obverse movement of Negro and white population inside and outside the central cities of the standard metropolitan statistical areas (SMAS's). Indeed, central-city concentration continues even within the city. "In most of the 12 large cities where special censuses were taken in the mid-1960's," according to the U.S. Bureau of Labor Statistics, "the percent of Negroes living in neighborhoods of greatest Negro concentration had increased since 1960."[9]

As indicated by the 1970 Census, Negroes continue to leave the South at a rate of about 1.5 million per decade. The effects of this emigration are illustrated by the area-of-birth data for the northern and western cities of greatest Negro concentration given in table 20. "About one-half of the Negro residents, in the 10 cities of the North and West that led in Negro population in 1960, were not born there.

116

Table 19

Population Inside and Outside Central Cities of Standard Metropolitan Statistical Areas by Race 1900–1970

Year	Percent of U.S. population in SMSA's		Population (in thousands)				Ratio: central city population to outside central city population	
			Central city		Outside central city			
	Negro	*White*	*Negro*	*White*	*Negro*	*White*	*Negro*	*White*
1900	27	44	1,281	18,467	1,071	10,932	120	169
1920	34	51	2,382	32,168	1,165	16,611	205	194
1940	45	56	4,358	40,971	1,482	25,517	294	161
1960	65	63	9,704	47,575	2,490	51,934	390	92
1970*	74	68	13,140	49,430	3,650	71,148	362	69

Source: U.S. Department of Labor, Bureau of Labor Statistics, *The Negroes in the United States*, 1966, p. 67.
*Projected.

Of this group, most were born in the South."[11] Due to natural increase, however, net out-migration has not reduced the actual Negro population of the South: in 1930 it was 9.4 million and, in 1970, 12 million.

Table 20

Area of Birth of Nonwhite Population in the 10 Northern and Western Cities of Greatest Negro Concentration, by City of Residence, 1960

City of Residence	Native nonwhite (in thousands)	Total native nonwhite	Percent		
			Born in state or region of 1960 residence	Born in South	Born in other regions or areas
New York	1,085	100	49	39	12
Chicago	828	100	42	44	14
Philadelphia	531	100	53	40	8
Detroit	483	100	45	48	8
Washington	413	100	44	43	13
Los Angeles	393	100	39	46	16
Cleveland	252	100	45	48	8
St. Louis	216	100	52	40	9
Newark	138	100	46	42	11
Cincinnati	109	100	52	41	7

Source: U.S. Department of Labor, Bureau of Labor Statistics, *The Negroes in the United States,* 1966, p. 75.

What kind of people leave the South to go North and West? Migrants, both black and white, tend to be more highly educated than the general population and this difference in education has been accentuated for Negroes. Only about 10 percent of Negro males in the South age twenty-five to twenty-nine had some college education, but 19 percent of the black migrants from that region between 1955 and 1960 had college training. Among whites the figures were 27 and 42 percent respectively. About one half, 53 percent, of the 1955–60 nonwhite male migrants from the South, twenty-five to twenty-nine years old, had some high school education as compared to 42 percent in the total southern population.

118

We therefore conclude that the South has been losing its more cultured group, and that migrants to the great cities cannot be reasonably characterized as the unsophisticated children of tenant farmers. Even so the total national effects of southern cultural deprivation, especially in the area of informal culture, should probably not be underestimated.[12]

"In 1970, four out of every ten Negroes in the United States [or 9.2 million] were living in the 30 cities with the largest Negro population."[13] In 1950 only three out of ten lived in these cities. Perhaps the most dramatic fact about this development, as shown in table 21, is the substantial percentage increase of the Negro population in the cities: it has more than doubled for many of the larger cities, including New York and Chicago, and increased about fivefold for Milwaukee.

Natural Increase

Historically, as chart IV illustrates, fertility rates of nonwhite women have been consistently higher than those of white women. With exception of the post-World War II more rapid rise, they have fluctuated commensurably with those of the women of the larger white population. In 1959, the high point since 1910, the fertility rates (births per 1,000 women aged 15–44 years) were 162 and 115 for nonwhite and white women respectively; in 1968, they had declined to 115 and 82. On this point the Department of Health, Education and Welfare concludes that since 1965 the rate for nonwhite women "has been declining somewhat more rapidly than the rate for white women, and the differential has decreased slightly."[14] The curves, as shown in chart IV, are by no means smooth.[15]

The relatively high fertility of Negro women accounts mainly for the characteristic age differentials of the two populations. "The Negro population is considerably younger than the white population."[16] In 1970 the median ages for Negro males and females were respectively 21.7 and 23.8 years, while those for white males and females were 27.8 and 30.5. With respect to migration, the percentage of the *rural nonfarm* population, age twenty-five to twenty-nine, of the total U.S. population in this age group and area declined from 16.0 to 10.1 percent between 1930 and 1960.[17] Table 22 shows that this age difference by race is emphasized in the population under fourteen years of age.

119

Table 21

Negro Population for 30 Cities with Largest Negro Population, 1970, and Percent 1970 and 1950

		1970		1950
Rank	*City and State*	*Number (thousands)*	*Percent Negro*	*Percent Negro*
1	New York, N.Y.	1,667	21	10
2	Chicago, Ill.	1,103	33	14
3	Detroit, Mich.	660	44	16
4	Philadelphia, Pa.	654	34	18
5	Washington, D.C.	538	71	35
6	Los Angeles, Calif.	504	18	9
7	Baltimore, Md.	420	46	24
8	Houston, Tex.	317	26	21
9	Cleveland, Ohio	288	38	16
10	New Orleans, La.	367	45	32
11	Atlanta, Ga.	255	51	37
12	St. Louis, Mo.	254	41	18
13	Memphis, Tenn.	243	39	37
14	Dallas, Tex.	210	25	13
15	Newark, N.J.	207	54	17
16	Indianapolis, Ind.	134	18	15
17	Birmingham, Ala.	126	42	40
18	Cincinnati, Ohio	125	28	16
19	Oakland, Calif.	125	35	12
20	Jacksonville, Fla.	118	22	27
21	Kansas City, Mo.	112	22	12
22	Milwaukee, Wis.	105	15	3
23	Pittsburgh, Pa.	105	20	12
24	Richmond, Va.	105	42	32
25	Boston, Mass.	105	16	5
26	Columbus, Ohio	100	19	12
27	San Francisco, Calif.	96	13	6
28	Buffalo, N.Y.	94	20	6
29	Gary, Ind.	93	53	29
30	Nashville-Davidson, Tenn.	88	20	20

Source: U.S. Department of Labor, Census of Population, 1970, *Negro Population in Selected Places and Selected Counties,* June 1971, table 1.

Chart IV

Fertility rates by color, 1920–1967

(Beginning in 1959 trend lines are based on registered live births; trend lines for 1920–59 are based on live births adjusted for underregistration)

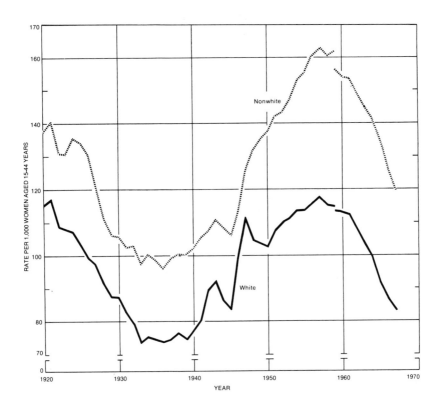

Source: U.S. Department of Health, Education, and Welfare, *Natality Statistics Analysis, United States,* 1965–67, May 1970, p. 12.

Table 22
Percent of Population by Age, Sex, and Color, 1970

Age	Negro		White	
	Male	*Female*	*Male*	*Female*
All ages	100	100	100	100
Under 5 years	11	10	9	8
5 to 14	26	23	20	19
15 to 24	19	19	18	17
25 to 34	11	12	12	12
35 to 44	10	11	12	11
45 to 54	9	10	12	12
55 to 64	7	7	9	10
65 years and over	6	7	9	12
Median age	21.7	23.8	27.8	30.5

In 1969, the National Advisory Commission on Civil Disorders came to the following conclusion regarding these racial age differentials:

> This rapid increase in the young Negro population has important implications for the country. This group has the highest unemployment rate in the nation, commits a relatively high proportion of all crimes, and plays the most significant role in civil disorders. By the same token, it is a great reservoir of underused human resources which are vital to the nation.[18]

There are, moreover, some well-known demographic facts that play a role in the long-run relationship of urbanization and fertility: advancement in occupational status, income, education—all tend to affect the birth rate negatively, and the resulting changes in age distribution will no doubt also tell in the same direction.

The U.S. Census projects population growth to the year 1990. Their estimate for the nonwhite population, based upon high assumptions, is 44.5 million and for the white population 255.6 million. Nonwhites would then be 14.8 percent of the total population, compared to 11.1 percent in 1970. "The difference in growth results primarily from the much higher birth rates of the nonwhite population, which are expected to remain above those of whites throughout this projection period while gradually approaching them."[19]

Health and Survival

It has been shown repeatedly that at any given time and environment, the extent of sickness and death among social groups tends to be correlated with their economic status, which is also related to their education. Economic status, moreover, has been positively associated with types of occupation. This paradigm seems logical since both healthful living conditions and care of the sick, especially in advanced societies, entails economic costs.

Table 23 gives us a general view of trends in racial death rates between 1900 and 1964: the dramatic decrease for both groups, and the nature and extent of closure of the gap. It should be observed, for instance, that "although death rates for the nonwhites have improved more on the average than for the white population since 1900, they were more than double the white rates for the prime ages twenty-five to forty-four in 1964."[20] Apparently, the lower rates for nonwhites over seventy-five are due to survival of the unusually viable black population after a more drastic elimination process in the earlier ages.

Although there has been a steep decline in maternal mortality (deaths per 100,000 live births) for both races during the last fifty years, the rate for nonwhites in 1964 was about four times that of whites: 89.9 and 22.3 respectively. Infant mortality (deaths from one to eleven months of age per 1,000 live births) was 14.6 for nonwhites and 5.4 among whites.

Table 24 shows differences in death rates for the ten leading causes of death among males in 1968. The rates for all causes of death per 100,000 white males was approximately 1,108; and for nonwhite males 1,159. The female rates, as we should expect were lower: 823 and 828 for white and nonwhite females respectively. Diseases of the heart and cancer were the leading causes of death for both white and nonwhite males, but, as the table shows, they were higher for whites. There are probably some racial bases for the fact that *suicide* appears as a leading cause of death only among white males and *homicide* only among nonwhite males. The homicide index, at any rate, suggests greater interpersonal conflict among nonwhites.[21]

123

Table 23
Death Rates, by Age and Color, 1900–1964

Age	1900		1964		Percent decrease 1900–1964		Nonwhite to white ratio of rates per 1,000 population	
	Non-white	White	Non-white	White	Non-white	White	1900	1964
All ages	25.0	17.0	9.7	9.4	61.2	44.7	1.47	1.03
Under 1	333.9	159.4	40.9	21.5	87.8	86.5	2.09	1.90
1–4	43.5	19.4	1.6	.8	96.3	95.9	2.24	2.00
5–14	9.0	3.8	.6	.4	93.3	89.5	2.37	1.50
15–24	11.5	5.7	1.6	1.0	86.1	82.5	2.02	1.60
25–34	12.1	8.1	3.3	1.3	72.7	84.0	1.49	2.54
35–44	14.8	10.1	6.6	2.6	55.4	74.3	1.47	2.54
45–54	24.3	14.8	13.2	6.8	45.7	54.1	1.64	1.94
55–64	42.1	27.0	27.1	15.9	35.6	41.1	1.56	1.70
65–74	68.9	56.2	50.6	36.7	36.6	34.7	1.23	1.38
75–84	120.9	123.3	69.9	82.8	42.2	32.8	.98	.84
85 and over	215.2	262.0	126.5	206.5	41.2	21.2	.82	.61

Source: U.S. Department of Health, Education, and Welfare, *White and Nonwhite Mortality Differentials in the United States*, June 1965, table 2, and unpublished data for 1964, same agency.

Table 24

**Death Rates for the 10 Leading Causes of Death for Males by Color,
United States, 1968
(Rates per 100,000 population)**

Rank Order	Cause of Death	White Male
	All Causes	1,108.3
1	Diseases of heart	451.4
2	Malignant neoplasms (cancer)	180.8
3	Cerebrovascular diseases	97.4
4	Accidents	77.7
	Motor vehicle accidents	40.0
	All other accidents	37.7
5	Influenza and pneumonia	39.1
6	Bronchitis	28.6
7	Certain causes of infant mortality	23.1
8	Cirrhosis of liver	18.8
9	Suicide	16.9
10	Diabetes	16.0
	All other causes	158.4

Rank Order	Cause of Death	Non-white Male
	All Causes	1,158.5
1	Diseases of the heart	327.1
2	Malignant neoplasms (cancer)	157.7
3	Cerebrovascular diseases	111.5
4	Accidents	108.2
	Motor vehicle accidents	46.3
	All other accidents	61.9
5	Influenza and pneumonia	59.6
6	Homicide	54.6
7	Certain causes of infant mortality	51.6
8	Cirrhosis of liver	22.8
9	Diabetes	17.3
10	Bronchitis	14.7
	All other causes	233.2

Source: U.S. Department of Health, Education, and Welfare, *Vital Statistics Report: Final Mortality Statistics, 1968,* March 29, 1971, table 4.

The death rate determines the average life expectancy of a population; thus the lower the death rate the longer the average life expectancy. Put otherwise, if the chances of death for newborn babies remain the same as they are during the year of birth, it is possible to calculate the number of years on the average that they will live. In 1965, for example, the life expectancy at birth for nonwhites was 64.1 years and for whites 71.0. But, through continuing conquests of disease in the United States, the death rate has been progressively declining; there has been a lengthening of average life expectancy not only for infants but also for persons of relatively advanced ages. Table 25 indicates differentials in life expectancy which are "lower for nonwhites than for whites at all ages in prime working years."

Table 25

Life Expectancy in Prime Working Years, Both Sexes by Color, United States, 1967

(Average number of years of life remaining at given ages)

Age	Nonwhite	White	Differences nonwhite to White (in years)
0	64.6	71.3	−6.7
24	43.5	48.8	−5.1
35	34.9	39.3	−4.4
45	26.9	30.2	−3.3
55	19.9	22.0	−2.1

Source: U.S. Department of Health, Education, and Welfare, *Life Tables, Vital Statistics of the United States,* 1967, vol. II, Sec. 5, table 5–4.

The Prospects

The Negro population in the metropolises is contributing to their growth at a faster rate through natural increase than through immigration. A critical incidence related to this development, emphasized in a definitive study on population growth, is the continued concentration and thus separation of nonwhites in the central cities of the United States. According to its authors:

Nonwhites, who were more heavily concentrated in metropolitan areas than whites in 1960, would be relatively even more

126

concentrated by 1985. In 1985 almost four-fifths of all nonwhites in the United States would reside in SMSA's (78 percent) as contrasted with seven-tenths (69 percent) of the whites. Ninety percent or more of nonwhites would be inhabitants of SMSA's three regions—in the Northeast, 94 percent, in the North Central states, 92 percent, and in the West, 90 percent. In the South . . . 64 percent would reside in SMSA's by 1985, as compared to 46 percent in 1960.

The concentration of nonwhites in central cities within SMSA's would rise to a level of 58 percent from a level of 50 percent in 1960. In contrast, the concentration of white population in central cities would diminish to reach a level of 21 percent in 1985 from a level of 30 percent in 1960.[22]

It has been further estimated that if this rate of growth continues together with the out-migration trend of whites, Negroes in some fourteen major cities of the United States will, by 1984, constitute more than 50 percent of the population. Already in Washington, D.C.; Gary; Atlanta; and Newark, New Jersey, Negroes outnumber whites.[23] Other cities will probably arrive at this stage in the following order: St. Louis; New Orleans; Richmond, Virginia; Baltimore; Jacksonville, Florida; Cleveland; Detroit; Philadelphia; Oakland, California and Chicago.[24]

Although the great city constitutes the most powerful magnet for Negro migrants, it presents, nevertheless, some of the most egregious frustrations. Here the phenomenon of relative deprivation becomes most glaring: individualism is heightened, education improved but increasingly segregated, employment opportunities beckon but the better opportunities remain closed, housing calls for occupancy but is still racially unavailable, and so on. The creative life of the city, the downtown entrepreneurial culture, seems automatically to push the Negro aside. He tends thus to be living in an animated social matrix but still not as a part of it. The population changes, which make it possible through the ballot for blacks to play significant roles in city politics, present a stupefying paradox, and thus exacerbate the increasingly urgent problems of social inclusion.

Chapter 9

The Ghetto: Structure

The outstanding fact about the Negro population during the last half-century has been its redistribution. A group properly characterized as southern and rural in 1910 has now spread at an accelerating rate among the great cities of the North and West. The Negro population today is over 90 percent nonfarm and approximately 50 percent nonsouthern. More specifically, the Negro urban population for the United States changed from about 27 percent in 1910 to 73 percent in 1960. In both the North and West it is about 95 percent urban.

It is this continuing resettlement in the great metropolises of the nation that has produced the phenomenon known as black belts or Negro ghettos.[1] They are essentially a consequence of racial discrimination and segregation.

At present we are interested in the competitive process of modern individualistic society in which race relations develop. In our society social classes, without arousing intergroup hostility, tend to live in identifiable communities. Ordinarily the middle and upper classes limit lower-class access to their communities not ordinarily by force, but by socially exclusive standards of living which include housing complexes beyond the economic reach and social aspirations of the lower class. The system does not normally deny *aspiration* to those standards. Such aspiration embodies the verve and enthusiasm necessary for support of the status-giving attributes.

The ghetto, however, is partly the result of an anomaly in the competitive process. It brings residential aspiration and its concomitant motivations to dead ends, and thus isolates the Negro community, separating the black from the white social class system. The Negro neighborhood tends to be more *socially* heterogeneous than the various white neighborhoods. The ghetto becomes therefore the most obvious physical symbol of the Negro's exclusion from the mainstream of American culture, and thus from normal operations of its pattern of social stratification.

Since racially restricted choice of residence constitutes the principal structural element in ghetto formation, two consequences must inevitably follow: (a) costs of comparable housing become higher for Negroes than for the rest of the population, and (b) available housing tends to be more densely used. Ordinarily the whole black community experiences the social implications of this isolation. It has been said:

> [Spatial segregation in the city] frequently limits the Negro consumer in his choice of such items as housing [and therefore] public services, transportation, supermarket facilities, recreation, banking, insurance, medical and legal services, and many others. Such artificial narrowing of consumer choice can and often does drastically reduce real income and curtail important increments to human, business, and community resource development.[2]

We should, in other words, expect overcrowding and its consequences to be a persistent characteristic of the ghetto. Ordinarily the ghetto area has been sharply bounded by some physical line—street, park, river, railroad, hill—which serves to make the larger area inaccessible to black residents.

Urban Concentration

The quality, quantity, and location of Negro residences in the great cities define the basic structure of their community, and their concentration intensifies cultural differences.

In most large cities in 1960, half or more of the Negroes lived in census tracts in which the population was 90 percent or more Negro [Negro tracts] and in which population density per square mile was especially high. Besides being confined to a disproportionately small space within the city, the Negro tracts were usually contiguous or formed one or more pockets within the city.[3]

The more rapid the migration of Negroes into the cities, the greater the piling up of population in Negro census tracts.[4] We should expect this increasing density to be a function of racial discrimination in the ghetto. In a primary sense, therefore, ghettos are a function of the relative absence of choice of place of residence in cities.

The Place of Housing

A critical fact of ghetto formation is housing restrictions. It is possible to argue, however, that no physical fact can be held responsible for the squalor and depredation which tend to follow Negro community "invasion"; that the ghetto is essentially the result of a peculiar way of behaving. And yet housing conditions define at least the ecological structure of the community with its distinctive interracial characteristics. Among manifest deficiencies has been the general shortage of housing for Negroes. The census of housing shows a much larger proportion of overcrowded residences for nonwhites.

Although overcrowding is greater in rural areas, both its pattern and cause vary from those in urban areas. For nonwhites especially, the effects of overcrowding are intensified by concentration in contiguous city blocks. Moreover, besides racial discrimination, poverty and overcrowding tend to go together. Almost all overcrowding among whites may be explained by poverty. If, however, discrimination accounts for the differential, the extreme seems to be, as shown in table 26, the seriously overcrowded rural areas most prevalent in the south, where nonwhite overcrowding is about six times as great as that of whites. In central cities of SMSAs, overcrowding among nonwhites is about two to three times that of whites. In Dallas, for example, the U.S. census index of overcrowding (1.01 or more persons per room) showed that nonwhite-occupied units, in 1960, were 19.3 percent overcrowded compared to 6.9 percent for white occupied units; in Philadelphia, the figures were 16.3 and 4.9 percent respectively.

Table 26

Percent of Housing Overcrowded or Seriously Overcrowded, United States, Urban and Rural, by Color, 1960

(Occupied by homeowners and renters)

Area	Overcrowded (1.01 or more persons per room)		Seriously Overcrowded (1.51 or more persons per room)	
	Nonwhite	White	Nonwhite	White
United States	28	10	14	2
Urban	25	8	11	2
Rural	41	13	25	4

Source: U.S. Bureau of Labor Statistics, Report No. 332, *Social and Economic Conditions of Negroes in the United States,* 1967, p. 57. Cf. *Census of Housing,* vol. 1, pt. 1, tables 22–30, for detail characteristics.

The quality of housing for nonwhites, though improving, is still highly inadequate. Table 27 shows that in 1966, the proportion of nonwhite households occupying housing that was either dilapidated or lacking in basic plumbing facilities was over three times as great as that for whites.

Table 27

Percent of Occupied Housing Not Meeting Specified Criteria,* by Color and Area, 1960 and 1966

Area	Nonwhite		White	
	1960	1966	1960	1966
United States	44	29	13	8
Central Cities**	25	16	8	5
Urban fringe	43	29	7	4
Smaller cities, towns, and rural	77	64	23	14

Source: same as table 26.

*"Not meeting specified criteria" if it is either dilapidated or lacks one or more basic plumbing facilities: hot running water, flush toilet, bathtub or shower.

**Of SMSAs, population 50,000 or more.

131

Data on regional differences emphasize the poorer quality of housing for nonwhites in the South. "Nearly half of all nonwhite households [in the South] live in dwellings that are either dilapidated or lack basic plumbing facilities compared to less than one-fifth in the North and West."[5] Moreover, as table 28 indicates, housing in smaller cities and rural areas is, on the whole, consistently inferior to that in metropolitan centers.

Table 28

Percent of Occupied Housing Not Meeting Specified Criteria,* by Color, *Region,* and Area, 1966

Area	North and West		South	
	Nonwhite	White	Nonwhite	White
All housing units	16	6	46	11
Central cities	15	6	19	4
Urban fringe	15	4	51	5
Smaller cities, towns, and rural	32	11	75	19

Source: Same as table 26.
*Dilapidated or lacking in basic plumbing facilities.

Cost of housing for nonwhites does not decrease *pari passu* with quality. This may be illustrated by differentials in expense for both house rent and ownership. "Negroes in large cities are often forced to pay the same rents as whites and receive less for their money, or pay higher rents for the same accommodations."[6] In demonstrating the first situation, the National Advisory Commission on Civil Disorders relied on relevant census tracts in Chicago in which "both whites and nonwhites paid median rents of $88, and the proportion paying specific rents below the median was almost identical. But the units rented by nonwhites were typically:

Smaller (the median number of rooms was 3.35 for nonwhites versus 3.95 for whites).
In worse condition (30.7 percent of all nonwhite units were deteriorated or dilapidated compared to 11.6 percent for whites).

132

Occupied by more people (the median household size was 3.53 for nonwhites versus 2.88 for whites).

More likely to be overcrowded (27.4 percent of nonwhite units had 1.01 or more persons per room versus 7.9 percent for whites). . . .

The second type of discriminatory effect—paying more for similar housing—is illustrated by data from a study of housing conditions in disadvantaged neighborhoods in Newark, New Jersey. In four areas of that city, nonwhites with housing essentially similar to that of whites paid rents that were from 8.1 percent to 16.8 percent higher.[7]

Discrimination in home ownership has probably been even more significant. The powerful financial institutions engaged in providing capital for home building have been able not only to determine cost but also location of nonwhite residences. According to data in table 29, nonwhites were less likely than whites to have their property mortgaged; indicating, no doubt, less willingness on the part of financiers to assist them; and "a smaller percent of nonwhite than white homeowners had government-assisted loans."[8] Nonwhites had loans of relatively short duration, and they paid higher interest rates.

Real Estate Associations as a Force

Probably the most persistent and well organized group of workers for racial segregation and thus ghetto conditions in housing has been the national, state and local white real estate associations. These organizations are highly expert, well financed, and maintain effective lobbies in national, state, and city legislatures.[9] They have been the mainstay of racial neighborhood zoning, zoning ordinances, and restrictive covenants. Negro real estate dealers are not ordinarily admitted to their membership. Blacks have, therefore, organized their own smaller National Association of Real Estate Brokers outside the powerful National Association of Real Estate Boards.[10] The latter maintains effective sanctions against any of its members who deviate from its principles of racial segregation.[11] The association has been among the most insistent and effective opponents of open-housing legislation; and it has supported and initiated restrictive covenants.[12] In the crucial *Shelley* vs. *Kraemer* case the National Association of Real Estate Boards, together with the Arlington Heights Property Owners Association presented themselves as friends of the court in support of the legality of covenants.[13] Ordinar-

Table 29

Financial Characteristics of Owner-Occupied
Single-Family Houses, 1960

Characteristics	Percent Homes Occupied by	
	Nonwhite	White
All properties purchased	100	100
No mortgage	51	42
Mortgage	49	58
Properties with mortgages:		
Total	100	100
FHA* insured	10	19
VA* guaranteed	19	24
Conventional	71	58
Interest rate 6 percent or more	56	26
Mortgage term less than 18 years	61	38
Mortgage loans as a percent of purchase price (median)	88	81

*Federal Housing Administration and the Veterans Administration.
Source: U.S. Bureau of Labor Statistics, Report No. 332, *Social and Economic Conditions of Negroes in the United States,* 1967, p. 58.

ily, however, the relationship between white real estate boards and neighborhood improvement associations has been

> informal and incidental and does not represent a planned and deliberate scheme of organizational tie-up. It is nevertheless sufficiently real to permit a substantial and effective degree of collaboration. . . . Membership of the improvement associations usually contains a strategic representation of real-estate men, generally those who live within the neighborhood district or carry on business there. In Chicago and Detroit the officers of many of the improvement associations are prominent real-estate men.[14]

Consequences of this relationship, of course, involve other major disadvantages of housing segregation, such as for example, closed access to the larger sources of capital for housing construction in the prohibited areas and systematization of racism in the community. Real estate brokerage, let us note, is primarily business activity, hence its principles regarding racial housing restriction have been based upon conclusions that democratic alternatives would result in reduction of income from investments and services. The basic rule, with respect to race, for members of the national organization, was as follows:

> A realtor should never be instrumental in introducing into a neighborhood a character of property or occupancy, members of any race or nationality, or any individual whose presence will clearly be detrimental to property values in the neighborhood.[15]

Although national and local real estate boards continued to oppose enactment of fair housing laws, open declarations on depressing effects of Negro residence in certain communities have been recently muted. Tradition had already established policy, hence racial discrimination could be followed systematically. Fair housing bills are still fought on grounds that they "deny home owners basic freedom to contract with persons of their choice."[16]

FHA and VA

Virtually all the present functions of the federal government in providing housing for private occupancy derive from the United States Housing Act of 1937, amended many times. As stated in Section I of this Rooseveltian law:

> It is hereby declared to be the policy of the United States to promote the general welfare of the Nation by employing its funds and credit . . . to assist the several States and their political subdivisions to alleviate present and recurring unemployment and to remedy the unsafe and unsanitary housing conditions and the acute shortage of decent, safe, and sanitary dwellings for families of low income in urban and rural nonfarm areas, that are injurious to the health, safety, and morals of the citizens of the nation.[17]

The various governmental services set up for this purpose are today centered in the U.S. Department of Housing and Urban Development. We are presently concerned with the racial policies of the Federal Housing Administration (FHA), the Veterans Administration (VA), and the Local Housing Authorities (LHAs). The FHA insures mortgage loans thus increasing their availability, while the VA guarantees such loans made by financiers to private individuals for the latters' housing needs.[18] The LHA administers low-cost housing, the ownership of which it acquires through federal aid and rents from low-income people in the community.

The FHA is by far the most important and prestigious governmental agency supporting housing for private use. In 1960 one official source asserted: "There can be little doubt that the low downpayment, long-term FHA or VA mortgage loan, which has helped bring about home ownership of more than 60 percent of the dwelling units in the United States, will continue . . . to provide a broad support for the housing market."[19]

The remarkable fact is that the history of the FHA and VA has actually been one of support for racially discriminatory covenants and residential segregation. Its emphasis has been on the business aspect, not the welfare design, of its original conception. Prior to the Supreme Court decision against racially restrictive covenants (1953), its orientation on interracial community housing was repeatedly stated in its *Underwriting Manual*.[20] For example, in its 1938 issue, under the section of "Protection from Adverse Influences," the following position was taken:

> Protection in the form of zoning restrictions is becoming more general. One of the best artificial means of providing protection from *adverse influences* is through the medium of appropriate and well drawn zoning ordinances. . . . Deed restrictions [restrictive covenants] are apt to prove more effective than a zoning ordinance in providing protection from *adverse influences*. . . . Usually the protection from *adverse influences* afforded by these means includes prevention of the infiltration of . . . lower-class occupancy, and inharmonious racial groups. . . . If a neighborhood is to retain stability, it is necessary that properties shall continue to be occupied by the same social and racial classes.[21]

The particular significance of the FHA's "harmonious racial" ideology and policy was that it bore the moral authority of the government; it was thus uniformly and nationally respected. It operated with an intensity and duration sufficient to confirm and institutionalize the segregation traditions of the housing industry. Abrams puts it emphatically:

> From its inception FHA set itself up as the protector of the all-white neighborhood. It sent its agents into the field to keep

136

Negroes and other minorities from buying homes in white neigh-borhoods. It exerted pressure against builders who dared to build for minorities, and against lenders willing to lend on mort-gages. . . . It not only insisted on social and racial 'homogene-ity' in all of its projects as a price of insurance but became the vanguard of white supremacy and racial purity—in the North as well as the South.[22]

Gradually, during the Supreme Court Decisions on restrictive covenants, FHA and VA changed their announced policies. Later manuals sought to make this clear: "Underwriting considerations shall recognize the right to equality of opportunity to receive the benefits of the mortgage insurance system in obtaining adequate housing accommodations irrespective of race, color, creed or na-tional origin. Underwriting considerations and conclusions are never based on discriminatory attitudes or prejudice."[23] There still re-mained, however, the question of whether practice had also changed. In its 1962 study of housing in Washington, D.C., the United States Commission on Civil Rights found that:

The Federal Housing Administration, which has been a princi-pal factor in the expanded supply of new housing in metropoli-tan Washington, has taken no action to assure that builders afford equal access to new housing regardless of race, color, religion or national origin. Those policies designed to encourage open occupancy, which the FHA has instituted on a nationwide basis, have not been adequately implemented. . . .[24]

Low-Rent Public Housing

The public housing program, through which the government provides living accommodations directly to renters, has been under the direct administration of Local Housing Authorities. It was initi-ated by the Federal Housing Act of 1937 to provide "an adequate supply of decent, safe, and sanitary dwellings" for families of low income who could not afford such quarters under ordinary market conditions.

The act offers to contribute a federal subsidy to local building programs which are also tied to slum clearance. "Rents in public housing are required by law to be set at least 20 percent below rents for 'decent, safe and sanitary' units in the private market. The differ-ence between a local housing authority's revenues and the amount required for meeting its financial obligations is made up by an annual federal contribution.''[25] A limit is set upon income, above which, families cannot enter nor remain in the low-rent projects. Those displaced by slum clearance are given priority. The U.S. Housing Authority in the Department of Housing and Urban Development (HUD), supervises local developments but ownership is vested in the local authorities.

The two principal motives for the program—provision of decent housing for low-income citizens and slum clearance or urban renewal—tended to identify it with the physical environment of a larger percentage of urban Negroes than urban whites. Neglect of Negro housing by private enterprise exacerbates the conditions. Moreover, there has been no consistent policy against discrimination in the Public Housing Administration: its general rule having been to follow local ''patterns and trends.'' As a result, nonwhites have ''shared much more in public housing than in the housing aids distributed through the private market. From the beginning, more than a third of all public-housing units were occupied by Negroes; in recent years this proportion has risen to about 44 percent.''[26] For many, the new housing was a godsend. As Robert Weaver puts it: ''Here was a program that offered about 3 percent of the colored families in the North their first opportunity to live in new, well-designed, and desirably surrounded shelter. Most of the developments that housed Negroes in the North were located on what had been slum sites.''[27] This could also be said of housing for Negroes in the urban South.[28]

Thus far, public housing has accounted for a relatively small proportion of the housing needs of the population. On the whole, however, it has been a salutary force not only because it provided housing where it was most urgently needed but also because of its experimental contribution to interracial living. Unlike the earlier ''racial homogeneity'' policy of the FHA, local housing authorities were left to work out racial policy. This meant inevitably segregation in the South, and mainly segregation in the North and West with some valuable experience in problems of interracial housing.

Besides the bias of specific local housing authorities, two social tendencies in public housing led to increased segregation of Negroes: (a) those structures built in Negro communities were ordinarily completely segregated, and (b) those built in marginal racial zones tended to alter rapidly from interracial to total Negro occupation.

White occupants, because of relatively increasing income, tended to pass the limit of eligibility more frequently than Negro

138

occupants. Moreover, when some critical racial ratio had been reached, it was the whites generally who tended to move away.[29] Developments in slum clearance and urban renewal programs tended also to limit the uses of these projects. "To a great extent," McEntire observes, "public housing no longer serves the general population of low-income and poorly housed families, but is tied to urban-renewal operations. Statutory preference in tenant selection must be given to families displaced by urban renewal, and these families are largely Negro because of the character of urban-renewal areas."[30]

Sometimes urban renewal, with its possibilities for racial zoning, has had the effect of displacing Negro residents without adequate provisions for their relocation. In his discussion of this development, Charles Abrams stressed the likelihood of a reduction in the supply of Negro housing: "If the public housing program did not increase the over-all housing supply for the underprivileged, it at least substituted good housing for bad. The urban redevelopment program provided no housing *for them* at all and deprived them of the housing they had."[31] In like manner, the U.S. Commission on Civil Rights concluded from its study of housing in the Washington metropolitan area that:

> The aims of urban renewal and other civil improvement programs in the District are being jeopardized by the failure to secure decent, safe, and sanitary housing for the displacees who are predominantly nonwhite. In one Washington suburban community where urban renewal is in operation, it is having the effect of forcing Negroes out.[32]

New Developments

Two current movements, steadily gaining momentum, promise to have fundamental effects on housing, especially the housing of minority groups. They are: (a) the Congressional "Fair Housing Law," of the Civil Rights Act of April 11, 1968, and the Supreme Court decision *Jones* v. *Mayer and Co.*, June 17, 1968, which climaxed previous juristic approaches to the unrestricted sale of housing to Negroes; and (b) the federal planned housing program intended to subsidize low-income home ownership and rental tenfold, which the Secretary of the Department of Housing and Urban Development declares will have "the most important impact on the mental health of those who are both poor and alienated," and "substantially end slum housing in this nation."[33] In a 1971 review of the situation, the U.S. Commission on Civil Rights spoke directly to the point:

139

Fair housing is the law of the land. All three branches of Federal Government have acted to assure that housing is open to all—without discrimination. The executive branch through issuance of the Executive order on equal opportunity in housing in November 1962. . . . Congress, in 1964, added the support of the legislative branch by enacting Title VI of the Civil Rights Act of 1964, proscribing discrimination in programs of activities receiving Federal financial assistance. Four years later, Congress passed the Civil Rights Act of 1968, including a Federal fair housing law (Title VIII), which prohibits discrimination in most of the nation's housing. And later that year, the Supreme Court. . ., in *Jones* v. *Mayer and Co.,* . . . ruled that racial discrimination is prohibited in *all* housing, private as well as public. . . . Title VIII places principal enforcement responsibility in the Department of Housing and Urban Development (HUD).[34]

It has been repeatedly recognized, however, that while law and courts may insist upon equal access to decent housing facilities, a primary condition of success is availability of such housing and capacity to pay for it. As the Secretary of Housing and Urban Development puts it: "Open occupancy is right, but it is not an assurance that poor families now searching for better housing . . . will be able to find it at prices they can afford." It was indeed essentially this concern which led President Lyndon B. Johnson to put before Congress in the spring of 1968, the multibillion dollar housing program which promised to increase by tenfold previous federal efforts in the field.

This program called for the building of some 26 million housing units and rehabilitation of two million units during the next ten years. Six million units of the construction were to be "Federally-assisted housing for low- and moderate-income families, 300,000 to be started the first year" compared to 530,000 started during the past ten years.

The projected means of providing federal financial assistance differed from those of previous programs. Under the new design the federal government subsidized the monthly mortgage payments for poor families by paying all the interest charges needed above one percent. The family would pay up to 20 percent of its monthly income toward the mortgage payment.

Chapter **10**

The Ghetto: Community Characteristics

Its Culture

Racial Ostracism as a Factor

The core of the Negro subculture in American metropolises constitutes an unassimilated way of life: the conjunction of black, southern plantation conditioning and the individualistic, highly motivated, racist spirit of modern urban society. Ecologically, the ghetto is the outcome of nation-wide physical mobility and racial ostracism.

The "free air" of the American city attracts the ambitious underprivileged, but popular white exclusiveness enforces social disjunction and thus black concentration. The city, however, is the locus of commerce and industry: without these there can be no capitalist city. Labor here is auxiliary and residence supportive. The size of the urban population is a reflection of the magnitude of commercial and industrial processes. In other words, the great city is the product of businessmen acting individualistically but conforming nonetheless to

141

a societal tradition conducive to a high degree of capitalist cultural achievement and progress. It is primarily from this tradition that ghetto blacks are largely alienated or excluded.

The growth of the Negro urban population does not, therefore, reflect a concomitant rise in the capacity of blacks to operate the city. Negroes are free to organize their labor and thereby insist upon greater recognition as workers. This fact, however, does not necessarily involve them commensurably in the process of urban creativity and identity. For whites, on the other hand, such organization may be sufficient to relieve frustration because white labor tends, at least theoretically, to constitute business apprenticeship and thus a functional continuum with management. The ghetto is very much a product of the relative unavailability of this dynamic, associational cultural outlet.

Dependence upon political power has therefore been largely illusionary. Attempts to force political power already in the hands of urban blacks to yield the economic base of central cities necessarily results in social confusion, even for the Negro community.

Ghetto culture is not critically lower-class despite its poverty, substandard housing, family disrepute, static outlook, storefront churches, slum conditions, and so on—it is lower-class culture subject to implicitly planned degradation and repression. By and large, the cultural failure and low reputation of Negroes may be thought of as the desiderata of the white ruling élite especially in the traditional homeland of the Negro, the plantation South.

"Deviant behavior" in Negroes confined to their communities thus demonstrates arguments that Negroes are unfit for normal cultural opportunities. Over the past one hundred years the Negro masses have experienced forces of cultural repression such as, for example, the unschooled European immigrant never had to face. Toward the end of the Civil War, Frederick Douglass defined some of these culturally repressive influences as follows:

> we cannot conceal from ourselves . . . the fact that there are many powerful influences, constantly operating, intended and calculated to defeat our just hopes, prolong the existence of the source of all our ills—the system of slavery—strengthen the slave power, darken the conscience of the North, intensify popular prejudice against color, multiply unequal and discriminating laws . . . consign to oblivion the needs of heroism which have distinguished the colored soldiers, deny and despise his

claims to the gratitude of his country, scout his pretensions to American citizenship, establish the selfish idea that this is exclusively the white man's country, pass unheeded all the lessons taught by these four years of fire and sword, undo all that has been done toward our freedom and elevation, take the musket from the shoulders of our brave black soldiers . . . exclude them from the ballot-box where they now possess that right . . . overawe free speech in and out of Congress, obstruct the right of peaceably assembling . . . revive the internal slave-trade . . . reverse the entire order and tendency of the events of the last three years, and postpone indefinitely that glorious deliverance from bondage, which for our sake, and for the sake of the future unity, permanent peace, and highest welfare of all concerned, we had fondly hoped and believed was even now at our door.[1]

The cultural pathologies of the ghetto may thus be thought of as a projected achievement of white power groups. The extreme form of today's racial system was, of course, slavery; and it is revealing to cite again Douglass's reproach: "As to the second point," he said in argument, "viz.: the Negro's ignorance and degradation, there was no disputing either. It was the nature of slavery, from whose depths he had risen, to make him so; and it would have kept him so. It was the *policy* of the system to keep him both ignorant and degraded."[2]

To see clearly the sources of behavior in the ghetto is to recognize the factors involved in change. Thus Rembert W. Patrick is sensitively revealing when he writes of social changes since World War II;

In human relations some southerners worked to ease the burden placed upon Negroes. Hands were shaken; last names were used and Miss, Mr., and Mrs. placed before them; efforts were made to pronounce Negro correctly; and the first letter of that word was capitalized. These were not unimportant concessions by white southerners with deep rooted prejudices. Various forms of discourtesy were and still are the psychological weapons of racial discrimination. Like Thomas Jefferson did in the wisdom of age, liberal southerners realized that environment, not heredity, was the principal reason for the lowly station of the Negro. Still they shuddered at Uncle Tomism without acknowledging their part in forcing the Negro into a degrading obeisance.[3]

Except for this inherent societal pressure, there would be no racial ghetto; and, let us not forget, the pattern is by no means van-

143

quished. There are powerful interests all over the nation continually devoted to its perpetuation. One could, for example, cite the continuing popularity of the racist tactics of Governor George C. Wallace of Alabama, in his quest for the presidency of the United States and the nature of his popularity to illustrate the remarkable strength of anti-Negro sentiments. His almost gleeful depiction of the pathologies of life in the ghetto seem to demonstrate their political value. And many agreed with him that abrogation of the open housing laws would be an important means of remedying this situation.[4]

The Unwanted

Perhaps no phenomenon so profoundly characterizes the mentality of the core ghetto Negro as a sense of not being wanted, included, and accepted in the larger American society. He is not likely to feel encouraged to participate in the legitimate social order. The dominant society tends to speak over his head whereas a member of the Negro middle class is more likely to make this breakthrough.

The core ghetto tends to constitute an external society, racially identified. Thus, from the point of view of the dominant society, the behavior of ghettoites may seem illogical, erratic, or contradictory. If, for example, we study the life of Malcolm X, we observe three principal stages: his youthful ghetto behavior which made him the prey of policemen and jails; his nationalistic transformation during the relative quiet of his incarceration; and finally, his attempts at societal inclusion and identification with the larger community following his experience abroad.

This tendency to exclude Negroes from the dominant social processes goes back, of course, to pre-Civil War days. Frederick Douglass said of it: "The worst enemy of the nation could not cast upon its fair name a greater infamy than to admit that Negroes could be tolerated among them in a state of the most degrading slavery and oppression, and must be cast away, driven into exile, for no other cause than having been freed from their chains."[5] Such difficulties are no doubt at the seat of the irresponsibility openly manifested among Negroes of the core ghetto.

After the 1954 Supreme Court school decision, it seemed to the leaders in many southern states that the time for legally enforcing the social assimilation of Negro Americans had arrived. To be sure, every means of traditional resistance to this purpose were brought into play.

Negroes were encouraged to leave the South. It was felt that if the North really knew the Negro, it too would be revolted by the thought of assimilating him. The following Associated Press report from South Carolina reveals the nature of this attitude:

> Northern advocates of racial integration were challenged today by Gov. George Bell Timmerman, Jr. "to cast off their hypocrisy and accept the Negro into their communities, their institutions and their families." He called on "the integrationist to prove his sincerity" by supporting a program of voluntary migration of Negroes from the South to communities "where racial mixing is acceptable. A Federal program of financial aid to enable those who want to mix to move to other areas," he said, "would cost only a fraction" of the billions advocated for foreign aid.[6]

All over the Deep South there were similar acts of encouragement to those Negroes who were discontent with their status. In a number of deep southern cities Negro families were actually put on buses for transportation to the North, their fares paid, and their debts cancelled on condition that they promise never to return. On March 1, 1956, the Alabama State Senate "unanimously passed a resolution calling on Congress to appropriate funds to move southern Negroes to the North and Midwest 'areas where they are wanted and needed and can be assimilated.'"[7]

Robbed of a normal sense of belonging, clothed with the anonymity and the physical freedom of the metropolist, the ghetto Negro develops a contrary, alienated subculture that is both isolated and self-isolating. As Morton Grodzins puts it:

> Negroes and whites meet each other across separate societies rather than within a single group. The Negro shares with whites the better things of life, but he does so in isolation with other Negroes. The disadvantaged segregated community even produces advantages for some individuals within it, providing protected markets for Negro professionals and businessmen and protected constituencies for Negro political and church leaders. Yet even those who profit from segregation suffer from it. They feel the pin-pricks as well as the sledges of discrimination, and they must suppress their dissatisfaction in accordance with standards of conduct expected of all "better" people, whatever their race.[8]

And yet, the ghettoite does not "suppress his dissatisfaction" in accordance with norms of middle-class society.

145

The Ghetto and Social Classes: Crime as an Index

Improvement of the social status of Negroes in the United States means especially a broadening of the scope of their functional opportunities on the one hand, and removal of barriers to upward achievement and mobility on the other. To the white racists segregation is the most comprehensive and effective device for repression.

Ghetto crime and delinquency rates are objective indices of the social situation. It is true that in the South especially, Negroes are more likely to be unjustly arrested and punished for some crimes, especially those affecting apparent interests of the white community.[9] After all such allowances are made, however, the data probably underestimate actual conditions. Only about 25 percent or less of the crimes against property are cleared by arrests. Table 30 is a compilation of selected criminal acts in which Negro offenders rate inordinately high (over 50 percent of the total) and low (mainly white collar). The abnormally high expectation of crimes of violence and robbery in the core ghetto tends to become a constant source of fear, insecurity, and anguish. Although the regular data show that crime and delinquency among ghetto Negroes are multiples of their incidence among whites, the figures frequently obscure the gravity of the situation. Again, as the U.S. Commission on Civil Disorders points out, "official statistics normally greatly understate actual crime rates because the vast majority of crimes are not reported to the police. For example, a study conducted for the President's Crime Commission in three Washington D.C. precincts shows that six times as many crimes were actually committed against persons and homes as were reported to the police."[10] Table 31 illustrates the situation by actual data for Chicago. The authors conclude in part: "Variations in the crime rate against persons within the city are extremely large. One very low-income Negro district had 35 times as many serious crimes against persons per 100,000 residents as did the high-income white district. . . . Low-income Negro areas have significantly higher crime rates than low-income white areas. This reflects the high degree of social disorganization in the Negro area. . . ."[11]

An important reason for relatively limited official records of criminal acts in the ghetto is that they are regarded as normal, a way of life. They involve techniques of defense and retaliation which may be in themselves unlawful, but are locally expected. Thus the incidence of deviant behavior falls most heavily upon typical inhabitants

Table 30

Urban* Arrests, Selected Offenses, By Race, 1970

Offense Charged	Arrests			
	Total White Negro and Others	*White*	*Negro*	*Percent Negro*
Gambling	65,360	17,021	45,277	69
Murder and non-negligent Manslaughter	9,784	3,167	6,424	66
Robbery	66,436	19,790	45,321	68
Prostitution and Commercialized vice	40,323	13,387	26,498	66
Forcible rape	11,237	4,869	6,171	55
Aggravated assault	93,079	44,137	47,147	51
Forgery and counterfeiting	31,043	19,919	10,842	35
Fraud	52,401	36,373	15,618	30
Embezzlement	6,501	4,658	1,808	28

*3,891 cities over 2,500; 1970 population 102,647,000.

Source: U.S. Department of Justice, *Uniform Crime Reports for the United States,* Washington, D.C., 1970, table 38.

Table 31

Number of Index Crimes* and Patrolmen Assignments per 100,000 Residents in 4 Chicago Police Districts, 1965

Index crimes* and patrolmen	White district Income		Negro district Income	
	High	*Low-middle*	*Very low No. 1*	*Very low No. 2*
Against persons	80	440	1,615	2,820
Against property	1,038	1,750	2,508	2,630
Patrolmen assigned	93	133	243	291

*Index crimes: homicide, forcible rape, aggravated assault, robbery, burglary, grand larceny, and auto theft.

Source: *Report of the National Advisory Commission on Civil Disorders,* 1968, p. 267.

of the core ghetto. It has been shown, for instance, that almost nine-tenths of the crimes committed by Negroes in Chicago between September 1965 and March 1966 "involved Negro victims."[12]

The Ghetto Environment

Although most of the crimes in the ghetto are committed by a minority of its residents, the group as a whole is exposed to its consequences (Chart V). The pathologies tend thus to become an element of the subculture.[13] The physical environment of the community presents overt proof of the behavior that may be expected. Its very aspect alarms the middle class.

Our concern here, however, is mainly with certain recognized conditions. A list of these would include squalor, noise, physical deterioration, adult idleness, profanity, children unattended roaming the streets, vandalism, rape, theft and robbery—all of which are likely to produce a sense of fear and insecurity; the critical point, however, is that core ghetto inhabitants tend to become inured to the situation. David R. Hunter states:

> the slum is more than any of its parts, more than you can see. It is more than the crowded buildings . . . more than the dirty streets, the lackluster people sitting on the steps, the shrieking children running up and down, the sullen boys hanging on the corner, the stupefied addicts leaning against the wall, the cruising patrol car. It is a way of life, and it is a way of looking at the future, or perhaps looking away from it.[14]

Noise in core ghettoes comes not so much from industrial operations as from the very process of living. The blare of soundmaking, amusement machines, the use of automobile horns as a means of social communication, and inconsiderate boisterousness are examples. The uproar which ordinarily goes with ghetto card-playing or drinking parties constitutes particularly distracting forms of noise.

Noisiness and loudness tend to follow the child and the student into the school; and, as we should expect, they tend to engender culture conflict.

The way residential property is kept up is an indication of certain personality and cultural traits. The ghetto situation is no exception. Two principal forces lead to speedy deterioration of core ghetto property: neglect by landlords, and both neglect and destructiveness by occupants. At this point we are concerned not so much

Chart V

Number of Victims (per 100 population) of Serious Crimes by Race and Income Group, 1966.

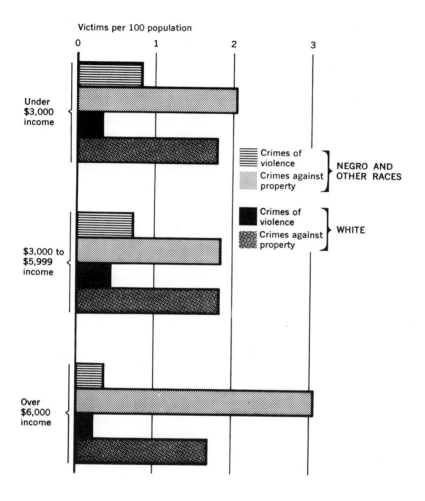

Source: U.S. Bureau of Labor Statistics, 1971.

with landlord neglect as with tenant limitations—the immediate process of ghettoization.

As low-income Negroes move into housing vacated by whites or into subsidized apartments, a process of stripping its environs of articles of value is likely to begin. All moveable decorative items including utilities may disappear: "even garbage cans . . . are sometimes stolen as fast as landlords can replace them."[15] This tendency to strip ghetto housing areas frequently gives them an appearance of ominous bareness.

One of the most tragic aspects of ghetto society is its obvious dissipation of adult time and energy. The spectacle of men in the prime of life, in full daytime, sitting or lying or leaning about ghetto premises is a stark example of the effects of societal isolation. These men seem not to be affected by the cultural spurs toward efficiency and achievement. To them, obviously, nothing seems worth doing. This, of course, may be easily explained as cultural lag, a continuation of work attitudes consistent with the historic culture of slavery. But the phenomenon persists.

One of the marks of the ghetto is the sight of children busily exploring the public community—running in and out of stores, crossing streets, climbing up trees, unattended. This manifestly is ideal preparation for the toughness and excitement of "street corner society." As one observer puts it: "With the father absent and the mother working, many ghetto children spend the bulk of their time on the streets—the streets of a crime-ridden, violence-prone and poverty-stricken world."[16] To these children regular school rooms would appear simply to be drab forms of punitive institution. Moreover, granting the restrictive obligations of poor parents, questions about the nature of concern for their childrens' discipline still remains.

A continuing danger to peace and security in the ghetto is the existence of thievery and robbery. Indeed, burglary tends to be a settled preoccupation of residents. The thief is constantly inventing pretexts and physical devices for entering homes and businesses. By way of protection, windows and doors, especially those of stores, are frequently barricaded. Police officers tend increasingly to be stationed in self-service shops, in elevators, buses, subways, and lavatories. Handbag snatching and muggings are common. More and more, the firearm has been replacing the knife as the principal weapon of assault. Thievery may be regarded as justifiable behavior and sometimes even as a right. This sort of burglary sometimes leads the white retail merchant to withdraw in despair. Moreover, it limits the chances of Negro merchants in filling the void. The civil rights movement and recent protest riots seem to have augmented the boldness of the thief.

Explanations, of course, are not necessarily justifications. Negroes of the ghetto are the immediate sufferers from its social pathologies. It has been a socially limiting milieu for them. Their methods of solving its problems have been spontaneous and frequently self-defeating. It seems clear that the only lasting solution within the larger societal context is the abandonment of ghetto culture—elements of which tend to be consistently related to each other. And, since that culture has begun to overflow into the front room of the larger society, it has been increasingly recognized that its defects can no longer be tolerated.

Chapter 11

Baptism and Intermarriage as Racial Policy

Probably no subject in the field of race relations is more likely to be influenced by personal and propagandistic positions than interracial marriage. This is understandable. In our society, there is a strong, romantic presumption that only two individuals are involved in the choice of mates.

The argument by Negro leaders against legal prohibition of interracial marriage provides an opportunity for faceless groups to take action and focus the race problem on the white woman as the ultimate prize of Negro manhood. On such a basis has racial segregation and discrimination been justified.

Restrictions on intermarriage, however, have constituted an underlying part of the stratagem of racial exploitation, along with negative attitudes toward interracial education, "freedom of the ballot," and equality of opportunity. The total effect has been to limit cultural assimilation and thus to create a social gap powerful enough to prolong indefinitely the vested interests and purpose of the ever-watchful ruling class. In this situation, of course, the cultural consequences of intermarriage tend to be disruptive regardless of the social status of mates. The racists and their laws have made this patently clear.[1]

Endogamy

Endogamy, like any other major social trait, can be categorically differentiated only from the point of view of a particular social system. There may be, for example, tribal endogamy based upon intertribal invidiousness and religious solidarity. In western society Jewish endogamy is a case in point. It seems to have had its origin in ancient Semitic tribalism. The high priest Ezra, after listing specific tribal groups in the region, admonished the Hebrews: "Give not your daughters unto their sons, neither take their daughters unto your sons, nor seek their peace or their wealth for ever (9:12)." The trait has had its historical vicissitudes especially in situations involving Jewish nationalism.

In cases of estate endogamy the broad strata of a pyramidal status structure—slaves, serfs, freedmen, and traditional grades of vassals and lords—maintain their integrity through in-marriage. In caste endogamy, a multiplicity of status groups, functionally identified, constitutes the larger societal structure. Endogamy helps to maintain the solidarity of noncompetitive groups and to provide a dependable milieu for the welfare of their membership—with the upper castes, of course, always securing the greatest advantage. In a caste society there is no social impulse toward intermarriage.

The endogamy with which we are presently concerned, *capitalist endogamy,* entails a more or less calculated policy of imperialistic expediency.

Baptism

Investigation of the beginnings of proscriptions against interracial marriage in North America reveals further the peculiar content of race relations: the withholding of the culture from Negroes so that they might the more easily be exploited. The crucial achievement of the colonial oligarchy was to make interracial marriage appear not only immoral but criminal. Upon this accomplishment depended the structure of racial separation and cultural disparity. In the early history of race relations, another identifying institution, baptism, presented similar and related problems.

153

Baptism, like intermarriage, raised questions inimical to the clear purpose of slavery. It sought to define the Negro as a human being with elementary rights of entry into the stream of cultural development. It made slaves Christians and thus one with the human brotherhood. As James C. Ballagh explains: "It was clear that involuntary slavery of Christians to Christians was inconsistent with the freedom and equality of man involved in the true profession of Christ."[2] Indeed, slavery itself was in part originally justified as an effective means of converting non-Christian peoples and thus serving the humanizing purpose of God:

> The freedom of Christianity was in theory shared by all members of the Christian State, and the name "Christian," in opposition to "heathen," embraced the inhabitants of a Christian land. Consequently the enslavement of Englishmen or persons born in Christian lands was abhorrent. No such feeling was extended to the heathen, whether Jew, Mohammedan or Indian. Slavery was but a just means to a pious end, the salvation of the soul. But when the heathen slave became a convert, a Christian, the inconsistency of a theory that kept him in subjection was apparent. Baptism thus involved a dilemma.[3]

To understand the nature of race relations in its present context it is necessary to keep constantly in mind the interest group to whom this "dilemma" was directly presented: the "traders" who constituted the effective power structure in early colonial America. The problem, squarely faced, involved either a denial of Christianity to those who could be enslaved or a direct abrogation of the humanizing power of Christianity itself. Both solutions were considered. The first was tried perhaps with greater determination in the British West Indies. However, it met with considerable reaction. As Frank Tannenbaum observes:

> This persistent refusal of baptism "touched the English conscience to the raw," but custom, tradition, hostility, and fear on the part of the planters proved stronger than missionary zeal. As one writer puts it, "I sincerely believe and am well assured that the slaves being instructed would be less attentive to labor, less inclined to obey their overseers and other deputies, and would be more anxious and more easily enabled to throw off the yoke of slavery altogether."[4]

This, no doubt, constitutes the essence of the Negro's handicap in North America. In colonial Virginia the second alternative was eventually chosen: the state reluctantly allowed the Negro to be baptized but voided the sacrament of its power to liberate. Again, James C. Ballagh describes the predicament and its solution:

> if enfranchisement was a possible result [of baptism], Christianization was certain to be retarded or completely stopped. The wisdom and the conscience of colonial assemblies were equal to the emergency. They held both to their justification and to their slaves. The Virginia Assembly in a law of 1667 . . . settled the question by the naïve declaration, worthy of the metaphysician that rightly separates the spiritual person from bodily form: "Baptism doth not alter the condition of the person as to his bondage or freedom; in order that diverse masters freed from this doubt may more carefully endeavor the propagation of Christianity."[5]

The conclusion of this logic shows that the oligarchy was conscious of its obligation to placate a doubting, censuring public. And yet, as Ballagh remarks further: "If their consciences at all troubled them, they were easily quieted by the reflection that they were traders and not missionaries, and that the demand was based upon economic necessity."[6]

Economics and Baptism

Having taken the critical step, the propagation of racism as social support of the exploitative purpose now arose as a logical consequence. In other words, this decline of Christianity as an assimilative force led increasingly to a general tendency to regard all Negroes as a group apart characterized by the degrading status of bondage. The implicit liberating power of religion was "supplanted by the more profitable social principle of fundamental racial difference."

> So by a [Virginia] act of 1682 the benefits of Christianity as a mode of securing freedom were definitely denied all Negroes, mulattoes, hostile Moors and Turks, and to such Indians as were sold by other Indians as slaves where original heathenism could be affirmed.[7]

Perhaps for our present purpose—to show that the intrinsic effect of baptism was similar to that of intermarriage—the work of Morgan Godwyn, the Negro's and Indian's advocate, is most revealing. He was an English minister who served as a missionary in Vir-

ginia where he observed the exploitation of Negroes on the plantations. In 1685 he published in London a long "sermon" in which he
pointed out the difference between the practices of French and Spanish colonizers and those of the English regarding baptism of Indian
and Negro slaves.[8] His critique is significant because it seems clearly
to identify the forces in opposition: the interests of businessmen versus the rights of peoples. His censure was addressed to the King of
England, and he was under no illusion about the reactions of the
powerful group he attacked. In opposing them, he said, "I have put
my life in my hand."

It is also interesting to note that Frederick Douglass had no
doubts about the place of baptism in the economic order. In 1881 he
wrote:

> Two hundred years ago, the pious Doctor Godwin dared affirm
> that it was "not a sin to baptize a Negro," and won for him the
> rite of baptism. It was a small concession to [the Negro's] man-
> hood; but it was strongly resisted by the slaveholders of Ja-
> maica, and Virginia. In this they were logical in their argument,
> but they were not logical in their object. They saw plainly that to
> concede the Negro's right to baptism was to receive him into the
> Christian Church, and make him a brother in Christ and hence
> they opposed the first step sternly and bitterly. So long as they
> could keep him beyond the circle of human brotherhood, they
> could scourge him to toil, as a beast of burden, with a good
> Christian conscience, and without reproach.[9]

The appeal, therefore, against Christianization was based essentially on the economic interests of the masters. Eventually, however, Cotton Mather provided a way out:

> "if the Negroes are Christianized [it is argued], they will be
> baptised; and their baptism will presently entitle them to their
> freedom; so our money is thrown away. . . ." There is no such
> thing. . . . Christianity directs a slave . . . to satisfy himself that
> he is the Lord's freeman, tho' he continues a slave. . . . The
> way is now cleared, for the work that is proposed: the excellent
> work, the instruction of the Negroes in the Christian religion.[10]

Accordingly, wherever such instructions and baptism were allowed,
the slave had to accept as basic the teaching that obedient and faithful
service to his master was primarily the will of God.

The sacrament of marriage presented the master class with the
same kind of alternatives as baptism; and it was resisted on inherently

the same principles. Marriage limited control over the slave population as a commodity. Normally, marriage entails family ties and obligations which produce marginal effects institutionally limiting the master's economic power over the individual. He was thus faced with the alternative of doing away with an elementary human institution among the slaves—procreation through the moral sanction of matrimony—and thus abandoning any measure of economic accountability, or allowing marriage and family ties with the consequent limitations of their use as chattel. He chose the former alternative.

Not that marriage and the normal family were completely abolished; rather, the master retained the right either to allow or to forbid them. The situation, as it developed, is related by Tannenbaum:

> Under the law of most of the Southern states, there was no regard for the Negro family, no question of the right of the owner to sell his slaves separately, and no limitation upon separating husband and wife, or child from its mother. That this was so may be seen from the following advertisements:
> NEGROES FOR SALE.—A Negro woman, 24 years of age, and her two children, one eight and the other three years old. Said negroes will be sold SEPARATELY or together, as *desired*. The woman is a good seamstress. She will be sold low for cash, or EXCHANGED FOR GROCERIES.[11]

One profound result of this practice by the oligarchy was to induce utter irresponsibility in the father of slave children. As one court put it: "the father of a slave is unknown in the law."[12] The law thus encouraged Negro promiscuity. Negro women ordinarily became free game for white and black men alike—indeed for white men particularly since they were the more authoritative and possessive.

In another case, to illustrate, the children of a slave husband and "a free woman of color" (in Virginia, 1848) were held as slaves. "On behalf of herself and her three children the woman applied for a writ of *habeas corpus* . . . charging that they were illegally detained." The court held that "the apprentices in question are bastards, their father being a slave, and therefore incapable of contracting matrimony in the mode prescribed by our law."[13] Thus the necessities of thralldom logically determined the status of the children.

Intermarriage did not present a distinctly new problem; it merely constituted an aggravation of the basic dilemma. And yet, an element of white popular disloyalty to the ruling class was introduced. The white person who intermarried became racially disloyal.

157

According to a Kentucky court in 1841—after reviewing precedent going back one hundred years—"our local law should be understood as prohibiting such [interracial] marriages, as inconsistent . . . with decorum, social order, public policy, and the national sentiment; and . . . they must, therefore, be deemed unlawful and, of course, void."[14] This was the law. But it should be differentiated from any assumption of inherent antipathy between the races. The law strove for consistency with the major facts of the slavocracy.

Sex and the Racial System

Intermarriage between a white woman and a Negro man presented a greater threat to the system than the reverse relationship. The oligarchy, therefore, gave it special attention and provided extremely heavy penalties for the white woman. Early in the history of Maryland, when the subject of interracial marriage was still in flux, a law (1663) declared: "That whatsoever freeborn women (English) shall intermarry with any slave . . . shall serve the master of such slave during the life of her husband; all the issue of such freeborn women, so married, shall be slave as their fathers were."[15] She might also be banished, sold into servitude, separated from the child and castigated.

And yet, she sometimes stood her ground, but this only made matters more severe for her. Around 1700, the following case in Pennsylvania suggests the severity of the punishment:

> David Lewis Constable of Haverfoord Returned A negroe man of his And A white woman for haveing A Basterd Childe . . . the negroe said she Intised him and promised him to marry him: she being examined, Confest the same: . . . the Court ordered that she shall Receive Twenty one laishes on her beare Backe . . . and the Court ordered the negroe never more to meddle with any white woman uppon paine of his life.[16]

It has been repeatedly argued, even by those who are not detractors of the Negro people, that the critical force in race relations is a peculiar sexual drive of the Negro male toward the white female. Ordinarily the argument has been kept on a biological plane with its gravamen centering about some implicit fear among whites of "mongrelization." An explanation of race relations, however, should always involve the social system and a given situation. Intermarriage is essentially cultural, not biological. From the latter point of view, it has not been the Negro man but the white woman who presented the greatest problem to the oligarchy.

Since the law did not recognize the Negro man as a husband, it could have left the white woman who bore him children to suffer the consequences. That, no doubt, would have been punishment enough. The system, however, could not endure the status of her children as freedmen. In such a relationship, the white woman would constitute a most effective cultural bridge. The white mother was more likely to transmit the culture of the dominant society to her children than the Negro mother.[17] Moreover, if she married, she could exert powerful influence upon her Negro husband directly, contrary to the essential purpose of the white ruling class. She could help him to discard his tradition of racial obsequiousness and narrow occupational outlook. Her acceptance of her role as wife and cultural leader would create a social situation antithetical to Negro slavery. Thus the white woman's freedom to marry became one of the most challenging forces in the system.

In that situation the obvious duty of the oligarchy was that of separating, as far as possible, white women from colored men. This was accomplished partly by putting her upon a psychological "pedestal," and insisting that it was her elementary wish to be there. The oligarchy maintained that it was inconceivable that any affectionate relationship could develop between white women and black or mulatto men. Moreover, since most Negro men could not marry, any incidence of interracial coition tended automatically to be defined as Negro rape. Indeed, the artificial tension of the situation sometimes led to neurotic dreams among white women of having been ravished by Negro men.

In a sense, then, it was not essentially the Negro male's sexual desire which was feared and restricted but rather the sexual freedom of white women. An early Maryland law (1715) warned her as follows: "Any white woman who shall suffer or permit herself to be got with child by a negro or mulatto . . . shall be sentenced to the penitentiary for not less than eighteen months nor more than five years" (Maryland: Rev. Code, art. 72, § 113).

The counterpart of the "pedestal" was the pit of degradation to which the Negro male was consigned. He had to be taught to accept a conception of himself so debased and was threatened by penalties so frightful that he could form no design regarding white women as normal sexual objects. Thus it became a criminal offense

159

for a Negro or mulatto male, even by ocular or verbal means, to conceive of sexual attraction to a white woman. The infamous Scottsboro trial illustrates the continuity and the lengths to which this determination of the white power structure of a state might be carried in order to exact its proscription against Negro-male-white-female sex relations.

This general situation provided the classic rationale for the formal and informal lynching of Negroes, especially in the South. Intercourse between white men and Negro women produced a less direct danger to the social system. Cohabitation without marriage left mulatto children mainly in the hands of slave mothers, and they were reared to take their place in bondage. Marriage, of course, produced families and this had the effect of establishing a primary allegiance of the white male basically opposed to slavery. Although this allegiance was not so pervasive as that of the white mother, the state oligarchies still condemned it outright.[18] Promiscuous sex relations with Negro women were difficult to prove and were carried on undercover.

The problem was one of eliminating the mulatto as a force for social change. Since, because of his biracial parenthood, he tended to have a double allegiance, he could not be given full status in the dominant society without the prospects of his utilizing it in opposition to thralldom. But he could be given a special intermediate status sufficiently attractive to alienate him from the blacks; and, in some states, Louisiana especially, this was actually tried; or he could be pushed back into unabridged slavery; and, with the shortage of labor in colonial America, this course seemed most attractive to the ruling class. As Ballagh puts it with regard to the norm-setting situation in Virginia:

> In the recognized impossibility of completely checking the growth of a mulatto class the only alternative left was to reduce this class as far as possible to the status of the lower parent, so we find that as long as a trace of the inferior blood was commonly recognizable the person was socially, as well as legally, treated as far as possible as a full blooded Indian or negro. Thus mulattoes, like negroes and Indians, could not hold office nor could they bear witness except against persons of their color.[19]

Even in bondage, however, mulattoes tended to occupy privileged places. They were likely to get the more desirable jobs, to be trained in some skill, and to be made the concubines of the masters. They thus became a "fertile source of new bastards." "Their position,'' says Ballagh, ''rendered them especially eligible for gross purposes, both in their intimate contact with the Negroes and in their relations to their employers.''[20] The definition of the mulatto came to be accepted as any person of known Negro ancestry.

The Cultural Gap

We now have an intimation of the essential nature of the Negro problem in the United States. He does not suffer merely from the disadvantage of a lower-class subculture but rather from a hollowed out, distorted, and perverted version of that culture. He has been made to accept a definition of himself as unworthy of dignity and respect; he has been made to observe laws that require a built-in accommodation to degradation. By contrast, in Latin America, ''the slave was married in the church, and the banns were regularly published. It gave the slave's family a moral and religious character unknown in other American and slave systems.''[21]

The Negro subculture thus lacked vital elements, a situation still insisted upon by the oligarchy even long after freedom. The culture itself served to restrict assimilation. It was, no doubt, knowledge of this pathological cultural conditioning which led some of the colonies to fear the disorganizing presence of the manumitted slave or the free Negro, and thus sought to compel their emigration from the territory.

Status of Intermarriage

Historical Patterns

Alexis de Tocqueville, writing in the middle of the nineteenth century and taking his bearings from the American slavocracy and the Haitian revolution, declared:

> Those who hope that the Europeans will ever be amalgamated with the Negroes appear to me to delude themselves. I am not led to any such conclusion by my reason or by the evidence of facts. Hitherto wherever the whites have been the most powerful, they have held the blacks in degradation or in slavery; wherever the Negroes have been strongest, they have destroyed the whites: this has been the only balance that has ever taken place between the two races.[22]

It seems obvious now that Tocqueville's view, by no means limited to him at that time, was too nearsighted. One hundred years

161

later, after long and intensive study of race relations, W.E.B. DuBois explained:

> If white and black in the South were free and intelligent, there would be friendship and some inter-marriage and there ought to be; but none would marry where he did not wish to, and there could be no greater intermingling in the future than in the shameful past, unless this union of races proved successful and attractive.[23]

All through the history of race relations in the United States there has been white and black miscegenation both through inter-marriage and informal relationships. Thus far, however, slavery presented the most favorable situation. The economic and political re-conquest of the Negro during the post-Reconstruction period tended to continue a situation conducive to interracial cohabitation. Up to about 1940, the pattern of miscegenation involved predominantly white males and Negro females. For the period of thralldom, John H. Franklin summarizes some of the points we have been making:

> The extensive miscegenation which went on during the slave period was largely the result of people living and working together at common tasks and the subjection of Negro women to the whims and desires of white men. There was some race mixture that resulted from the association of Negro men and white women, but this was only a small percentage of the total. Despite all the laws against the intermingling of the races, the practice continued; and its persistence is another example of the refusal of the members of the dominant group to abide by the laws which they themselves created.[24]

As the economic and social status of Negroes improved, the pattern of interracial sex relations tended to change from promiscuity and concubinage between white males and Negro females to marriage between Negro males and white females. However, this apparent reversal in the traditional order of mating became much more restricted not only because of its institutionalization but also because of prohibitive regional legislation. And yet the prospects may become more significant for a development of stable race relations.

Data from the 1960 U.S. Census (see table 32) seem to question the general conclusion about the racial pattern of intermarriage: that white females predominate. In a closely reasoned discussion, Lewis F. Carter argues that those researchers who emphasize Negro-male-white-female marriage ("hypogamy" instead of "hypergamy") gathered all their facts from large, urban centers and not from the nation as a whole nor from smaller communities. Their work thus introduces an "urban and regional bias" which tends to show a reversal of the actual relationship.[25] And, as we have just intimated, the census data seem to concur.

Table 32

**Negro-White Married Couples for the United States
and Selected Areas, 1960**

Area	Negro Husband	Negro Wife	Total Couples
United States	25,496	25,913	51,427
Central cities of Urbanized areas	12,295	10,871	23,166
Rural Farm	1,609	2,714	4,323
The South	8,624	11,808	20,432
Rural farm	1,589	2,294	3,883

Source: United States Census of Population 1960, *Marital Status,* Report PC (2)–4E, table 10. (Based on 5 percent Census sample.)

Of the approximately 50,000 interracial marriages in the United States, there appears to be no significant difference in the racial pattern of mates; in the central cities, however, there were a larger number of Negro-male-white-female couples while the rural areas (mostly in the South) showed a preponderance of white-male-Negro-female marriages. Obviously there remains very much to be explained if these data are to be accepted. Until 1967, all the southern states prohibited interracial marriage. We should expect, moreover, rural areas to be most conservative and thus to limit the chances of white men marrying Negro women.

An index on the momentum of race mixture is suggested by data on the mulatto population. In 1850, 406,000, or 11 percent of the Negro population were recorded as mulatto; in 1910, the figure reached 2,051,000, or 21 percent. Both the changing definition of the term *mulatto* and the mating of mulattoes with blacks and whites should be taken into consideration. The census has discontinued its record of this characteristic of the population. "Passing," obviously,

163

is a concern of mulattoes. It has been estimated that if those "passing" were counted, the figure on intermarriages would be closer to 600,000 than 50,000.[26] Mulatto males, it is thought, pass more frequently than females. Females tend to be more family-bound than males.

Attitude of Negroes

The fact that these numbers are small when compared to the totals for intraracial marriages is not of primary significance. The trend of social attitudes regarding the practice is far more revealing. Intermarriage has never been opposed by responsible Negro leaders; indeed, it has been advocated not only as a right of free men but also as a means of protecting Negro women from the sexual irresponsibility of white men.

The proscription, moreover, tended to remain as a standing insult to Negroes, a fact which prompted W.E.B. DuBois to declare: "[This] impudent and vicious demand that all colored folk shall write themselves down as brutes by a general assertion of their unfitness to marry other decent folk, is a nightmare." In a 1967 report on the argument before the U.S. Supreme Court in the Loving case, this point was brought out:

> Loving's lawyers told the Court that antimiscegenation laws are all that remain of the once elaborate legal structure of segregation in the South and that they continue to symbolize "the Negro's relegation to second-class citizenship. . . . White racists can still point to these laws to support their appeal to the ultimate superstition fostering racial prejudice—the myth that Negroes are innately inferior to whites."[27]

Intermarriage has been dignified by such outstanding Negroes as Frederick Douglass, Walter White, Richard Wright, Edward Brooke, Lorraine Hansberry and many others. Those who intermarry are probably of a higher average social status than that of the general population. Freedom to intermarry does not mean, of course, that the races will become totally fused.

Since we may assume that opposition to intermarriage is not the critical aspect of race relations but only one important means to further other basic objectives, we should expect antagonism and propaganda against it to subside as the economic, political, and educational opportunities of Negroes are normalized. The Negro breakthrough in these areas since the early 1950's has tended to circumvent the propagation of antimiscegenation propaganda. Results of a general survey of popular sentiment on interracial marriage, particularly the marriage of the daughter of the United States Secretary of State, Margaret Rusk, to Guy G. Smith in 1967, seem to indicate a definite weakening of the opposition. Perhaps the following response summarizes the tenor of its conclusion:

> Judge Vaino Spencer, a Los Angeles municipal court judge who viewed the [Smith-Rusk] marriage both as a Negro and a woman, observed: "That two young, attractive, well-educated people, both from such nice families, should be able to marry today with their parents present is a very special thing. It shows a tremendous change in attitude on the part of people from both groups."[28]

A few years later, announcement of the engagement of Ralph J. Bunche, Jr., son of the late U.S. undersecretary for special political affairs, to Patricia Hittinger, daughter of William Hittinger, an outstanding businessman, was made on the society page of the *New York Times* (Sunday, Jaunary 2, 1972) but no mention was made of racial difference. The incident was not reported as a news item.

Modern Law and Intermarriage

The trend of the legal status of interracial marriage expresses a change in attitude even more concretely. Historically, antimiscegenation state statutes have been standard governmental policy. The United States Supreme Court avoided confrontation of the issue since 1883 when, in *Pace* v. *Alabama*,[29] it supported the state law against interracial cohabitation. Beyond doubt, the majesty of those laws has had a powerfully deterring influence since they defined an intermarriage contract as criminal and void. The authorities assumed that, like the attitude toward incest, only the abnormal would deign to question the ban.

By 1930, some forty states had experience with anti-intermarriage laws; and attempts had been made to make such proscriptions legal in twelve others, in addition to the District of Columbia. The total effect of these laws on the rest of the country was not negligible. Knowledge of the "indecency" became part of the general American culture. Physical attacks on Negro-white couples in the streets of New York and Chicago by outraged or revolted whites were not uncommon.

Soon after World War II, however, cracks began to appear in the "cake of custom." The movement involved two trends: states began to repeal their restrictive laws with such momentum that by 1967 they remained only in the southern region; and both state and federal courts moved with increasing determination against them. The latter trend culminated, on June 12, 1967, in a declaration by the United States Supreme Court that:

> "these [restrictions] cannot stand consistently with the [Equal Protection Clause of the] Fourteenth Amendment. . . . the freedom to marry or not to marry a person of another race resides with the individual and cannot be infringed by the State."

The effect of this decision was to abrogate all legislation making intermarriage illegal. It involved in the process some seventeen state jurisdictions.

The court found it necessary to overrule the opinion of the Virginia trial judge (Leon M. Bazile) who had written in part:

> Almighty God created the races white, black, yellow, malay, and red, and he placed them on separate continents. And but for the interference with His arrangement, there would be no cause for such marriages. The fact that He separated the races shows that He did not intend for the races to mix.[30]

In this leading case, a white man, Richard Loving from Virginia, married a Negro woman, Mildred Jeter, in the District of Columbia—where the laws permitted intermarriage—and then returned to live in Virginia where they faced a nonintermarriage statute and resultant conviction.

Two cases preceded it: one in California in 1948 (*Perez* v. *Lippold,* 32 Cal. 3d 711) in which the California State Supreme Court held that the statute restricting marriage because of race violated the Fourteenth Amendment; and another in Florida which was finally decided by the U.S. Supreme Court in 1964, anticipating the *Loving* decision. In the Florida case, *McLaughlin* v. *Florida,* (U.S. Supreme Court, Oct. Term, 153 So. 2d 1, 1964) an unmarried Negro man and white woman occupied the same room at night, in violation of the state law which "made criminal a white person and a Negro living together in adultery or fornication." The Court said: "It is readily apparent that [the law] treats the interracial couple . . . differently than it does any other couple. No couple other than a Negro and a

166

white person can be convicted under [it].'' The Court, therefore, struck down the specific statute but left intact ''the State's prohibition of interracial marriage.'' In the present case, however, the concurring opinion of Justice Stewart enunciated the precedent even more definitively. Said he:

> I cannot conceive of a valid legislative purpose under our Constitution for a state law which makes the color of a person's skin the test of whether his conduct is a criminal offense. The [couple] were convicted, fined, and imprisoned under a statute which made their conduct criminal only because they were of different races. . . . I think it is simply not possible for a state law to be valid under our Constitution which makes the criminality of an act depend upon the race of the actor. Discrimination of that kind is invidious *per se*.

This, then, has been the legalistic fate of statuary restrictions on interracial mating in the history of American race relations. The ultimate frontal attack upon it by the courts has logically followed the progress of more elementary aspects of the problem: education, economic opportunity, access to the ballot, housing. And yet, the effects of its use as a diversion and foil to progress have been tremendous. Much of the difficulty in overcoming the emotional residues of the tradition still remains.

The Prospects

In the foreseeable future we should expect the Negro-male-white-female pattern of intermarriage to continue. The white woman, representative of the larger superordinate culture, and the Negro man's assimilation to that culture, besides his primary role as initiator of matrimony, may establish the basis for that pattern. The white-man-Negro-woman marriage will depend upon the rising social status of Negroes, the larger cultural interracial contacts incident to desegregation, and the normal attraction of personalities.

Two negative forces must be reckoned with: the rise of Negro nationalism and the still obdurate white racism, especially in the South. Black nationalism tends to add difficulties to acceptance of the intermarried family in the Negro community. White racism, of course, not only rejects the family but also actively manifests displeasure. Ordinarily the social life of the couple and that of their children are conspicuously identified with the Negro community; and this is affected by social class affiliation.

In time, however, we should expect all these negative indices to subside. Negro group negativism has been largely a response to the reactions of whites; and these reactions now tend to be directly confronted by other more fundamental trends in race relations. For example, we should expect white employers to be far less ready to discharge an intermarried spouse merely because of the marriage; housing should be more readily available than in the past; aggressive staring and even violence by whites against an interracial family in public may find increasingly less social approval. Moreover, as these public sanctions abate, we should expect the parental families, especially that of the white spouse, to be more readily reconciled to the interracial marriage.

There has been no spectacular rise in interracial marriages following the Supreme Court's nullification of statutory prohibitions in June 1967. About a year later, July 1968, a survey by the Associated Press to determine its effects, especially in the southern states, concluded: "On the basis of records and estimates, it is likely that the number of interracial marriages in these states during the first year of freedom to marry falls below 100."[31]

The significant fact inheres not so much in the frequency of intermarriage as in the disposition of society to take such marriages for granted. This desideratum will be hastened as the need to maintain interracial cultural disparity continues to diminish.

Chapter 12

The Family

Place and Significance of the Negro Family

In any large-scale society, the family does not determine the characteristics of the system; society does.[1] To understand the institutional role of the family, therefore, the society and its elements must be understood. In other words, the family, with different degrees of perfection, responds to the constitution and objectives of the social system. "The modern democratic family," explain Burgess and Locke, "to a great extent is a product of the economic and social trends accompanying and following the industrial revolution."[2]

Ordinarily, and especially in Western society, it is an institution whose function is that of procreation (sanctioned by marriage), maintenance and socialization of the young, and conservation of the elementary welfare of its adult components. The family has been traditionally respected, even by the state, as a haven for its members, whose privacy should not be thoughtlessly breached by any authority. In the West, this attitude is symbolized by the adage that a man's house is his castle.[3]

169

The significant social fact for the Negro family—the great average family descending from slavery—is that it has been denied the normal, idealistic attributes of the institution. The basis of this denial is the determination of the white ruling class to exclude Negroes from participation in the culture. The family tends to constitute a subculture of the larger culture. It ordinarily seeks to recreate the cultural milieu in microcosm for the socialization of its members, the aim being their most effective out-group participation.[4]

In our social system, it is right and proper that the man—husband, father—assume leadership in the family's cultural orientation, especially in its economic and vocational aspects. The man ordinarily takes the initiative in its constitution, and thus fulfills his primary societal role—his calling. It is this role which identifies him with the vital processes of society, and thus makes his family societally adjusted.

The family is ordinarily considered successful if the wife is cooperative and supports her husband's career. The greater the opportunity for the realization of a man's career, the greater the trend toward a man-centered type of family. The ascendancy of maleness in the family is not derived primarily from the male-female interrelationship within the family, but rather from the larger society. In times of crisis, in war, in masculine games, in "frontier" movements the male brushes aside women and children, defines the problem, and acts for the whole society. Attitudes acquired through such functions also define his headship within the family.[5]

But that social attribute in our society which commends responsibility, self-reliance, competitiveness, and achievement, especially among males, has been traditionally unavailable to Negroes. This point has been emphasized by Professor J. H. Scanzoni who writes, in reference to the Negro lower-class family, that whatever provisions devised for its welfare, "they must be based on the cardinal theoretical principle that the conjugal family is inextricably linked to the American economic-opportunity structure, chiefly through the *husband's* occupational role."[6]

It is, of course, higher education that determines the dynamics and growth of the economic system. It is here, therefore, that we should expect to see the male involved. It is here also that he consistently develops the personality characteristics necessary for the assumption of his position as head of the family. Masculine control of the larger society is consistent with assumption of leadership in education. We observe, however, in table 33, the racial anomaly. The Negro male adult shows the lowest percentage of advanced education—lower even than that of the Negro female—while the white male is by far, and logically, the most highly educated.

Table 33

Percent of Population 25 to 34 Years Old Who Completed 4 Years of College or More, by Sex, 1960, 1966, and 1970

Year	*Negro*			*White*		
	Total	*Male*	*Female*	*Total*	*Male*	*Female*
1960	4.3	3.9	4.6	11.7	15.7	7.8
1966	5.7	5.2	6.1	14.6	18.9	10.4
1970	6.1	5.8	6.4	16.6	20.9	12.3

Source: U.S. Department of Commerce, Bureau of the Census, *The Social and Economic Status of Negroes in the United States,* 1970, p. 81.

In a sense, then, the Negro woman may be considered better prepared for leadership in the Negro family. As we shall see, this and other causes wreak havoc in the Negro family. The lower the social class the more evident is this fact. The purest illustration of this goes back to thralldom. Where, in that situation, cohabitation was allowed, the master ordinarily bypassed the Negro man and dealt directly with the woman of the cabin concerning such matters as supplies and care of the children.

Freedom and Marriage

After the Civil War, marriage among the freedmen assumed new meaning to the reconstituted white employer class. During the time of bondage, let us recall, the institution of marriage tended to limit the chattel interests of the master, hence he relied upon his legal power to disregard it. He controlled procreation; and children inevitably became his property. In the process, the basic social rights and duties infringed upon were particularly those of the Negro man. Coition for him lost its customary significance. Indeed, sexual promiscuity was often encouraged; he thus gained a degree of sexual freedom but lost self-respect, a sense of possession, and the responsibility of manhood. Since these values had to be societally supported and learned, the majority of Negroes, no doubt, became accommodated to a pattern of sexual irregularity. It is to this important fact that Tocqueville referred, when he wrote: "The Negro has no family: woman is merely the temporary companion of his pleasures, and his children are on an equality with himself from the moment of their birth."[7]

When freedom came, this penchant for nonfamily life had to be lived down. The process of change was assisted by the new attitude of the dispossessed whites toward Negro marriage and by missionary work in the field. For the dispossessed employer class the marriage of Negro workers now had two positive values: it tended to tie more securely wives and children to husbands as units of labor—to employ the man on the plantation was to employ his family—and it assured the dependability of the male worker.[8]

The family headed by the man was especially desirable under the system of share tenancy, generally adopted after the war, in which the family furnished all the labor in the production of crops for a share of the income from their sale. The landowner deducted from that share the cost of the family's annual maintenance. Family tenancy of some form, into which the majority of freedmen gravitated, thus became a new source of economic pressure and labor exploitation.

Initially, there seems to have been no great eagerness among the majority of freedmen for conventional marriage. Males, particularly, appear to have become accustomed to the looser sexual patterns. Here, moreover, was an insistence upon responsibility without the motivation of freedom of opportunity or rewards of success. As Henderson H. Donald explains:

> at first the freedmen had a marriage system that was peculiarly their own. It was cohabitation, that is, common-law marriage, an arrangement whereby men and women lived together as husbands and wives without taking the trouble to procure marriage licenses and to have themselves joined in wedlock by appropriate ceremony. Their marital unions, therefore, were hardly different from those which they were accustomed to form under the slave regime.[9]

In one particular respect, however, the new system of marriage was different from that characteristic of the slave regime: it was free *by law* from the master's direct determination. This fact allowed a number of forces to come into play to regularize the institution: persuasion by missionaries and by the newly established churches, mild punitive sanctions from legislatures and local courts,[10] rules and advice issued by the Freedmen's Bureau,[11] and the planter's preference for families as prospective tenants.[12]

By 1890, the date of the first general census showing "conjugal conditions" of the population, about 32 percent of the Negro population were married compared to about 35 percent for native white of native parentage. Table 34 makes this comparison.

Table 34

Marital Status of Negro and Native White of Native Parentage Population for the United States, 1890

Status	*Negro*			*Native White*		
	Total	*Male*	*Female*	*Total*	*Male*	*Female*
United States	100.0	100.0	100.0	100.0	100.0	100.0
Single	62.5	65.7	59.3	59.8	62.7	56.7
Married	31.7	31.6	31.7	35.4	34.5	36.3
Widowed	5.5	2.5	8.6	4.5	2.5	6.6
Divorced	0.2	0.1	0.3	0.2	0.2	0.3
Unknown	0.1	0.2	0.1	0.1	0.2	0.1

Source: *The Eleventh Census of the U.S.*, Pt. 3, 1890, pp. 115 and 116.

Although opposition to formal marriage among Negroes ceased, adverse racial pressures upon the family were by no means removed. Indeed, the Negro family tended to be the reservoir of all the pathological consequences of race prejudice and discrimination peculiar to the system. During the Reconstruction period, the Negro male was rarely allowed to achieve true manhood. He was never "mistered," he could still be addressed "Sambo" or "boy" with impunity, his posture before whites of any consequence had to be that of cringing obsequiousness; he could not speak up to whites in assertion of his interests as a normal citizen should nor was he allowed to compete occupationally with whites; various economic devices, sometimes culminating in peonage, were officially sanctioned to prolong his exploitation; the public education of his children was relatively limited and structured so as to maintain their lower-class position; they could expect little or no systematic discipline from him; his wife still sought employment in domestic service or in the cotton and tobacco fields.

On entering the "white man's" house he had to use back doors, but his home was entered from the front with hardly a knock by landlords or other whites. The limited cultural motivation in his family usually sprang from the women. Indeed, the unrelenting social pressures upon the man and his normal world tended to leave the onus of responsibility for stability of the family in the hands of women.

And yet, it should be emphasized that the behavior of the Negro family man was not merely a consequence of negative social pressures. He was not, on the whole, a connoisseur of family ideals. The culture of slavery left him with disreputable habits of companionship and fatherhood.[13] At the Civil War's end there were so many "reputed" cases of polygyny and polyandry that special laws had to be enacted to enforce monogamous relationships.[14] The family had thus not yet become the man's customary source of motivation and self-realization. As Henderson H. Donald relates it:

> Very soon the Federal government took action to check this tendency. . . . On May 15, 1865, General John M. Schofield, commanding in North Carolina, decreed that able-bodied Negroes must support their families, and might not go away from home leaving aged persons helpless. . . . Two weeks later, the military authority at Lynchburg, Virginia, issued an order to the effect that husbands must labor for the support of their wives and families, sons for their parents, and brothers for their younger brothers and sisters. The order especially emphasized that the freedman must recognize his responsibility to live with and support his family; he must provide the members thereof with a house, food, clothing, and all in his power for their comfort; he must be responsible for their conduct; must compel his sons and daughters to perform such work as they were capable of; and that he was entitled to receive their wages and obligated to provide for their support.[15]

These, manifestly, are normal traditions of husband and father responsibility. However, the generative force of masculine family responsibility emanates chiefly from outside the home. A father cannot be socially conditioned to regard himself as puerile, indecisive, and without ambition in the society at large and yet be expected to exercise responsible mastery in the home.[16]

Discipline of Children

The relative absence of traditional authority and cultural pur-
posiveness in the Negro father tended to play havoc with his constituted role as disciplinarian. In the social situation deriving from the
Civil War, he was likely to reach the conclusion that he had no social
aspirations strong enough to serve as a constructive basis for the
discipline of his children. Indeed, the little formal schooling available
to the young led him to believe that the children knew best.[17] It was
the obdurate problems of integration, which this society presented
the freedmen, that mainly determined his inconsistency and irresolu-
tion in the exercise of parental control. The following observation
suggests this:

> Although widespread among the Negroes was the custom of
> chastising the young as a means of regulating their behavior,
> there seemed to have been many parents who were not at all
> inclined to discipline their children in any way. Thus in the
> eighteen-eighties, it was noted that even the most respectable
> parents allowed their children to grow up without steady in-
> struction in lessons of propriety and morality. In the Gulf States
> the children were permitted, for the most part, to act as they
> pleased. The father could not govern them. Hence they were
> growing up in idleness and shiftlessness. When necessity con-
> strained them to labor, their services were reluctant and proved
> of little value.[18]

And yet, the cardinal difficulty inhered not so much in laxity of
parental discipline as in the problem of devising self-respecting "lessons in propriety and morality." To be consistent with the existing
demands of the oligarchy, the Negro parent would have been con-
strained to give his children dishonorable lessons in social subordination—lessons contrary to those given the neighboring white
children. The master had become the father surrogate.

Place of the Woman

Another factor characteristic of the structure of the Negro
home from that in society as a whole was the peculiar place occupied
by the woman. In white society, one important source of the man's
authority over his wife was his normal control of the purse strings. As
we have seen, slavery virtually turned this function over to the
woman of the cabin: "supplies" were ordinarily delivered to her. But
more importantly, she had obligations to work in the field or in the

master's "big house" similar to those of the man. When freedom came, this tradition of the Negro woman as a worker continued. On the other hand, the white woman was ordinarily regarded as a "home-maker."

The Negro wife tended to continue her tradition of work outside the home, and the husband ordinarily showed that he expected it. H. H. Donald cites an extreme example:

> In some of the cities and towns of the South, the idle Negro obtained his food from the kitchens of white families where his wives were employed—for he generally had two or three wives, to make sure of something to eat when one quarreled with him. His clothes were old garments stolen or begged by the women from their employers, and his spending money for tobacco and whisky he got by pilfering whatever he could lay his hands on of dark nights that was salable to the junk dealers.[19]

Some time ago the writer attempted to indicate the relationship between marriage and employment for Negro women compared to that of white women.[20] There was a decided difference between the marriage and employment curves for the two groups. In 1930, at all ages, Negro women in the United States were not only more highly employed than white women but also far less likely to give up the job with the coming of matrimony. Between ages twenty and thirty-four white female employment dropped precipitously; but Negro employment continued to rise until age forty when it tapered off gradually with advancing age.

Now let us turn to the significance of poverty as it affects the family. In 1969, as table 35 shows, 28 percent or 1,326,000 Negro families in the United States were below the low income level as defined by the census. In the central cities of metropolitan areas, 21 percent of the Negro families were below this poverty line. The non-metropolitan areas of the south showed the highest incidence: 50 percent of all the Negro families were below the low income level.[21]

Stability of the Family

Although marriage and family obligations are, today, clearly the basis of Negro life, they are still, for the group as a whole, relatively fragile institutions. The signs are, moreover, that they are probably becoming more so.[22] Since 1950 the percent of all Negro families with husband and wife present fell from about 78 percent to 67 percent in 1971. During the same period the percentage of white

176

Table 35

Families by Sex of Head, and by Income, 1969

Family income	Negro		White	
	All families (thousands)	*Percent of all families Female head*	*All families (thousands)*	*Percent of all families Female head*
Total	4,774	28	46,024	9
Under $3,000	1,015	58	3,713	29
$3,000 to $4,999	947	39	4,453	19
$5,000 to $6,999	831	26	5,428	14
$7,000 to $9,999	934	12	10,098	7
$10,000 to $14,999	706	7	12,871	4
$15,000 and over	341	6	9,462	3

husband-and-wife families tended to remain constant at about 88 percent of the total.

The correlate of this situation among Negroes has been the rising percentage of families with female heads. This figure rose from approximately 18 percent in 1950 to about 29 percent in 1971. White families with female heads tended to remain, for the same period, at about 9 percent of all white families.

A comparison of the marital status of female heads of families helps to define the cause of the phenomenon. Table 36 shows that for 1970 the single and separated accounted for 50 percent of the female heads of families among Negroes but only 20 percent among whites. It has been shown also that the percentage for both the single and separated increased for Negroes from 41 percent in 1960.[23]

Size of family income tends to be inversely related to the percentage of families headed by women. This relationship holds for both Negroes and whites. In every category, however, the percentage of families with female heads is larger for Negroes than for whites. The effect of a change in income on the type of family head seems decisive enough; obviously, however, there still remains an abiding

Table 36

Marital Status of Female Heads of Families, 1970

Marital status	Negro	White
Total, female heads (thousands)	1,349	4,186
Percent, total	100	100
Single (never married)	16	9
Separated or divorced	48	37
Separated	34	11
Divorced	14	25
Married, husband absent	6	7
In Armed Forces	2	3
Other reasons	4	5
Widowed	30	47

cultural difference. Is the extent of marriage and family stability among Negroes associated not only with economic status but such factors as cultural assimilation, differences in morbidity and mortality?

Maintenance of idealistic values of the family entail various types of costs. These values are largely realizable within the social context of the family itself and in the larger community. Many types of social participation presuppose the family; and the higher the social status, the more important the social and economic values of the normal family. Perhaps the consistent difference in family stability between whites and Negroes, in spite of economic variations, has been due to differences in opportunity for family-value realization. The higher percentage of divorce relative to separation among whites, as shown in Table 36, is probably indicative of the greater significance of social involvement for white families.

The relatively greater incidence of illegitimacy among Negroes may also be defined in terms of societal inclusion. From about 1940 to 1960 illegitimacy among Negroes has been about ten times the rate for whites. Since that time, as indicated in Table 37, a decreasing rate among Negroes and a gradual rise among whites have tended to narrow the difference. Like female heads of families, illegitimacy for both Negroes and whites correlates negatively with rising income and education. A census-tract analysis for Washington, D.C. (table 38) shows that the rate of illegitimacy for both races declines with increasing income and education.

Table 37

Estimated Illegitimacy Rates* by Color, 1940 to 1968

Year**	Nonwhite	White
1940	35.6	3.6
1950	71.2	8.6
1960	98.3	9.2
1961	100.8	10.0
1965	97.2	11.0
1968	86.6	13.2

*Illegitimate births, regardless of age of mother, per 1,000 unmarried women 15–44 years old.

**Years selected to show trend.

Source: Bureau of the Census, *The Social and Economic Status of the Black Population in the United States,* 1971, table 88.

Table 38

Illegitimacy Rates as Related to Income and Education, by Color, in Integrated Census Tracts (30 to 70 percent nonwhite), in Washington, D.C.[1]

Median family income[2]	Nonwhite		White	
	Illegitimacy rate (per 1000 births)	Median years of school completed	Illegitimacy rate (per 1000 births)	Median years of school completed
$3,000–$3,999	336	8.7	(3)	(3)
$4,000–$4,999	280	9.3	(3)	(3)
$5,000–$5,999	(3)	(3)	203	12.1
$6,000–$7,499	190	11.7	91	12.2
$7,500 or more	138	12.5	42	12.2

Source: U.S. Bureau of Labor Statistics, *Negroes in the United States,* June 1966, p. 194.

[1]Birth data relate to 1963; other data to 1959–60.

[2]Relates to the group for which illegitimacy rates are given.

(3)No census tracts in this income class, for the group shown.

The effects of unemployment, to which Negroes are particularly susceptible, has been also studied. The same census-tract data on nonwhite illegitimacy were correlated with unemployment rates to yield results indicating a direct positive association. When the nonwhite male unemployment rate for tracts was 12 per hundred and over, its percent of illegitimate births was 40.8. When, however, the unemployment rate was 2.0 and below, the illegitimacy rate declined to 17.6 percent.[24] The Office of Policy Planning and Research had this to say regarding the results of unemployment: "The conclusion from these and similar data is difficult to avoid. During times when jobs are reasonably plentiful . . . the Negro family becomes stronger and more stable. As jobs become more and more difficult to find, the stability of the family becomes more and more difficult to maintain."[25]

Children and the Family

Opportunity for children to live in unbroken families seems to be an index of their state of wellbeing and their chances for favorable societal adjustments. Data for nonwhites during the sixties show progressive disruption of parental unity. Table 39 shows that at the beginning of the decade, 75 percent of the children of nonwhite family heads were living with both parents; by 1970, however, the figure had declined to 67 percent. During this same period, over 90 percent of the children of white families lived with both parents.[26]

Table 39

Own Children Living with Both Parents as a Percent of All Own Children, 1960 to 1970

Year	Nonwhite	White
1960	75	92
1965	71	91
1970	67	91

In this situation also, social class, as represented by size of income, correlates positively with percent of children living with both parents. The percentage for nonwhites, however, is lower regardless of the size of income. For example, in 1969, own children living with both parents as a percent of all own children, for families with income under $3,000, was 24 and 44 percent, nonwhites and whites respectively. A similar disparity remains throughout the higher categories of income.[27]

The Prospects

The racial significance of the Negro family tends to be intensified as we move down the social status pyramid. The relatively large base of poverty among Negroes and the deleterious effects of racism lead us to the conclusion that the future of the Negro family and, of course, the socialization of the masses of Negro children depend mainly upon prospective changes in the way of life among the lower class.

In spite of recent plans for improvement, the means and direction of change remain in question. Thus, according to one distinguished source: "...a national effort toward problems of Negro Americans must be directed toward the question of family structure. The object should be to strengthen the Negro family so as to enable it to raise and support its members as do other families."[28] The critical question seems to be whether fundamental changes in the family can be accomplished by direct approaches to its problems.

The strength of the Negro family ordinarily derives not essentially from operations within the family itself but from less direct social gains which are still limited and opposed by elements in the larger society—especially those determined by southern leaders. Prospective benefits must include such values as freedom of economic opportunity, educational equality and encouragement, societal respect for open housing, political equality, and freedom from racism.

It seems reasonable to conclude that both Negro and white family trends are affected similarly by larger societal changes. There remain, however, consistent differences: the extraordinary increase in Negro illegitimacy since about 1950 (probably a form of Negro societal aggression); the percentage decrease in husband-wife heads of families; and the increase in percent of female heads of families.

We may venture the hypothesis that the peculiar differences in family trends are part of the syndrome of modern racial alienation and aggression.

Chapter 13

Nationalism and the Schools

Black Nationalism Enters via the Schools

In New York City two contradictory forces—desire for community control and need for desegregation—converged unexpectedly in the fall of 1966 and apparently established a malignant precedent for racial confrontation in the schools. These forces arose from the difficulties involved in desegregating schools in residential areas. The larger cities especially, with concentrations of blacks and whites, plus the opposition of Negro separatists, were forced to implement all forms of desegregation. No dependable way of fully integrating the metropolitan schools has been found. "Busing," free-choice open enrollment, zoning, school-pairing, and so on are plans tried in New York City with some creditable results but without significant solutions to the problem.[1] The idea of metropolitan school desegregation, however, has not been officially abandoned, and it continues to be the aim of leading civil rights protest groups.[2]

The general position of the black nationalists, the separatists, has been that the legitimate aspiration of Negroes should be self-determination in autonomous Negro communities supported financially by the government. The ghettos are thus regarded as colonies on their way toward liberation. This belief, postulated unequivocally by Elijah Muhammad and Malcolm X, animates the Negro masses. The New York City schools inevitably became a direct target. The idea implicitly rejects the 1954 Supreme Court decision on public school desegregation. In a relevant statement Robert C. Maynard explains:

> Black nationalism has other goals at the community level, principally concerning commerce and the police. But the schools are being focused upon as all important to the fostering of the ethic of black pride and black self-determination since a people who seek their liberation from a colonialist system must control what is being taught to the young. Because the foundation of nationalism is that blacks are a nation within a nation, it rejects the notion that integration is synonymous with equality. It argues that demanding a place for black children in a white school system is an admission of inherent black inferiority.[3]

The Black Muslims and other nationalist groups have established their own private schools in which they "control what the young will be taught"; but, thus far, public schools have avoided the incursions of specialized ideologies. Even so, clashes came when, in September 1966, a group of Negro parents and "community leaders" urgently demanded that the New York City Board of Education either desegregate the schools or allow the "black community" to control them.

Because of the ecological situation, the board could not, upon demand, desegregate the schools—a feat which would also call for disbanding the ghetto. And even if this were feasible, black nationalistic interests would probably nonetheless have offered resistance. It was, therefore, in the area of administrative decentralization that the drive for community control took root.[4]

The long, severe struggle which developed was complicated by a confusion of purposes: community control directed toward improvement of the quality of education in the ghetto—admittedly the worst in the city—or the achievement of the black nationalist goal of racial separatism.[5] There were protracted, frenetic arguments about such matters as: the value of community involvement in education; progress of educational decentralization in other states; experience with community control in the suburbs; rights of parents with respect to the selection of teaching personnel and the content of their children's education; the failure of previous plans for school improvement; the peculiar educational needs of Negro children; and the duty of the government to give an autonomous school district a trial since it "could hardly be worse than previous efforts."

At first, the New York City Board of Education, the United Federation of Teachers (UFT)—a union of white and Negro public school teachers—and white liberals regarded this surge of Negro interest in the schools as a situational manifestation of the civil rights movement.[6] Perhaps, it was thought, the movement would arouse the ghetto family to work with school teachers and administrators for improvement of the quality of their childrens' education. This indeed was a type of involvement very much needed in the black community. Already Head Start had recognized the value not only of giving disadvantaged children an early orientation toward the norms of the larger society but also of convincing their parents about the nature of education in relationship to those norms. At its inception, the movement was therefore generally encouraged.

The movement received a decided stimulus when, in the spring of 1967, Mayor John V. Lindsay appointed a panel, headed by Mc-George Bundy of the Ford Foundation, to report on decentralization of the city's schools. On November 9, 1967, in a letter transmitting its very comprehensive report, the panel said:

> So many children are not learning what they need to know to take part in modern society that there is a growing loss of confidence in our public schools. The premise upon which we were appointed was that effective decentralization could help. . . . The essence of the plan which we propose is that the present centralized system should be reformed by a clear grant of new authority to *Community School Boards.* . . . We believe these School Boards should have power to appoint and remove Community Superintendents, should have a new and wider authority over curriculum, budget, personnel, and educational policy in the schools of the district. . . . The liberating force for the urban education of the Negro and the Puerto Rican must be a new respect, a new engagement, a new responsibility. [And in the "preface"]: Community School Districts should receive a total annual allocation of operating funds . . . a Community School System consisting of a federation of [30 to 60] large autonomous school districts. . . .[7]

The report obviously straddled the interests of those groups basically in conflict. The board of education of the city of New York

184

and the teachers' union were apparently primarily interested in ideas for improving the *quality of education,* while the black nationalist leadership sought *control* of the community school districts, especially exclusive authority over curriculum, personnel, and budget.[8] As Martin Mayer puts it: "From the beginning, the two groups had different objectives. The people's board was interested in 'community control'. . . .and the union was interested in the expansion of its More Effective Schools (M.E.S.) program. . . . M.E.S. was extremely popular with communities where it had been tried. . . ."[9] Clear lines of battle were thus drawn.

The report of the panel suggested this: "We have met men and women in every interested group whose spoken or unspoken center of concern was with their own power. . . . We believe in the instrumental value of all these forms of power—but in the final value of none."[10] It was, nevertheless, power—especially black power—which asserted itself as never before through a community educational system plan. As the Reverend Milton Galamison (pastor of a Negro church in Brooklyn) observed:

> It was almost historically providential that the concept of school decentralization and community control emerged. . . . It presented the Black Community, which had lost its way, with a hope and a cause. The community determined that Black people would no longer suffer the twin evils of segregation and colonialism. . . . Nonresident whites could not reap the economic benefits of working in a Black community while Black children suffered the degradation of unwantedness.[11]

The mayor of the city approved the plan but, as we have intimated, it ran forthwith into direct opposition from the Board of Education and the UFT.

The confrontation, which became a white-black issue,[12] resulted in a succession of teacher strikes, city-wide school closings, abandonment of the Bundy Plan by the state legislature in May 1968, and ultimately discontinuance of the "demonstration school" projects in Negro communities. The long struggle with the union over dismissal of a number of white teachers by the school district was interspersed with terroristic acts of violence, threats of violence, and overt racial abuse by Negro militants. The upshot was that this attempt to establish a nationalistic power base in the Negro community through exclusive control of the three demonstration public school districts was first limited by the State Department of Education; and then, on April 30, 1969, as part of its decentralization law, the New York State legislature merged them into larger zones. The eight-school Ocean Hill-Brownsville district was enlarged to include twenty-five schools.

Nature of Community Control

Black community control of the schools is essentially part of the political program for Negro "liberation" and nationalization of the community. It is a vital part of the movement which advocates racial separation, counter-integration, and black self-government in the ghetto. Ideologically, it is essentially a continuation of the Garveyite protest movement—nationalism modified by the experience of Elijah Muhammad and Malcolm X. According to Galamison, the governing board of the Ocean Hill-Brownsville "demonstration district" could not "extricate itself from the colonialist structure of the New York City school system" until it had acquired certain rights such as "the right to control funds and fiscal policy" and "the right to hire and fire superintendents, teachers, and principals."[12a]

This nationalist ideology was not, of course, universally accepted. It was not the position taken by such civil rights organizations and leaders as the NAACP and Martin Luther King, Jr. Like other aspects of black separatist protest, it tended to have ready currency among Negro groups.

"Black Educational Needs"

It was among this group that the idea of "black educational needs" can be defined as culturally distinct and as having primacy in the child's learning over the requirements of standard American education.[13] It was argued that black educational needs could be transmitted only by black teachers. "If the glories of European culture and the Renaissance are being taught to white children," says Robert C. Maynard typically, "then the glories of African culture, of the Dahomeans and Ashantis, must be taught to black children. Beyond that, the role of education in the nationalist scheme is to interrupt the cycle of self-agnegation, the forces that cause young black children to see themselves as less than human. . . . For the nationalist, the restoration of black pride is all important. . ."[14]

Perhaps the Arabs may be regarded as a people who accomplished too much too early. Their phenomenal medieval civilization became rigidly traditionalized and thus kept them bound to their past while the revolutionary engine of European culture moved forward inexorably. Today, they remain among the most lamentable of the backward peoples. The Jews, on the other hand, emigrated mainly to the centers of Western society, absorbing its vital elements so that they can now return to the area, ready to utilize profitably its natives and their resources. The ability to look back "with pride," therefore, is not necessarily the hoped-for open sesame to Negro progress; it may not always be a blessing.

The Black Panthers realized the sterility of this argument and called it "cultural nationalism." In order to make Negro children believe that the culture of ancient Africa is directly comparable to that of present-day United States, they must be socially isolated and deliberately propagandized. Moreover, they should not be allowed to go to Africa where they might see that the consequential culture, the *dynamic culture* of modern African cities, is conspicuously Western, "European" culture—all the way from religion and the arts to mathematics and physics, and indeed, even to the very architecture and ecology of the new communities. And inevitably so. Any residue of "native culture" must either be "modernized" or remain static and primitive.[15]

It is Western culture, mainly that of the United States, which African universities essentially teach. My own observations in West Africa would seem to verify Pierre L. VandenBerghe's point that "what determines class position in the modern sector of Nigeria is the amount of formal Western education a person possesses. . . . The new ruling class of Nigeria is overwhelmingly Christian . . . and Western."[16] Moreover, the American Negro child who has been indoctrinated to magnify the "ancient glories" of Dahomey would be so culturally misled that, as an adult, he would very likely not be able to rest in peace or to find employment in such places as Accra, Lagos, or Abidjan. Both the pyramids and the Aswan Dam are, for instance, wonderful cultural achievements. But only whites can build the dam. To have the child concentrate upon the former but close his eyes to the latter fact is obviously to insist upon a self-image constantly subject to disillusionment. As a black American engineer, however, he might participate in erecting such cultural monuments—without losing interest in the achievements of ancient Africa.

The great damage and disservice that the black-controlled, community school ideologists inflict on the developing personality of the Negro child contribute to his limitations for living effectively in the larger American society. The implicit message of these ideologists is that the child should also be psychologically ghettoized. Their insinuations may even stultify the child's attitude toward learning.

The American Negro child cannot develop self-respect by learning to look askance on the culture in which he must live. Self-respect is achieved through one's concept of one's role in the culture and the ability to excel in it. Obviously, the means toward this end is freedom of opportunity. The traditional civil rights struggle has increasingly made its contributions. On the other hand, the road of social withdrawal, adopted by black nationalists, widens the cultural breach between Negroes and whites; and, by its very operation, causes the Negro child further to lose self-respect. Inevitably, therefore, that road must be retraced.

The Black Community School and the Dynamic Culture

The black-community school movement may be partly a subconscious result of social fright, "cultural shock," due to the sudden exposure of the group to relatively large cultural opportunities precipitated by the recent civil rights adventures. This is borne out by the tendency of black nationalists to shun the movement. Perhaps it may also be seen in their attitude toward "quality education." Obviously, Negroes must now be primarily concerned with the quality of their education so that they may effectively compete for the emergent opportunities. The arguments of the black-community school leadership, however, seem to reverse the process. First social status must be coerced through black nationalistic power, then cultural opportunities should be considered; quality of education will then follow.

If due emphasis were given to quality of education, much of the racial struggle within the ghetto schools would probably evaporate. Parents can be most helpful by concentrating upon the dominant culture and showing their children, through education, how to move into it. The segregated ghetto school would be, on the face of it, the most unlikely place for the accomplishment of such a purpose.

What the civil rights movement demands of whites is that the American culture be made open—that the chance to learn and opportunity to teach be made available to blacks. Negroes have no distinctive culture to learn or to transmit in isolation—unless it be the weak southern plantation derivative.

188

Black Nationalism and Busing

Some whites, including members of the power structure in the South, have been particularly opposed to busing for public school integration. What seems most ironic and inconsistent, however, is the position taken by Negro separatists. They embarrass the movement by relying upon reasoning similar to that commonly employed by white segregationists.

The following situation, chosen at random, is typical of this attitude. In July 1969, the board of education of University City called a public meeting to consider redistricting of the city's ten elementary schools to achieve "interracial balance." University City is a western suburb of St. Louis with a population of about 51,000 in 1960. "Black enrollment ranges from one-half percent at one school to 78 percent at another. Three schools are more than half black. Total elementary school enrollment is about 30 percent Negro."[17] Controversy arose over a report to the board suggesting that pupils be assigned to the schools by grade rather than by neighborhood. The plan involved busing of pupils of both races.

Opinions were divided at the meeting—some whites insisting that many citizens would leave the community if the plan were put into operation. The point here, however, is that, according to news reports, one Felix Garth, a Negro resident of "a neighborhood [in the area] with an elementary school that is nearly 80 percent black, told the board that he supported a centers plan but was opposed to a limited busing program that would move black children out of their neighborhood into white schools where they would not know the other children. Many people have the idea that because a school is all black it's all bad. That is not necessarily so. Black children can get a better education in a high quality black school than they can if they are bused into a white school that may provide a hostile environment."[18] It seems obvious that if reliance had been put upon similar arguments, Little Rock, for instance, would never have occurred.

In group situations, where black nationalist feelings may be aroused, appeals such as this may be very cogent. They seem to declare to white leaders—implicitly even to federal courts—that desegregation is a supererogation, an unwanted imposition upon Negroes. Thus, the effect may be one of disrupting practical considerations. It would be ironic if concerned white authorities were forced to digress in order to convince Negro audiences of the value of becom-

189

ing immersed in the American culture and of the contribution which an unsegregated elementary school system might make toward achievement of that end. The tradition of racial isolation has created problems of integration, but such problems are sometimes inadvertently regarded as justifications for continued isolation—or indeed for backsliding into intensified racial isolation.

Important as they are for each group, the values of school integration are still not the same for whites as for blacks. It is the culture of the ghetto and not that of the suburbs which is disadvantaged and restrictive. It is, in other words, the Negro residential area and its schools which are shut off from the influence of the larger, dynamic society, a society open to elementary schools in white residential areas. And, as James Coleman and his associates conclude, "A pupil's achievement is strongly related to the educational backgrounds and aspirations of the other students in the school."[19] It is particularly the Negro child, therefore, who develops self-isolating attitudes, attitudes which limit his cultural orientation to American life. Indeed, isolation itself may become entrenched as a social value in the Negro subculture.

Negro children now have, as never before, a real opportunity to acquire the culture at its normal level. As the U.S. Fifth Circuit Court pointed out in March 1967: "The class [most affected] is all Negro children in a school district attending by definition inherently unequal schools and wearing the badge of slavery [which] separation displays."[20] Indeed, attendance at schools in the white area, and insistence that all the children be given an equal chance to participate, should prove of greater cultural advantage to Negro pupils than the reverse movement of achieving racial balance by busing white children into predominantly Negro schools. In reality, all life for Negroes in the United States must, hypothetically, for the most part, involve "busing" into the larger society.

It is in the dominant white culture that significant achievement in any field must be sought. It is there that the norms of competition, the standards of production, and the universal ideals in sports and recreation are to be found. By protecting children from the racial problems involved in "busing" them into the larger society, Negro parents may be exposing the younger generation to more aggravated experiences later on. The records show that one important place of confrontation is the registrar's office in white elementary schools and universities. Withdrawal is not a solution but an exacerbated postponement.

Chapter **14**

Negro Protest and the Subculture

The Negroes' protest is based fundamentally upon a conflict between economic interests peculiar to a type of social situation that involves subjection to industrial protection, cultural isolation, and opposition to the composite status. The material interests of the system demand their subservience; but the social ideals inherent to the system are morally inconsistent with the process of degradation. The history of their protest reaches back to their forebears' involuntary emigration from West Africa. Even then, their resistance to special interests was constantly manifest. It is not slavery *per se*—a condition known to both Europe and Africa during the precapitalist era—which generates protest but rather bondage under peculiar social circumstances. Slaves do not *protest* in all types of social organization. In some they accept the status with resignation.

Since this critical point has been frequently overlooked, we emphasize again that the movement which initiated the "age of dis-

191

covery'' was uniquely a development of the capitalist system that originated in the European medieval cities. "The conjunction in a single half-century of the discovery of an immense new labor supply and of a new and comparatively empty continent in which such a supply could be profitably utilized gave an importance and a permanence to'' the slave trade which it could never have attained otherwise.[1]

Given this type of society, the only means of maintaining and utilizing the reluctant labor force was unremitting physical and psychological coercion. Observe, for example, Alexis de Tocqueville's moving logic on personality and bondage in the United States:

> The Negro, who earnestly desires to mingle his race with that of the European, cannot do so; while the Indian, who might succeed to a certain extent, disdains to make the attempt. The servility of the one dooms him to slavery, the pride of the other to death.[2]

Recognition of this fate, however, should not obliterate the functional nature of the European purpose. Tocqueville, no doubt, had seen the typical Negro, broken in by the constraints of thralldom.

As a group, however, the Negro people were never completely broken in. Their masters and the community organizations always had doubts about the reliability of their apparent contentedness. Herbert Aptheker has devoted a major part of his research career to demonstrating this fact. His definitive work on Negro slave revolts points to the ever-present concern of masters about latent unrest among the bondsmen.[3] In 1831 the recorder of Nat Turner's "confessions," Thomas R. Gray, lamented:

> whilst every thing upon the surface of society wore a calm and peaceful aspect; whilst not one note of preparation was heard to warn the devoted inhabitants of woe and death, a gloomy fanatic was revolving in the recesses of his . . . overwrought mind, schemes of indiscriminate massacre to the whites. Each particular community should look to its own safety, whilst the general guardians of the laws, keep a watchful eye over all.[4]

But racial protest has its heritage not so much in the slaves' surreptitious uprisings but rather in the public, accusatory contentions of the abolitionists. The argument remains essentially that of an insistence upon complete inclusion of all men, Negroes specifically, in the American society. Frederick Douglass, an untiring abolitionist, who survived the Civil War to become the outstanding Negro assimilationist protest leader in the latter half of the nineteenth century, declared in an 1856 public address in Boston:

> I have had but one idea for the last three years to present to the American people, and the phraseology in which I clothe it is the old abolition phraseology. I am for the "immediate, unconditional, and universal" enfranchisement of the black man, in every state of the Union. . . .
> We may be asked . . . . why we want it. I will tell you why we want it. We want it because it is our *right,* first of all. No class of men can, without insulting their own nature, be content with any deprivation of their rights. We want it, again, as a means of educating our race. Men are so constituted that they derive their conviction of their own possibilities largely from the estimate formed of them by others. If nothing is expected of a people, that people will find it difficult to contradict that expectation. . . .
> Everybody has asked the question, and they learned to ask it early of the abolitionists, "What shall we do with the negro?" I have had but one answer from the beginning. Do nothing with us! Your doing with us has already played the mischief with us. . . . If the negro cannot stand on his own legs, let him fall. . . . All I ask is, give him a chance to stand on his own legs! . . . If you see him on his way to school, let him alone—don't disturb him! If you see him going to the dinner-table at a hotel, let him go! If you see him going to the ballot box, let him alone—don't disturb him. If you see him going into a workshop, just let him alone—your interference is doing him positive injury. . . . If you will only untie his hands, and give him a chance, I think he will live. He will work as readily for himself as for the white man.[5]

Since the Civil War, this is what protest has been essentially about; neither the NAACP nor the mid-twentieth century Supreme Court has contravened its essence—indeed they have sought piecemeal to realize it. In 1917 Kelly Miller wrote: "The Negro feels that he is not regarded as a constituent part of American democracy. This is our fundamental grievance and lies at the basis of all the outrages inflicted upon this helpless race."[6] We are still sobered by Tocqueville's prediction that: "If ever America undergoes great revolutions, they will be brought about by the presence of the black race on the soil of the United States; that is to say, they will owe their origin, not to the equality, but inequality of conditions."[7]

The Mainstream and the Subculture

Protest seeks to remove the status of outsider assigned to the Negro. Involved here, however, is the social structure of the dominant culture and its trailing, limited subculture. A critical objective of the southern ruling class has been to assure the integrity and continuity of the latter. It seems necessary, therefore, to refer briefly to the rise of this subculture.

At the time of emancipation, the Negro had retained very little if any of his original African culture.[8] He was dependent upon his master's tutelage for effective plantation labor. As Stanley M. Elkins observes:

> Much of his past had been annihilated; nearly every prior connection had been severed. Not that he had really "forgotten" all these things—his family and kinship arrangements, his language, the tribal religion, the taboos, the name he had once borne, and so on—but none of it any longer carried much meaning. The old values, the sanctions, the standards, already unreal, could no longer furnish him guides for conduct for adjusting to the expectations of a complete new life. Where then was he to look for new standards, new cues—who would furnish them now? He could now look to none but his master, the one man to whom the system had committed his entire being: the man upon whose will depended his food, his shelter, his sexual connections, whatever moral instruction he might be offered, whatever "success" was possible within the system, his very security—in short, everything.[9]

What the Negro acquired, however, was not a normal derivative of his master's culture. In 1865, 95 percent of the Negro population lived in the South and 90 percent of them were newly-emancipated slaves. It was, therefore, the culture associated with American bondage that Negroes brought into freedom. And this, let it be noted, was not merely the culture of a lower class but of an extremely perverted lower-lower class.

The Negro *masses* became freedmen conditioned to a tradition of the most degraded form of family irresponsibility, with a distorted conception of the nature of property, with relatively little personal motivation for work, with the slave's orientation toward division of the day regarding rest, work, and relaxation; with feeble and restricted powers of reaching out toward the motivating forces of the larger culture. The Negro was almost entirely illiterate. He had a telltale drawl, servile rhetoric, and comparatively little use for quiet and cleanliness; he was trained for the crudest form of agricultural manual labor, and subject to the ambivalent control of his former master. All this was bound up in a cultural pattern that held him outside the normal structure of the American social status system. And yet, his was inherently an American culture with an American future.

What is more, the old, white power structure exerted itself to perpetuate this ineffective way of life. It isolated Negroes through segregation, put them in "their place" with formal and informal rules and violence, and thus contributed to the perpetuation of thralldom in the United States. As C. Vann Woodward puts it:

> In America the Negro . . . faced his ordeal as an isolated minority newly emerged from two and a half centuries of a bondage that had stripped him of his native culture and left him defenseless before his enemies. That he survived at all is remarkable, but that some should regard the achievement with shame is even more so. Only a people who have endured such an ordeal and could draw upon the collective wisdom of the experience could have marshalled the patience, the restraint and the discipline under the most intense provocation in their great movement of protest. . . . Before the Negro turns his back on his own history, or exchanges it for the tradition of another people, or invents a false history for himself, he might try to appreciate the value of the special heritage that is his own.[10]

Negro culture, then, is peculiarly of American origin and development. Urbanization has not effaced this fact: the Negro "went from the lowest status in the Southern countryside to the lowest status in the urban areas."[11] The immemorial past of this inherited culture must be sought largely in Europe, not in Africa.

"Equality" has meant not physical identity but the acquisition of ability so to behave in the larger American culture that the handicap of Negro culture would appear to have completely lost its restrictive conditioning effects. It is the latter achievement which the white detractors of Negroes in the South have sought most assiduously to forestall. We need hardly cite in illustration their determined resistance to prevent the simultaneous education of white and Negro children.

Many Negroes are so thoroughly submerged in their pattern of lower-class culture that they seem to think of it as inherently Negro

195

and thus worth conserving. "This world of the lower class," observe Drake and Cayton in their Chicago study, "is, to lower-class people, the normal and familiar context of daily life."[12] Since the culture is the result of Americanization under singular social restraints and limitations, the normal avenues of escape for anger and aggressiveness have been largely blocked. A characteristic of the culture, therefore, has been in-group irrationality, conflict, and violence, with the constant threat of external explosion.

We may assume that all viable cultures have their built-in norms of social control. The operation of these norms tends to be accepted voluntarily. Persons belonging to the culture, therefore, "know how to behave," and corrections for any deviation are ordinarily supported by the group. But one of the great problems of Negroes—the Negro masses especially—has been the feeble operation, in their subculture, of the norms of the dominant society.

Since they do not have fully effective cultural controls of their own, and are more or less excluded from the purview of the dominant culture, their behavior tends to become erratic, frequently criminal, without compunction in terms of the dominant norms. Observe, for example, with what equanimity H. Rap Brown, who was reared on the streets of a Negro community, describes his behavior during an audience with President Lyndon Johnson at the White House in 1965: "I stole some stuff out of the White House. . . . I was trying to figure how to get a painting off the wall and put it under my coat. I figured it belonged to me anyway."[13] Brown, incidentally, employs the scatological vernacular of the lower levels of ghetto culture.

Culture Conflict and Protest

The social variation which characterizes the lower class of the Negro subculture tends to be irreversibly incompatible with the dominant culture. What is more, the Negro subculture had to be largely negative, defensive, reactionary—with inherent processes such as "getting by" and "getting away with." In situations calling for positive, creative living it is , therefore, a culture which must be deliberately unlearned.

An important current definition of Negro self-respect is total American respect for the Negro lower-class subculture. The size of this class is relatively so large that its ethos, rather than that of the Negro middle class, has been frequently assumed to be the dominant orientation of all Negroes. American culture and society, of course, is middle-class oriented. Its educational system is devoted largely to middle-class motivation and American cultural dynamics. It seems, therefore, that to be successfully included in the larger culture, the ambition of Negroes, like that of whites, must be middle-class directed. Indeed it should now be clear that the whole world, including the socialist countries, has to develop in its people attitudes for hard work, honesty, efficiency, sobriety, and upward cultural motivation such as that which made possible the development and maintenance of the phenomenal American productive system. Both modern Russia and China agree on this point. There is no alternative if progressive maximization of the peoples' welfare is the objective.

Indecision about this notion among certain Negro leaders has involved race relations in a conflict of cultures. Some leaders seem to be asking that black, lower-class recognition constitutes a stable form of social organization in contradistinction to the larger middle-class socio-economic system. Accordingly, the subculture has been thought of not in dynamic terms—not as progressively entering into the continuum of American social mobility—but rather in static, self-sufficient terms. The Negro's peculiar "language," food, plan of production and government, and complement of obscenities are all considered worth preserving against incursions of influences from the larger society. Nationalism normally calls for group solidarity, and this solidarity can be most conveniently developed by pointing to the enemy at the gates.

Black English

Since a people's language tends to constitute their primary mark of cultural distinction, attempts have been made to conceive of "black English" as a "separate language." The Center for Applied Linguistics in Washington, D.C., has made special efforts to study characteristics of the Negro dialect and to suggest that it should be taught in schools to all Negro children. Teaching standard English is not, it is assumed, like teaching standard mathematics. "English teachers," the argument runs, "try to wipe out all traces of a kid's right to continue speaking the dialect of his home."[14] According to this logic, red English, hillbilly English, Yoruba English—all should be taught respectively along with standard English.

In order to give prestige and national significance to "black English," its origin has been sought in Africa, the West Indies, the ghetto—indeed everywhere but in its proper place: the southern slave

197

plantation. One official from the center asserts: "A sentence such as 'He be at work' is a well-known stereotyped characteristic of black English . . . [meaning] 'he is at work all the time.'"[15] Ordinarily the black-English advocates cite no vestigial use of African languages among American Negroes, but rather concentrate on the latter's allegedly peculiar conjugation of certain defective English verbs. The derived structures are then said to have been determined by the Negroes' African origins.

Leaving aside the question of whether all Negro lower-class persons employ identical usage—and whether Negro school teachers speak the language in their informal gatherings—it seems clear that the slave who attempted to use standard English on the plantation would be a marked man. The dialect and idiom may well be studied for its servile characteristics. What is being sought as a nationalized language is a devious cultural development; and, perhaps, a subtle means of perpetuating the Sambo image.[16] For example, a Howard University Negro nationalist states:

> Just as the Afro hair styles, the Afro dress and the way blacks address each other as "brother and sister" have given black people a greater amount of racial pride, black English will also work to unify American blacks.[17]

What is not always realized by those who propose to organize Negro lower-class culture as a counterpoise to the larger American culture is that its material base is, in a sense, more completely dependent upon operations in the larger social system than that of any other social group. Its problem is that of the particularly disadvantaged poor. As the discriminatory laws which formerly limited cultural participation are removed, the handicap and impermanence of Negro lower-class culture will become the more glaringly manifest.

Attempts to "Africanize," standardize, and applaud these cultural handicaps will only magnify them and thus aggravate the general cultural gap.[18] That, no doubt, is precisely what the most determined white detractors of the Negro people would do if they had a clear opportunity. The Negro is thus merely committing himself to the status of a cultural outsider in his own country—apparently something no other group of Americans has found profitable. The traditional social strategy of Jews, on the other hand, has been devotion to mastery of the dominant culture and achievement of societal inclusion on their own terms.

Structure of Negro Protest

Now that we have reviewed the cultural basis of interracial conflict in the United States, it seems appropriate to consider the ways in which protest has been expressed and the nature of its opposition.

Historically, protest has taken different forms but these forms have not always been mutually exclusive. We will attempt to bring them together under the following headings: aims, methods, and leadership. We shall consider the consequences of protest as characterized mainly by assimilation, nationalism, and anarchy. Emigration from the United States as a solution was realistically abandoned with the emancipation proclamation and the thirteenth Amendment to the Constitution. Table 40 is a suggestive outline.

The Protest for Assimilation

The protest for assimilation has been oriented toward the federal government and its courts, as the power capable of producing positive results, and toward the South and its leadership as the germinal force in the United States devoted to the suppression of the Negro race.[19] Moreover, the Negro people were generally known to be southerners, hence there could be no effective liberation until the hand of the southern oligarchy was restrained. It was in the South particularly that the Negro was driven back into his limited subculture. And it was normally to be expected that southern representatives in Congress and among the great leaders of business in the North would watch for any evidence of action leading to the social integration of Negroes and strike it down.

The first great battle after the Civil War, fought in the tradition of the abolitionists, resulted in amendments to the Constitution defining Negroes as citizens, and in federal civil rights laws designed to grant citizenship status. At this point, Negroes theoretically became assimilated Americans; the forces of public alienation were *legally* removed, and they now had to find their places competitively in the social status system. We have seen, however, the way in which nullifying devices and federal court decisions in a post-Reconstruction set of reactions virtually nullified the Reconstruction gains. Protest, therefore, tended to be spontaneously initiated against these obvious deprivations.

From the beginning—from the writing of the Constitution itself—the situation of the Negro has involved the federal government.

199

Table 40
Characteristics of Negro Protest

Aims	Methods	Leadership and Ideology
(1) *Assimilation:* abolition, suffrage, civil rights, social rights, economic opportunity	(1) Action directed to specific ends: appeals to federal and state governments, to courts, and to private influential groups—boycott and picketing, sit-ins, freedom rides, marches and mass demonstrations, civil disobedience, "demands," voter registration	(1) The abolitionists, Frederick Douglass and members of Congress, William M. Trotter, the NAACP, W.E.B. DuBois, Roy Wilkins, M.L. King, Jr., the original SCLC, SNCC, CORE
(2) *Emigration:* colonization, Garveyism's "back to Africa"	(2) Personal enterprise; settlement in Liberia and Sierra Leone by free Negroes and manumitted slaves with Western governmental assistance	(2) Paul Cuffe, Martin Delany, the American Colonization Society, state colonization societies, Abraham Lincoln, Marcus Garvey
(3) *Nationalism:* Garveyite, Muslimite, separatism, self-determination	(3) Nationalistic propaganda, racial pride, black racism, exotic religion, Garvey's UNIA, regalia and uniforms, patriotic business enterprise, ghettoization, strategic violence	(3) Marcus Garvey, Elijah Mohammad, Malcolm X, more recently SNCC, CORE
(4) *Anarchy:* liberation, revolt and rebellion, chaos, induced fear, and destruction (Ends and means tend to converge.)	(4) Conspiracy, police confrontation, rioting, looting, arson, shooting, bombing—utilizing cover of darkness and escape	(4) Malcolm X, mobs, gangs, Black Panthers, Marx-Lenin, Frantz Fanon, Che Guevara, Mao Tse-tung's Red Book

At the turn of the century, there was no place to look for help save the national government. In 1909 the NAACP organized for active protest; and the federal courts seemed to be the only avenue open to action. Appeals to the courts regarding removal of the obstacles to political participation, to equality in public accommodations and in education gradually brought positive results. It was, of course, in 1954 that the Warren court, upon the petition of the NAACP, handed down its historic decision on desegregation in public education.

The decision implicated the federal government directly. The Court, moreover, obligated itself to supervise the desegregation of public schools in the United States and especially in the South; and it implicitly bound the administration to use force in the process. Thus, race relations suddenly became headline news; the public was awakened, and protest leaders became champions of the national morality. The decision involved so wide an area of racial discrimination that the NAACP seemed to have its hands full merely in helping to support the mandate of the Supreme Court. For the first time resolution of the "Negro problem" had become an obligation of the United States. And blame for the social conditions of Negroes became increasingly centered upon "American institutions."

Indeed, the pace quickened so markedly that, to many Negroes, the NAACP had become backward and conservative. In the Deep South, however, the organization was still being hunted down and banished. Its representative in Mississippi, Medgar Evers, was waylaid and shot in 1963. The times, at any rate, seemed ripe for some form of direct action by Negroes against the static pattern of discrimination in the area.

One of the most effective types of mass behavior is certain forms of the boycott. It is difficult to locate and punish. By peacefully withholding patronage, it may compel concessions. An opportunity arose in 1955 to test this strategy against racial segregation in public transportation in Montgomery, Alabama, the "cradle of the Confederacy." The movement gradually gained momentum, affecting more and more of the southern power structure and gaining the attention of the nation.

As a form of protest, the boycott had already become traditional among Negroes. It started in Chicago in April 1929 when James H. Porter, a public-spirited individual, wrote the president of the Metropolitan Life Insurance Company complaining that no Negroes were employed by the corporation either in its offices or as agents. He received a long answer, which read in part:

> You ask why we do not employ colored people to look after the large amount of business which we have in force in colored lives. The reason is that we know from experience that better service is given our colored policy-holders by white people than would be given by colored agents.[20]

Porter took the letter to the editors of the Chicago *Whip,* Joseph D. Bibb and A. C. McNeal, who published it in full with an editorial denouncing the Metropolitan and calling for a boycott. They said:

> After you read the letter below you will understand why colored people are poverty-stricken, in need of the necessities of life, and unable to do the great things they have in mind.

The campaign continued with increasing intensity from May 1929 to December 1930. Although the company did not capitulate, Negro insurance companies in the area admitted that they used the argument and publicity in sales talks and thus experienced some transfer of business to their own establishments.

During the drive against Metropolitan, almost all other businesses in the area were also brought under attack and most of them agreed to employ Negroes. The F. W. Woolworth five-and-ten-cent stores held out stubbornly, but they too eventually gave in and began to employ Negroes as clerks. The motto was "Don't spend your money where you can't work"; and the pickets carried signs reading "this store unfair to colored labor." Discrimination against black labor by the public utilities and labor unions was also challenged as never before but with only partial success. This, let us recall, was during the nadir of the Great Depression.

The boycott and picketing spread rapidly among Negroes in other cities—New York, Cleveland, Baltimore, Detroit, Washington. It did not openly penetrate the South. Here and there *businessmen* resorted to legal injunctions. In 1938, however, the U.S. Supreme Court held that the boycott was a proper instrument in the Negro's struggle against discrimination in employment. Both the NAACP and the Urban League actively supported the movement although they did not assume leadership in organizing a national campaign. The movement hardly received attention in the metropolitan dailies.

When, therefore, early in December 1955, Mrs. Rosa Parks was arrested in Montgomery because she refused to give up her seat on a city bus to a white passenger, E. D. Nixon, a Pullman porter, who had had public experience as an officer of the local NAACP, was able confidently to announce to the Negro ministers of the community: "I feel that the time has come to boycott the buses. Only through a boycott can we make it clear to white folks that we will not accept this type of treatment any longer."[21] Over 90 percent of the habitual Negro bus-riders devised other means of transportation, and many buses cruised almost empty at rush hours.

On first consideration it may appear that this act constituted nothing more than the precedent-making desertion of Woolworth stores by colored shoppers in Chicago. On closer examination, however, it is clear that the Montgomery development represented a distinct phase in the rise of Negro protest. First, it involved the use of the boycott in the Deep South, and second, it directed the instrument against both the policies of business and the laws of the state. It is the latter aspect especially that distinguishes the Montgomery episode from the northern buying-power boycott. Before the leaders had fully developed their line of action, they became aware that their major antagonist was not merely a private business but rather the government of a state and its laws. Martin Luther King, Jr., relates that at one of their first meetings the strategists became almost "crippled by fear."

Without originally intending it, therefore, the boycott constituted a form of civil disobedience. Indeed, the boycott had hardly begun when a sympathetic white librarian, Juliette Morgan, in a letter to the *Montgomery Advertiser,* compared the act of Negroes walking rather than using the buses to Gandhi's salt march to the sea. From then on the leadership, especially that of the Reverend Dr. Martin Luther King, Jr., progressively defined its program in terms of Gandhian non-violent ideology.

As the campaign developed, public officials became almost the sole adversaries. They kept all the leaders under continuous surveillance and eventually summoned them into court to answer not only the charge of creating a public nuisance by the operation of a "car pool," but also a plea for damages accruing from alleged loss of tax revenue to the city as a result of the reduction of earnings by the bus company.

Adoption of Gandhian principles—which are altogether com-

203

patible with the teachings of Christianity—provided a foundation for the group's discipline as it confronted the political power of a Deep South state. For the first time since the Civil War Negroes *en masse* were defying legalized racism in the South. The struggle gained nation-wide and international publicity. Sympathetic whites encouraged and supported it liberally. By November 13, 1956, when the U.S. Supreme Court handed down its decision invalidating the bus segregation laws of Alabama, a new form of protest, nonviolent direct action, had been devised and tried in the South. The leadership, in January 1957, formed the Southern Christian Leadership Conference (SCLC) to propagate and encourage the practice. In speech after speech, King spread the following doctrine:

> If the Negro is to achieve the goal of integration, he must organize himself into a militant and nonviolent mass movement. . . . We will take direct action against injustice without waiting for other agencies to act. We will not obey unjust laws or submit to unjust practices. We will do this peacefully, openly, cheerfully because our aim is to persuade. . . . The way to nonviolence may mean going to jail.
> If such is the case the resister must be willing to fill the jail houses of the South. It may mean physical death. But if physical death is the price that a man must pay to free his children and his white brethren from a permanent death of the spirit, then nothing could be more redemptive. . . . This then, must be our present program: nonviolent resistance to all forms of racial injustice, including state and local laws and practices, even when this means going to jail. . . .[22]

Up to 1960, however, the movement had not increased sufficiently to test the capacity of the region's prisons. Clearly, to do so would require Negroes to act *en masse,* something more difficult than would appear at first sight. The movement called not only for a repetition of the negative action taken in the buy boycott—although this type of withdrawal was then being imitated in other cities of the South—but also for open resistance to racial exclusion. For this further step, King needed, at least initially, a special kind of Negro group: one selected for its ability to assume a dignified posture, for its ability to understand the subtleties of nonviolence, for its interest in sustaining an attack upon segregated facilities that are chiefly of middle-class concern, and for its physical stamina and courage in the face of public violence and formal punishment.

An indiscriminate mass of Negroes—the larger the better—would no doubt have served the purpose of a typical Gandhian, nationalistic struggle; but not one designed to achieve the more limited goals of desegregating, say, the public facilities of a southern airport, of a library, or a restaurant. It was not clear that SCLC had evolved a plan of action to meet this problem.

By February 1960, however, the problem seemed to have solved itself. On the first of the month, at Greensboro, North Carolina, four Negro freshmen students, seventeen to eighteen years of age, from North Carolina Agricultural and Technical College, quietly took seats at the lunch counter of a Woolworth variety store and waited for service. They were not served; but they held their places for about an hour until the store closed, as usual, at 5:30 P.M. On the following day, accompanied by some twenty other students, they returned to occupy seats and read textbooks while they waited at the counter, but with no better results. The strategy, however, gained instant national publicity, and it quickly spread to other parts of the city and beyond. Students from white and Negro colleges in the area joined in the campaign. In April 1960, a group of students meeting at Shaw University in North Carolina, organized the Student Nonviolent Coordinating Committee (SNCC) under sponsorship of Dr. Martin L. King, Jr., and SCLC.

The force of the sit-in inheres in the public embarrassment and inconvenience it occasions. The Greensboro incident was of critical importance because it sparked the contagion which directly activated other groups in the South. It should be observed, however, that this was not the first sit-in. Probably the first deliberate, nonviolent attack upon racial segregation in public places was that which the newly-formed, biracial Congress of Racial Equality (CORE) successfully leveled against a Chicago Loop restaurant in October 1942. From that time on, the organization continually employed the method of small-group, biracial pressure against segregation in border states. The leadership of CORE, with its home base in New York, was therefore already accustomed to this form of nonviolent action. But it had not challenged the Deep South.

The most common reaction to sit-in requests for service was the closing of lunch counters. In a few cities, such as Charlotte and Raleigh, proprietors of variety stores removed their counter seats and the public was served standing. In a few instances Negro customers were forced to pay exhorbitant prices. Almost everywhere the protestors were subjected to harassment by white persons or groups. Some were dragged from their seats and beaten, as in Nashville and Jackson. There were hundreds of arrests for trespass, vagrancy, loitering, disorderly conduct, or, as in Nashville, "conspiracy to disrupt trade and commerce," and, in Baton Rouge, "criminal anarchy."

Sit-ins of various types assert civil rights that are either implied or clearly expressed in statutory law. The Civil Rights Act of 1964 produced widespread desegregation in the South; in many places, however, resistance to Negro pressure took the form of severe violence. White leadership, especially in rural areas and small towns, expected Negroes to abide by custom, not to assert rights based on legal mandates. The sit-in protest was used to oppose such attitudes.

Freedom Rides were started by CORE in March 1961, and followed by others, in the Deep South to test desegregation in interstate traveling facilities.[23] The activities of the Mississippi Freedom Democratic Party (MFDP), sponsored by SNCC, may be thought of as forms of sit-ins. At the 1964 Democratic National Convention in Atlantic City, for example, the latter sat in the seats of the Mississippi delegation. The march and demonstration, however, embody special characteristics.

The March-Demonstration

Unlike the sit-in, which ordinarily addresses itself to specific discriminations, the march-demonstration attempts to appeal to the public over the heads of racists and their officials or to sympathetic but apathetic whites. It also seeks to uplift and encourage Negroes, thus relieving them of the pressures of social isolation and a sense of hopelessness. When it is peaceful, it may find Negro communities sympathetic; in the South especially, it has been generally regarded as a challenge, an open answer and an act of resistance to the entire structure of white racial superiority. In racist communities, therefore, the march-demonstration either drives whites away from the scene or arouses them to violent opposition.

The execution of the march-demonstration must necessarily be nonviolent and nonretaliatory or it will almost certainly be transformed at its inception into a riot or a fight against superior forces. When, during World War I, President Wilson proclaimed his purpose of making the "world safe for democracy" and Negroes were being lynched in the South and violently molested in the North, W.E.B.

DuBois led the first protest march (1917) in New York. In an open letter to President Wilson, Kelly Miller said:

> Ten thousand speechless men and women marched in silent array down Fifth Avenue in New York City as a spectral demonstration against the wrongs and cruelties heaped upon the race. Negro women all over the nation have appointed a day of prayer in order that righteousness might be done to this people. The weaker sex of the weaker race are praying that God may use you as the instrument of His will to promote the cause of human freedom at home. I attended one of these 6 o'clock prayer meetings in the city of Washington. Two thousand humble women snatched the early hours of the morning before going to their daily tasks to resort to the house of prayer. They literally performed unto the Lord the burden of their prayer and song, "Steal Away to Jesus." There was not a note of bitterness nor denunciation throughout the season of prayer. They prayed as their mothers prayed in the darker days gone by, that God would deliver the race. Mr. President, you can help God answer their prayer.[24]

The march did not become generally popular, however, until around 1960. Since then they have numbered in the thousands. Between August and December 1967, for instance, in Milwaukee alone, more than one hundred marches were led by Father Groppi, a white Roman Catholic priest, in support of demands for racial reforms in that city. They survived violent opposition and imprisonments. The march-demonstrations that draw national and international attention have been few but they have served as bellwethers. Perhaps the following are the most significant: the Birmingham sit-ins and march-demonstrations, beginning in the spring of 1963; the March on Washington, August 28, 1963; the Selma-Montgomery marches in March 1965; and the James H. Meredith Memphis-to-Jackson march in June 1966.

Each of these events publicly exposed and emphasized different aspects of racial conflict. In Birmingham it was the dramatic exposure of southern police brutality in their dealings with Negroes. The Washington demonstration, 200,000 strong, including many leading Americans, emphasized interracial concern over discrimination in the United States. It was climaxed by King's memorable "I have a dream" speech. The Selma-to-Montgomery march showed most clearly how nonviolence, strategically employed in protest demonstrations, could arouse the nation to help carry the contest to the very doorstep of the capitol of southern racism. And James Meredith's almost fatal individual attempt to march into Jackson against "fear and for the right to vote" made clear to the nation and the world what extreme hazards confront Negroes in their struggle to exercise civil rights in the South.

As we should expect, scores have been injured, thousands jailed, and many murdered in these march-demonstrations. On April 4, 1968, Martin Luther King, Jr., himself was cut down by the sniper's bullet while preparing for such a march in Memphis. The murderers are usually aware of the tacit approval of white officials in high places. When, to illustrate, on Sunday, March 7, 1965, state troopers, on orders from Governor George C. Wallace, violently turned back the first attempt to march from Selma to Montgomery, the governor said to reporters: "We saved their lives by stopping their march. If they had gone on they could have been attacked by angry whites along the highway."[25] At least two persons lost their lives by engaging in that march: the Reverend James J. Reeb and Mrs. Viola Liuzzo; the former beaten to death and the latter run down and shot in her car while driving on the Montgomery-Selma highway. Violence resulting in death was even more atrocious in Birmingham.

And yet, this violence must be reckoned as small compared to the unrequited injury and death which Negroes continually suffered in the Deep South at the hands of whites and which the demonstrations were intended to expose and change.

No other form of protest could have created so much concern and positive action on the part of the news media, the Congress, the presidency, the Supreme Court, and religious organizations. It was, no doubt, the Birmingham police severity and the worldwide publicity it received that led President John F. Kennedy, in 1963, to take effective steps in the promotion of a civil rights law which finally became the basic Civil Rights Act of 1964. "Moved by that emotional crisis, and seizing that sympathetic moment to go to Congress, the President [on June 19, 1963] proposed the broadest civil rights legislation ever seriously suggested."[26] In admittedly the most persuasive speech of his career, President Lyndon B. Johnson on the evening of March 15, 1965, during the crisis period of the Selma-Montgomery march-demonstration, addressed the Congress and the nation in support of the Civil Rights Act of 1965. Said he in part:

> I speak tonight for the dignity of man and destiny of democracy. I urge members of both parties, Americans of all religions and colors, from every section to join me in that cause. . . .

The real hero of this struggle is the American Negro. His actions and protests—his courage to risk safety and even life—have awakened the conscience of the nation. His demonstrations have been designed to call attention to injustice, to provoke change and stir reform. . . . At the heart of battle for equality is a belief in the democratic process. . . . Their cause must be our cause, too. It is not just the Negro but all of us who must overcome the crippling legacy of bigotry and injustice. And we shall overcome.

One remarkable fact about assimilationist protest is that it is middle-class oriented and led. This does not mean that the lower class does not benefit directly. In the United States lower-class individuals can benefit permanently only by the provision of such means as would reduce its numbers. The availability of the ballot is of elementary assistance; the opening up of skilled labor to Negroes relieves economic pressure on the lower class; and the wider availability of education should attract the more energetic of the lower class. But protest can only help the permanently lower class by seeking for them equitable poor relief. According to American standards, if the poor are helped, they will no longer be poor.

It was no doubt the criticism that his concerns were for the middle-class that led Martin Luther King, Jr., to plan, before his death, a Poor People's March to Washington. During the summer of 1968, "A-frame" shelters near the Reflecting Pool in the heart of Washington were set up to form "Resurrection City" under the leadership of the Reverend Ralph Abernathy and SCLC. The project collapsed late in June because of fragmented leadership and an absence of concrete purpose. And yet, it called attention to the problems of the poor—especially among Negroes in the South. The Department of Health, Education and Welfare was repeatedly brought into the spotlight. At the final cleanup of the fast-decaying "city," an editorial in the *Washington Post* took the attitude of good riddance; but in the same issue Jean M. White in her article, "Resurrection City: Symbol that Soured," concluded: "The question now is whether the poor people's leaders can move on from Resurrection City to . . . 'creating a sensitive enough country to deal with the problem of poverty.'"[27] Since then the problem of poverty has loomed ever larger. It commands the attention of the nation.

Chapter **15**

Other Forms of Negro Protest

Nationalism

The nationalist movement among Negroes in the United States gives up, avoids, and opposes the Negroes' quest for civil rights and full American citizenship. To the extent that Negroes make political and economic gains in the larger society, however, to that extent also the elasticity of the system itself presents an answer to Negro nationalism. The nationalist must therefore insist not only that no changes for betterment of race relations have taken place since the Civil War but also that no changes can be expected in the future. This position, adopted by all Negro nationalists, obviously contravenes the civil rights movement.

Nationalism strives to leave nothing derogatory unsaid, hence it is particularly attractive to the northern urban masses—recently arrived from the South—who have direct scores to settle with the "white man." If by constant reiteration, the belief that *white is evil and hellish* while *black is good and beautiful* could be drilled into the minds of all Americans, then, according to the theory, major race problems would become manageable. Since, moreover, nationalism calls for black patriotism, group solidarity, and hatred of the enemy, those Negroes who do not go along with the exclusionist position are regarded as traitors, spies, or "Uncle Toms."

Negro Americans As Colonials

The essence of the nationalist contention seems to be that Negroes are not Americans; they constitute a colonial people exploited by a foreign American nation as an imperialist power. This concept has been adopted by or attributed to both Negroes and whites. Like all the largely black colonies of Africa and the West Indies, it is assumed, Negro Americans must eventually liberate themselves by revolution if necessary, and thus establish an independent nation. Such terms as "liberation," "self-determination," and "territorial control," are inherent in this type of argument.[1] Frantz Fanon's polemic, *The Wretched of the Earth,* based especially on his experience in Martinique, his birthplace, and on French North Africa during the early stages of the Algerian revolution, has been frequently cited as theoretical confirmation of the position. Fanon himself, however, cautioned American Negro nationalists on the likelihood of their eventual disillusionment, because of such false comparisons. Referring to the outcome of "the first congress of the African Cultural Society . . . held in Paris in 1956" where an attempt was made to identify universally the status of all Negroes, he observed: "Little by little the American Negroes realized that the essential problems confronting them were not the same as those that confronted African Negroes."[2]

In March 1968, at a meeting of the National Black Government Conference held at the Shrine of the Black Madonna in Detroit, "black separatists, who hoped to form an all-Negro nation in five southern states, voted . . . to affirm 'the principle that we are not citizens of the United States.'" A "declaration of independence" was issued and negotiations were to be started with the United States for, among other things, land to establish the "Republic of New Africa" in the following southern states: Mississippi, Louisiana, Alabama, Georgia, and South Carolina, and for "reparations." Milton R. Henry, national chairman of the Malcolm X Society and first vice-president of the new government, told reporters that the 100 delegates "feel no sense of allegiance" to the United States. On March 28,

1971, the new nation was formally launched on twenty acres of land in Hinds County, Mississippi. Its career, however, followed a rough path.

If the black American citizen insists that he is an "American subject" and that he lives in an American colony despite his relative freedom, he expresses his personal alienation; and that is an understandable privilege. As one nationalist puts it: "American blacks are Africans in exile."[3] But Negroes in Angola or Mozambique, for example, are manifestly not seeking the same ends as those of Negroes living in the United States.

The American Negro nationalist would probably contend that both groups are struggling for territorial independence. We shall have to assume that, for Americans, this is an unrealizable objective. It should be remarked that the American Communist Party dissociates itself completely from the idea that American Negroes are colonials.

Another argument against the concept of "colonialism" is that capital investment in the underdeveloped countries by exporting countries—led by the United States, Great Britain, West Germany, France, and Japan—is a new form of colonialism: neocolonialism. Such events as, for example, the double-page advertisement in the *New York Times* on August 16, 1970, showing the president of Zaire, the former Belgian Congo, openly appealing to American private enterprises for investments in his country, tend to stimulate this kind of thinking. If nationalistic critics hope to find a form of socialism in the Congo, they may be severely disappointed.

But the importation of capital in itself need not mean a return to colonialism. It is merely the obvious means of furthering self-development. Capital is a costly factor of production. What Furnivall had to say in 1941 regarding progress in Southeast Asia has long since been recognized by most of the new nations. Thus Furnivall explains:

> In a capitalist enterprise there are four distinct elements: the shareholders, the directors, the management, and the employees. In a tropical dependency [a colony] all four elements may be mainly or exclusively foreign. . . . The fact that the owners or shareholders are foreign is of small importance, as in practice these exercise no control over business. But if we could replace the foreign management and employees by natives, we should do much to bring enterprise into line with social life. The management would recognize more readily their social obligations, and the public would come to understand that, although earning

212

dividends for foreign shareholders, the enterprise was nevertheless a part of the national economy. But we would be doing more than that; we would be promoting economic efficiency.

At present the management and higher employees draw large salaries to compensate them for the cost and disadvantages of exile and, by retiring early, they deprive the country of their experience just when it is becoming most valuable. Natives could serve longer and for lower pay and, if they could be trained to do the same work about as well as foreigners, there would be a large reduction in costs. The change would conduce not merely to social welfare but to economic progress, and is desirable both on humanitarian and on utilitarian grounds.

Obviously one could not make the change suddenly or by decree; the result would only be that enterprises built up under foreign management would go bankrupt under native management. The thing must be done gradually. Any firm that could solve the problem of replacing its European staff by natives would gain an advantage over its competitors that would enhance its profits and strengthen its position. But one could hardly expect European managers voluntarily to adopt a policy which might seem prejudicial to their interest, and some form of pressure would probably be needed.

One possible expedient might be to require all foreign enterprises to work under license and, as a condition of the license, to report nationalization of the enterprise. The renewal of the concessions and the grant of new concessions might be made contingent on the progress so achieved: and in the case of backward or recalcitrant firms, licenses could be cancelled and concessions forfeited.[4]

If the amount of capital invested in the country constitutes the primary criterion of colonialism, then Canada, a white man's country, must be considered much more a colony of the United States than all the countries of Africa together, including South Africa; and Cuba, Egypt, and India could then be defined as colonies of the Soviet Union. It is by no means conclusive that the loans currently made by Russia and China to the underdeveloped countries are always selfless, prudent, and productive.

The alternative to the use of capital and skill from abroad is not merely stagnation but also retrogression. Foreign capital, it is true, tends to be selective of investment opportunities but the greater the domestic development, the greater the national interests.[5] This entire process is unknown to natives under colonialism; and the antiwhiteism which obsesses so many militants in the United States seems quite inconsistent with it. We are not, of course, considering at this juncture the longer run, universal, socialistic tendency which would call for still another perspective.

Extension of the pejorative use of the term *colonial* in arguments of social protest tends ultimately to dissipate its meaning. If Harlem is an American colony, what shall we call the relatively few houses occupied by Negroes in some "white suburbs?" If all South America is a colony of the United States, then it could be said that "France and the rest of Western Europe are just American colonies."

> In fact, the American people have become colonized. At one time I thought that only Blacks were colonized. But I think we have to change our rhetoric to an extent because the whole American people have been colonized, if you view exploitation as a colonized effect, now they're exploited. They support the super-capitalist through taxation. . . . Therefore, the whole American people are colonized people and even more so than the people in these developing countries. . . ."[6]

It would be as reasonable, it seems, to speak of psychological colonialism. Perhaps a university may be thought of as a colony of the state; and the Negro American, regardless of residence, would remain a colonial. Moreover, since we expect him to remain black, he would remain a colonial forever. There is an alternative view, however. Just as, for example, we do not consider all *labor* in capitalist nations "disadvantaged," so too we should not condemn each case of capital investment in the underdeveloped countries. If foreign capital is not forthcoming, their land and labor may remain untapped and, therefore, largely wasted and useless.

Nativism

Since nationalism presumes separate existence, nativism normally is resorted to as a means of substantiation. The genius of a group, so the argument goes, has had an enviable existence in the past. Why should we not expect it to have it again? The present drive toward teaching African languages, especially Swahili, in schools attended by Negroes, and the wearing of certain African styles of hair and clothing are attempts to revert to nativistic origins. "Militants [argue] that Afro-Americans deprived of cultural roots in America can find self-identity in African culture.[7] Certain groups also advocate tribal patterns of social organization. The Muslim religion, of course, has been adopted as a nativistic counter to Christianity; and African art has been particularily prized.

214

There is a mystical American Negro culture, sometimes referred to as "soul," deriving from racial experience, which some nationalists identify as the unifying ethos. At the first World Festival of Negro Arts held at Dakar, Senegal, in April 1966, Langston Hughes explained that "soul" is like "negritude"; it is "the essence of Negro folk art redistilled—particularly the old music and its flavor, the ancient basic beat out of Africa, the folk rhymes and Ashanti stories—all expressed in contemporary ways so emotionally colored with the old that it gives a distinctly Negro flavor to today's music, painting or writing."[8] "Soul" certainly will not be found in scientific, political, or economic achievement. It probably centers in the southern rural Negro church and, as Hughes emphasizes, in the arts. Decades ago, E. B. Reuter wrote:

> Another thing making for the increase in this spirit of nationality is the growing literature of the race. This is a focal point about which the sentiments of the race crystalize. As it increases in volume and in quality and comes to be more widely read, the sentiment of pride correspondingly increases. There is also some effort being made by the Negroes themselves to create a Negro history. A tradition of musical genius already exists among the race, and outside musical circles, is generally accepted by the whites. The gift which so many Negroes have for effective public speaking is another thing of which the race is exceedingly proud. The point here is that regardless of the slender basis of fact upon which many of these things rest, they have an immense effect upon the thinking of the race. It is the opinion that a race has of itself that counts in the growth of a nationalistic spirit.[9]

Establishment of the independent Negro church by Richard Allen and Absalom Jones in Philadelphia at the end of the eighteenth century was itself a protest reaction to racial discrimination. The Negro spiritual and folk songs are indeed well-known forms of Negro art.

Racial Separatism

Racial separation, which may be psychological at first, is assumed to be a step toward black nation building. It is inevitably opposed to integration and assimilation. Separatism, however, is not new.[10] Abraham Lincoln frightened many Negroes, including Frederick Douglass, when he also became a serious separatist. In

August 1862, after having secured a grant of $100,000 to aid the emigration of freedmen, Lincoln

> called a group of prominent free Negroes to the White House and urged them to support colonization. He told them: "Your race suffer greatly, many of them, by living among us, while ours suffer from your presence. In a word we suffer on each side. If this is admitted, it affords a reason why we should be separated." Perhaps some of them pledged their support, for in his second annual message he was able to say that many free Negroes had asked to be colonized.[11]

The president's plans fizzled out as constitutional changes caught up with and outflanked the entire design.

In the past, separation has been mostly promoted by whites—though not by all white leadership. Incidentally, let it be noted that apartheid is not merely segregation; it is also separation; and one justification for it has been cultural difference and integrity.[12] It is especially this fact that has caused many Negroes to recognize the disservice done by the separatists. As one man of action put it, "I regard these existing Negro separationist movements as the biggest Uncle Tom movements in the country. Look beneath their castigation of white people . . . and you find the black incarnation of Governor Wallace's fondest dreams."[13]

Although the contentions of the separatists are many, they simmer down to the assumption that the American Negroes possess a distinct culture, that the larger American culture is foreign, that a people can achieve peace only in their own culture, and that this logic demands a separate country. Since, moreover, total emigration to Africa is not feasible, "a formal partitioning of the United States into two quite separate and independent nations, one white and one black, offers one way out of this tragic situation."[14] When the separatist has finally painted himself into a corner, he either stays smugly there or resorts to some fantasy such as the one above.

The Isolation of Black Nationalism

Perhaps many Negroes who advocate withdrawal from whites do not realize that they are responding largely to social compulsives built into their subculture by the old slave masters. Why, for instance, do Negro students on "white" college campuses form exclusive racial groups? W. Arthur Lewis makes the following observation:

Another attitude which puzzles me is that which requires black students in the better white colleges to mix only with each other; to have a dormitory to themselves; to eat at separate tables in the refectory, and so on. I have pointed out that these colleges are the gateway to leadership positions in the integrated part of the economy. . . . If we enter them merely to segregate ourselves in blackness, we shall lose the opportunity of our lives.[15]

In principle, then, black separatists look upon interracial associations as undesirable and evil. Implicitly, they and the extreme white segregationists serve each other's purposes: the white racists exclude blacks and the black racists withdraw from integrated situations and exclude whites. In each case, the results are essentially similar to those achieved by apartheid. This notion supports the 1896 doctrine in *Plessy* v. *Ferguson,* insisting upon social separation of the races. The recommended withdrawal of the twenty Negro colleges from the 430-member National Student Association at its August 1969 meeting in El Paso, Texas, is a direct instance of this.

The former Negro president of Morehouse College (Atlanta), Benjamin Mays, raised the following questions:

We need clarification on the Black University. Does this mean that no white students should be enrolled and no white faculty could teach? Does it mean that black men only would be on the Board of Trustees? Would the curriculum deal wholly or mostly with things having to do with black people? How much of the curriculum would have to be black to justify the name black curriculum? Would a black university get its money only from black people? If so, could it survive? . . . Would we expect white universities to respond in kind—a white university? As some clamor for a black university, how do we justify Negro students in Northern universities pressing the white administrations for more black students and more black faculty—which if carried successfully to the extreme, would so weaken Negro or black colleges that they could hardly exist?. . .[16]

Apparently Negro academic segregationists do not fully realize that the formal culture of the text book and classroom continues in informal relationships among students and teachers. To be deprived of the informal, primary group component, therefore, is to be engaged in unfinished business.

The ghettoized Negro youth with a formal education could hardly hold his own with a middle-class white of the same level of

217

education. Part of the disparity which ordinarily emerges when black and white schools are integrated is due, no doubt, to this difference.

The schools and colleges are the critical institutions in the service of the national culture, for the "social skills" go *pari passu* with work skills. As Charles Silberman reminds us:

> The kind of intellectual capital that is learned on the job is crucial for advancement. Some of that knowledge is transmitted by employers through formal training programs. Most of it is learned informally from fellow employees, who show new workers how to do the work, teach them what management expects, and so on.[17]

The AFL-CIO refer to their plans for assuring harmony in such informal employment relationships as their "buddy" program. Some writers resort to the mystique of "pluralism" in this connection. Karsten Prager explains:

> Integration—in the sense of accepting white values to the point where all black identity fades—is clearly no longer the immediate goal, not even for middle-class blacks who might once have aspired to it.
> The operative word today is 'liberation'—a push for *an open, pluralistic society* in which blacks can take their *rightful place* alongside other ethnic groups, a society in which . . . "you get yours and I get mine." What seems black separatism, such as the kind of self-imposed *apartheid* prevalent on many college campuses, is a temporary stage, a step in the march toward pluralism. Black college students are probably still in the van of the turning-inward movement, *of going back to black roots,* of finding comfort and security in blackness. . . . The major thrust remains the effort to carve out a healthy *black share* in a pluralistic society.[18]

Except for the word *apartheid,* we have added italics to call attention to concepts which may be both contradictory and confusing. Negroes cannot transform the American society to suit their limitations. The gist of this statement, however, conforms to the historic wishes of the southern oligarchy who have constantly insisted that Negroes in the United States ought to live in their own societal enclaves.

The Black Nation

West African people did not know nationhood in the modern sense until European imperalists introduced it. The colony was defined by a definite territory and governed as a separate entity on principles comparable to those by which a typical nation is organized. Independence has meant the taking over by natives of the right to govern. No such process operates under tribalism or feudalism. The quest for nationhood by black nationalists presents the basic problem of laying claim to territory.

In the United States Negroes may gain control of national territory through the elective process or through majority settlement. For decades they have had such control of many small places, ranging in population from a few score to a few thousand in a number of states. The nationalists seldom if ever refer to any of these as examples of what might be accomplished through self-determination or as nuclei for exemplary development and expansion. Then, too, territory might be acquired either by voluntary grant or by forceable seizure from the United States. The idea of the Negroes' right to a land base was perhaps first introduced in the early thirties by the Communist Party. The Party held:

> that Negroes in the United States constitute a separate nation, that the heart of this nation is geographically located in the South in an irregular area composed of those counties in which Negroes compose 50 percent or over of the population, and that Negroes should be given the right of selfdetermination in this interstate area, with an implied right to secede from the rest of the United States, thus assuming the responsibilities of a completely independent nation.[19]

The Communist Party, following Joseph Stalin's teaching on the subject, assumed that the Negro's position in the United States was similar to that of national minority groups in Europe and Asia or to that of colonial peoples. Today's Negro separatists would doubtless agree both with this definition of the situation and the plan for its territorial resolution. But, in the thirties, American Negroes, both communists and noncommunists, objected so strenuously to the view that the Communist Party eventually admitted its error and gave up the proposition.[20]

Another way of acquiring national territory is one currently proposed, and apparently being acted upon, of cordoning off all Negro neighborhoods and insisting that whites who enter them, to live or to establish businesses, recognize local black sovereignty: "black control of black communities." A dramatic illustration of the extent to which this idea has progressed was the curfew "proclamation" broadcast to the city of Chicago and to the nation on December 15, 1969, by the Negro nationalist, the Rev. C. T. Vivian. From 6:00 P.M. to 6:00 A.M., he declared, no whites would be allowed to enter the Negro areas of the city.

There was a quick negative reaction to this warning by both black and white residents, hence it was not carried out. But there can be no mistake about the violent nature of the street group to whom Vivian was appealing. It was the same group that has been helping to clear the ghetto of whites through burglary, vandalism, and sporadic violence. Through "fear and flight," whites have been progressively leaving the segregated areas. We are probably correct in assuming that something of this attitude remains. There is a "hard-core group in the ghetto," Chuck Stone observes, "who seek a violent confrontation between the races as the only solution. Out of this confrontation we can expect to emerge a new society of two nations—black and white—co-existing as co-equals."[21]

There is, furthermore, a clear echo of Marcus Garvey in the current suggestion that American Negroes should select a base on the African continent for development of a universal pan-African movement. While Garvey selected Liberia as the most likely landing place[22] for his Negro colonization project, Stokely Carmichael favors Ghana as the national center of pan-Africanization. As he puts it: "Our ideology must be Pan-Africanism, nothing else. . . . We have to have a land base. I think that the best place for that is Africa and in Africa the best place is Ghana."[23] Here the strategy for organizing all the black people of the world for action against the whites will be planned and implemented. Incidentally, the leader chosen as ideally suited to this purpose is Kwame Nkrumah.[24] Nothing, perhaps, would demonstrate more dramatically the utopian nature of these schemes than an actual attempt to put them into practice.

The Problem of Ghettoization and Power

The idea of thus constituting the territory of a nation from the multiplicity of black urban enclaves seems fantastic; it contributes, nevertheless, to the perpetuation of ghettos. The larger and more secure the Negro community, the greater the variety of black interest it encourages and supports. These interests in turn propagate the relatively weak and inferior ghetto subculture and shelter it from attack by those Negro leaders who attempt to point out its long-run disadvantages. Ordinarily, these interest groups seek cover in Negro nationalism. The idea of the ghetto as a temporary social situation similar to that experienced by other unacculturated immigrant groups is thus abandoned.

The white slums have been abolished as rapidly as their tenants have been able to acquire middle-class culture. It was assumed that the great struggle for civil rights—in occupation, in freedom of housing, in education—would produce similar effects on the Negro ghetto. Just as *individuals* of limited culture moved from the rural South to enlarge the urban mass, so too *individuals* were generally expected to leave that underprivileged environment as soon as they became identified with the mainstream of American culture.

Black nationalists insist, however, that this process of social mobility, characteristic of all Western society, should be halted. Negroes, it is argued, should retain their group solidarity until the whole ghetto is able to move up, which seems to mean that lower class must become middle class in spite of its lower-class ideals.

In an interview with Georgia state representative Julian Bond, reporter Roy Reed said, "[Bond] noted that black Atlanta had become a separate community, and . . . that was advantageous in gaining political power for Negroes."[25] E. Franklin Frazier gave special attention to the "vested interest" Negro business, professional, and religious leadership groups have in ghettoization. Life insurance, funeral parlors, personal services of all kinds such as barbering and beauty culture, religion and the cults, black politics, segregated education—these are some of the activities which depend for their prosperity upon progressive ghettoization. As Frazier puts it: "Only certain elements in the Negro community have a vested interest in segregation. . . . These groups in the Negro population enjoy certain advantages because they do not have to compete with whites." They could be expected, therefore, to "resist removal of the color line."[26]

What should not be overlooked, however, is the fact that the ghetto itself exercises the greatest pull; and the larger, the more insistent. It supplies warmth and security to the black masses despite its pathologies. And it tends to assuage evidences of subcultural inferiority, thus providing a haven for its weakest elements. It is here, for instance, that the urge to change one's name from, say, John Harrison to Muzumbo Alawala arises, so that cultural consistency might be achieved. The larger culture demands less of Mr. Alawala than of Mr. Harrison. Exotic names and dress implicitly beseech the

221

dominant society to grant concessions to cultural handicaps and limitations.[27] Conversely, white or Negro "foreigners," who desire to enter the fray of unlimited competition, frequently Americanize their names.

We consider the concept of power here because recently it has been brought into the protest movement with great impact. It was on the Memphis to Jackson continuation march, in June, 1966, that Stokely Carmichael shouted again and again to a mass Negro audience: "We want black power." The national television recorded the clamorous approval of the group. It was this event which dramatized the developing breach between the nonviolent and the violent approach to racial protest. It separated the ideology of M. L. King, Jr., from that of Carmichael and Floyd McKissick, spokesmen for SNCC and CORE respectively. The aim of the latter also changed from integration by way of civil rights to nationalism.[28] Moreover, King no longer provided social orientation for SNCC and CORE; this was henceforth supplied by Malcolm X and Frantz Fanon.[29]

It was this open breach, recognized and broadcast by the news media, which endowed the cry of "black power," (incomprehensible in itself) with mystical importance. If we could conceive of Negro Americans as a colonial people whose primary concern is that of gaining their independence from the United States, a foreign imperialist nation, then the yearning for black power among Negroes would appear obvious.

To know the significance of power we must know its purpose. If we know the desired end, then the most appropriate power available for its attainment can be discussed. For example, objectives may range from individual religious salvation to protection of South Vietnam from communist control. Marcus Garvey emphasized military power as the ultimate objective of his movement. He said in part:

> It is the commercial and financial power of the United States . . . that makes her the greatest banker in the world. Hence it is advisable for the Negro to get power of every kind. Power in education, science, industry, politics, and higher government. That kind of power that will stand out signally, so that other races and nations can see, and if they will not see, then FEEL.[30]

According to Malcolm X, power "produces insurrection against oppression. This is the only way you end oppression—with power."[31] This is an obvious but rather simple approach, operative among many species of the lower animals. It seldom answers such questions as why, through this means, serfdom and slavery had not been speedily ended everywhere. Have the scores of millions of traditional East Indian outcasts sought power? Power, the capacity to use violence, is one of the more inconsequential factors that determine social change. Carmichael, at any rate, developed a larger program for American Negroes than the one with which the James Meredith march was concerned. His vision has now been clarified. The purpose of black power is the organization of "the whole black world" to wage a fatal struggle against "Europeans. And that means that America is European." As he says:

> We have always been moving. Let's go back to the 1960's: we start a move for integration—a cup of coffee. Even before we got the cup of coffee, we recognized where else we were going. We were moving for the vote. By the time they were getting ready to give us the vote, we recognized that that was not it either. So now we recognize it is pan-Africanism.[32]

This, indeed, seems to be the ultimate fantasy of nationalist leadership. The mystical use of *we* and *they* allows the writer to conceive of himself as a leader of African unification without regard for the infinity of countervailing forces. It now seems clear that the black power demanded had nothing to do with enhancement of the drive for civil rights among Negroes in the United States. If anything, the call for black power was intended to counteract the civil rights movement as "pro-American" and thus antiblack. This is exactly what Roy Wilkins took it to mean as early as July 1966, in his address to the annual meeting of the NAACP.[33]

So far as compatibility with native Africa is concerned, Colin Legum records some of the positions on racial exclusion already expressed at the 1958 conference of the All African Peoples Organization meeting in Accra, Ghana:

> the question of the pan-African slogan "Africa for the Africans" was raised. The Accra conference chairman, Mr. Tom Mboya, announced from the platform, "Once the principle of 'one man, one vote' is established, we will not practice racism in reverse." Dr. [Kwame] Nkrumah went further: "When I speak of Africa for the Africans this should be interpreted in the light of my emphatic declaration that I do not believe in racialism and colonialism. The concept . . . does not mean that other races are excluded. . . . As Dr. [Nhamdi] Azikiwe has said: . . . it should

223

be obvious that unless we accept a broad definition of terms there can be no worthy future for Africanism. That being the case I would like to speak of the peoples of Africa . . . to include all the races inhabiting that continent and embracing all the linguistic and cultural groups who are domiciled therein."[34]

In the summer of 1959, on a research stint to West Africa, I was particularly interested in the problem of African unification. In Ghana I had a number of conversations with the late George Padmore, adviser to President Nkrumah, and author of *Pan-Africanism or Communism* (London, 1956). The central point we seemed to agree upon was that Africa's problem is essentially one of economic development and that, among other limitations, two basic obstacles, tribalism and nationalism, stood in the way. Padmore asked me to read a paper on "Factors in the Development of Under-developed Countries" before a select group, the National Association of Socialist Students' Organization, which met once every two weeks at the Castle, Nkrumah's residence. I made the statement, early in the question period, that Ghana was too small a country to establish a successful socialist economy. To my surprise, Nkrumah led a passionate majority reaction holding that Ghana was quite capable of developing such a system. It is just possible that his subsequent familiarity with the socialist debacle in Guinea has sufficed to clarify this point. Insistence on the position left me no opportunity for discussion of pan-Africanization. Incidentally, I found intermarriage, from George Padmore to public officials and university teachers, unexpectedly common in West Africa.

Any attempt by American Negroes to suggest policy or ideology to Africans, especially such stupendous political designs as plans for the unification of the continent, or the organization of all black people for an apocalyptic struggle with whites, should be regarded as the height of naïveté. Garvey, let us recall, was rejected even though he never set foot on the continent; and we may be certain that no better fate awaits the modern black racists. One thing seems certain: Africa can be unified only to the extent that it westernizes its culture: otherwise it remains tribal and therefore fiercely divided. Today, European and white American teachers and technicians are leading the way everywhere on the continent. I found constant lament over the lack of American or West Indian Negroes prepared to assist in this work.

We should remember, moreover, that the white missionaries

and philanthropists, who hastened to the South after our Civil War, were concerned primarily with the freedmen's lack of power. They debated the question of how to employ their resources most effectively: whether economic, political, or educational factors should be emphasized. While it seemed clear that work opportunities were essential for subsistence and that political power, the right to vote, could limit the forces of exploitation, they reasoned that only education would ensure progress in job opportunities and the franchise. In the very process of acquiring an education the Negro would be effectively integrated into American society. And to the extent that he sought employment in business or in any of the various occupational specialties, to that extent also he would become integrated. To withdraw physically is to set up problems of returning deviously.

Chapter **16**

The Projections of Nationalist Leadership

In this society Negro leadership is largely anomalous; it tends to be defensive and arises as a consequence of white racial hostility and deprivations fostered by white constituted leadership. It is not like, for example, Jewish leadership which functions within the Jewish community and has a well-defined, historic purpose and program. During the long period of Reconstruction, in the white South especially, to be anti-Negro was the best policy for anyone running for public office. Most presidents of the United States since the Civil War were probably thus affected.

Negro leadership, therefore, derives from this basic anomaly. It seeks to placate or eliminate the debilitating effects of racial repression advocated and exercised by white constituted leaders. The society, however, is not so structured politically as to include Negro leadership. In a sense, then, Negroes in the United States have remained largely leaderless.[1] Those who attempted to act positively, mainly black nationalists, have been separatists, and have therefore sought to remove themselves from the arena of interracial adjustment.

Blacks cannot be *the exclusive political leaders* of blacks in the United States unless Negroes are presumed to constitute a nation within the nation. In a period of generally rising concern about Negro intractability and lawlessness, intelligent white leaders should take the needs of the Negro citizenry into account. It is this kind of leadership that has been historically lacking. Today a political leader must be a leader of *all* the people.

John V. Lindsay, when he was mayor of New York City, was aware of this, whereas President Nixon virtually served Negroes notice that they could not look to him for that kind of leadership.[2] Let us consider certain movements among Negroes intended to fill this vacuum.

The Structure of Leadership

In a study made in 1950, we defined four major leadership movements among Negroes in the United States. We shall list them here in the light of subsequent developments. They are:

(1) *Assimilationism,* adhered to absolutely by such leaders and leadership groups as Frederick Douglass, the NAACP, and M. L. King, Jr. This movement has also been supported historically by some determined white Americans. It opposed slavery, it turned away from any idea of Negro emigration; it fought for the Negroes' civil rights as freemen during the whole period of the group's existence in this country; it has shown the way toward specific constitutional, educational, and economic advancement. In an incisive answer to Negro "isolationists," as early as the thirties, James Weldon Johnson remarked: "To say that in the past two generations or more Negro Americans have not advanced a single step toward a fuller share in the commonwealth becomes, in the light of easily ascertainable facts, an absurdity. Only the shortest view of the situation gives color of truth to such a statement; any reasonably long view proves it to be utterly false."[3]

(1) *Accommodation or compromise* called for postponement of political activity and social integration, and was led by Booker T. Washington. This ideology advocated devotion to education involving "work with the hands" and business enterprise. Assimilationism, which considered the struggle for political rights elemental, super-

seded the tendency toward exclusive reliance on primary economic development.[4]

(3) *Radicalism:* part of the world socialist movement had, and still has, its Negro advocates. Among the earlier leaders were such men as Chandler Owens and A. Phillip Randolph, editors of *The Messenger.* In August 1920, Owens said in an interview:

> Our Socialist movement among Negroes of America is for equality in all things with the whites, even intermarriage. We believe the Negro [to be] the equal of the white socially, and with education he will be the equal of whites from every standpoint. Therefore we do not think it will be necessary for the Negro alone to fight this war for freedom. If he joins with the Socialists of the world, he will share equally with the white in all things when Socialism becomes the order of the day.[5]

The assumption of radicalism is that a socialist system has the capacity to accommodate the change toward racial equality but capitalism has not.

(4) *Nationalism.* Even before the Civil War, those Negroes who for various reasons felt that they could not become adjusted to life in the United States chose "colonization." The "separatists" were most likely to be included among these. As early as 1815, Paul Cuffe, a Negro mariner, took some thirty-eight emigrants to Sierra Leone at his own expense.[6] All told, however, the repatriates constituted but a very small fraction of the American Negro population. It will be recalled that Liberia was founded in 1821 by the American Colonization Society, an organization initiated by whites for the return of American Negroes to Africa.

Black Racism

Black racism tends inevitably to constitute the ideological counterpart of white racism and the basis of Negro nationalism in the United States. African nationalism, on the other hand, is more realistic, territorially oriented, and nativistic. There has been a very decided tendency among most Negro nationalists to justify Negro racism by calling attention to previous or existing racism, nationalism, or other political deviations among whites. Normal standards of behavior for Negroes is thus supported and vindicated by citations of immoral or even criminal behavior among whites. Such Negro advocates seldom, if ever, realize that they have adopted and live by belief in the total superiority of "white" culture.

What seems good enough for the least of whites, they would argue, should be good enough as standard behavior for all Negroes. As it is commonly put: "whites do the same thing, or did it." "One of the greatest paradoxes of the Black Power movement," observes M.L. King, Jr., "is that it talks increasingly about not imitating the values of white society, but in advocating violence it is imitating the worst, the most brutal and most uncivilized value of American life."[7]

The origins of black racism stem in part from the noncompetitive nature of Negro subculture, fashioned during the age of thralldom. It is not to be found, for example, in the Jewish subculture; and, so far as we know, none of the previously unassimilated nationality groups in the United States has been identified with it. Because it is subcultural, its advocates could expect positive responses among an indiscriminate, mass Negro audience.

It seeks to match white racism at a time when the latter is under heavy attack. Thomas Gossett observes: "Racism, the most serious threat to the idea of equality before the law and to the individual development of one's own capabilities, is now on the defensive as it has never been before."[8]

Perhaps because of the absence of an independent economic power base and consequent frustration, black racism tends to be couched in terms of revenge, retaliation, and hatred of whites. We should recognize that invidious biological differentiation is an essential part of the content—though not the basis—of all racism.

Marcus Garvey as Nationalist

The most persuasive black nationalist and racist, Marcus Garvey, came to the fore during World War I, the period of the great universal efflorescence of nationalism when racism in general was first brought into serious contention. He encouraged whites to be racist so that his own black racism might be justified and accepted by American Negroes. "No real race-loving white man," he argued, "wants to destroy the purity of his race, and no real Negro, conscious of himself, wants to die, hence there is room for an understanding and an adjustment, and that is just what we seek."[9] Apparently, Garvey believed racism on both sides could be made to offset each other.

Although the idea of returning to Africa was never completely abandoned by Negroes, it was not until about 1920, with the advent of the dynamic Garvey, that Negro nationalism received definitive formulation. More recently Garvey was followed by such advocates as

229

Elijah Muhammad, Malcolm X, Stokely Carmichael, and others. Let us, however, briefly examine the strategy of the prototype. Garvey's program was contrived particularly for American Negroes and it was here that it enjoyed overwhelming success. West Indians and Africans were true colonials—they were already at home—hence the Negro nationalists of those areas would come into possession of their country merely through a normal grant of independence from the mother country. A black exodus differs from a black accession to power; hence the two groups' politics were not interchangeable. Garvey planned to lead an emigration movement, and he did this in the guise of a black savior. He never gave up his contention that a "repatriated" black population in a nationalized African continent was the only hope of Negro Americans. He declared:

> Until the Negro reaches this point of national independence, all he does as a race will count for naught. . . . If the Negro were to live in this Western Hemisphere for another five hundred years he will still be outnumbered by other races who are prejudiced against him. He cannot resort to the government for protection for government will be in the hands of the majority of the people who are prejudiced against him, hence for the Negro to depend on the ballot and his industrial progress alone, will be hopeless as it does not help him when he is lynched, burned, jim-crowed and segregated. The future of the Negro therefore, outside of Africa, spells ruin and disaster.[10]

Garvey's pamphlet, *An Appeal to the Soul of White America,* had two principal objectives: to point out to Negroes the futility of efforts to secure civil rights in America, and to ask the United States *not* to grant the civil rights demanded by "Negroes in positions of honor" but to help all Negroes to leave the United States for Africa. He said: "Let foolish Negro agitators and so-called reformers, encouraged by deceptive and unthinking white associates, stop preaching and advocating the doctrine of 'social equality' meaning thereby the social intermingling of both races, intermarriage, and general social co-relationship." Then, turning to the United States government he made this supplication: "The Negro must have a country, and a nation of his own. . . . We have found a place, it is Africa; and, as black men for three centuries have helped white men build America, surely generous and grateful white men will help black men build Africa."

It was no paradox, therefore, that Garvey should find in the

230

attitude and actions of the Ku Klux Klan an effective counterpart to his own designs. He praised the activities of that organization as "an honest expression of the white man's attitude toward the Negro; [which] prepares him to help himself."[11] In 1921 Garvey actually visited the Imperial Wizard of the Klan in Atlanta, Georgia, and came away seemingly further convinced that "the Ku Klux Klan had [no] other desire than to preserve their race from suicide through miscegenation and to keep it pure, which to me is not a crime but a commendable desire and [does] not supply the reason why Negroes should attack them. . . . I believe in the purity, honor, and pride, and integrity of each and every race."[12]

It was precisely on this point that the charismatic Garvey was able to drive home his nationalistic theories. As the *Amsterdam News,* a Negro weekly, declared in 1925: "In a world where black is despised, he taught them that black is beautiful."[13] Garvey would say to his audiences: "Negroes, teach your children that they are the direct descendants of the greatest and proudest race who ever peopled the earth . . . it is because of the fear of our return to *power,* in a civilization of our own, that may outshine others, [that] we are hated and kept down by a jealous and prejudiced contemporary world."[14]

It probably seemed obvious to Garvey that any demagogue who proclaimed the racial superiority of his group would have a large, fanatic following. Garvey would have had little to say to blacks had he not dangled the lure of power. "The Japanese," he pointed out, "would receive very little courtesy or fair play in any country if they had not a nation of their own to back them up in case of persecution. The Negro desires to have a nation of his own for identical reasons."[15] As soon as it became clear that he could not carry out his plans, Garveyism simply withered away.

More specifically, there seem to have been three immediate reasons for Garvey's decline: (a) He was dealing with an essentially fictitious world. The retarded Negro nations—Liberia, Haiti, Ethiopia—were not impressed by his declarations that blacks are descendants of the greatest powers on earth. Africa, in other words, rejected him.

(b) He apparently misunderstood the nature of the culture with which he was dealing. The British imperial system that he proposed to duplicate among African blacks—in his colorful street parades he usually dressed like a colonial governor—was not built by Marcus Garvey states but by private enterprise.

231

And (c) his exaltation of blackness, regarded as his residual contribution, had to be skin deep. In reality, "black is beautiful" (indeed, black can be beautiful) only insofar as black behaves beautifully; and blacks or whites can behave beautifully only to the extent that they are culturally prepared to do so. On the whole, the culture of the ghetto does not prepare blacks to behave beautifully; and the ultimate remedy seems hardly the blatant repetition of the slogan.

Moreover, his glorification of physical blackness was clearly a direct reaction to white racists in exactly their terms. As we should expect, therefore, the latter were more than a match for the black racist. The late Tom Mboya, in an article offering no comfort to American Negro nationalists, observed: "The objective of the black American must be the achievement of full and unqualified equality within American society. . . . The Black American should . . . not look to Africa for escape. He must merge his blackness with his citizenship as an American, and the result will be dignity and liberation."[16]

If, for example, the black tenant farmer tells his children that they are descendants of a mighty black race of historic African pre-eminence and, conversely, the white plantation owner tells his children that they are descendants of Aryans, the originators of the greatest culture known to mankind, the black children will, at most, still remain in their relative position. But then Negroes will have helped whites to concentrate on biological differences as determinants of cultural differences. Probably Negro achievers such as Benjamin Banneker and Frederick Douglass and white educators such as General O. O. Howard and the post-Civil War white missionaries in the South did incalculably more to impress permanently upon Negroes and upon the world that "black is beautiful" than the ideology of black nationalists. The "magnificence of Africa's ancient civilizations" is largely irrelevant to Africa's current problems of development. Preoccupation with it could even be a serious intertribal distraction.

The pride which Negro nationalists seem to experience in response to Garveyite exhortations emanates from psychological absorption in a more responsive mythical culture. They seem to turn their backs on the sophisticated culture in which they must inevitably live, the only culture from which they can derive pride of achievement, and thus they merely postpone the day of reckoning. Some of the same groups that castigate the Negro middle class, the "black bourgeoisie," for its middle-class behavior praise the Black Muslims for their advocacy of certain middle-class practices among their members—with the difference that the Muslim social structure has been devised peripherally by and for the societally underprivileged.

The Black Muslims

Garveyism declined almost completely with the collapse of its economic base and the deportation of its leader. What did not vanish, however, was the immemorial yearning among the Negro masses for a dignified existence. Thus the basis for other nationalistic movements persisted. The social situation conducive to the rise of black Muslimism was therefore already present. Although the Moorish Holy Temple of Science was founded in Newark, New Jersey, sometime in 1913 by Noble Drew Ali, Arthur H. Fauset says: "Marcus Garvey was to Noble Drew Ali what John the Baptist was to Christ."[17] Ali's system of Islamic Temples flourished in the ghettos of many cities before the advent of the Black Muslims. Since the latter have superseded the Moors, we shall consider their role among Negroes.

The Black Muslim cult may be thought of as a religious version of Garveyism:

(1) It seeks a separate *nation* for American Negroes, preferably outside of the United States but secured and maintained by this country:

> We want our people in America . . . to be allowed to establish a separate state or territory of their own—whether on this continent or elsewhere. We believe [whites] are obligated to provide such land and that the area must be fertile and minerally rich. We believe our former slave masters are obligated to maintain and supply our needs in this separate territory for the next 20 to 25 years—until we are able to produce and supply our own needs.[18]

(2) Like the prototype, it is firmly opposed to the Negroes' struggle for civil rights. "How can you make the slave and the master equal? The slave must first have what the master has to be the master's equal. What future [have] the so-called Negroes in integration, or social equality with their most deadly enemies?"[19] In saying "We want equal education but separate schools, [and] we believe that intermarriage or race mixing should be prohibited [by law]"[20] the

233

Muslims advocate the theories of the Ku Klux Klan. The Messenger of Allah, as the Honorable Elijah Muhammad is called, thought that when the Reverend Martin Luther King, Jr., said "he wanted to be the brother of white people, our enemies . . . what he wanted was to be white." Racial ideology is usually presented in a religious context. Thus Muhammad said: "God has given me the mission of separating you from your enemies, and setting you in heaven with money, good homes, and friendship in all walks of life."[21]

(3) Just as Garvey decided not to wait until the United States became disposed to sponsor the funding of a nation of Negro Americans at home or abroad but to begin nationalistic economic ventures forthwith, so too Muhammad embarked upon business enterprises in the United States as a critical activity of the Nation of Islam. Compared to the Black Star Line, however, Muslim economics are securely entrenched. The group entered the area of traditional Negro business, that of direct personal service within the ghetto. However, both depended upon membership financing with no strict accounting. Muhammad intended to link urban and rural production. In his column, "Muhammad Speaks," the Messenger declared that his economics

> goes to the essential root for self-help (farming). This back-to-the-earth movement puts the product in the hand that is most essential to becoming self-independent. Producing your own food; producing your own cotton and wool for your clothing, and producing your own clay and timber for building your homes, with the unity of followers, are some of the greatest steps that have been taken.[22]

We will not attempt here to examine in detail the Muslim economic ventures. They are now operating apparently praiseworthy restaurants in Chicago and other cities, grocery stores, bakeries, apartment buildings, barber shops, farms in the North and South involving an investment of probably over $5,000,000. Rather, we are concerned with the Muslims' idea of planning the economic structure of the black Nation of Islam within the United States.

The Muslims, moreover, have not hesitated to engage whites as agents in their commercial transactions and as technicians on their farms and in other businesses. The movement obviously is not competitive. For example, in a controversial purchase of farm land in St. Clair County, Alabama—a purchase surreptitiously negotiated through white intermediaries and actively resented by white residents of the county—the Muslims looked to white friends for support. One of them, a go-between who made a handsome profit on one of the deals and who called himself a "strict segregationist," defended the sect by saying: "The more I learn about the Muslims the more I admire them. They don't believe in smoking, drinking or adultery: they have no interest in white women; they believe in hard work and segregation."[23] Even this evidence, however, did not placate white antagonism. The rural people could not bear the thought of an "anti-Christian" black nation in their midst.

The Muslims seem now to have irreversibly entered the field of business, a dynamic phenomenon which will no doubt increasingly claim their attention, define their purpose, and establish their norms of success. Business, moreover, will hardly tolerate Muslim mysticism and racism. It will most likely cauterize the utopianism of the sect, identify it with the interests of the "white devils," and probably, like Garveyism, become the basis of the movement.

Unlike Garveyism, however, it has been able to collect untold sums of money through semi-religious appeals for contributions to establish and support these "businesses." So far as we are aware, no businesslike records have ever been shown to the membership. In reality, business seems mainly a means to establish a total subculture that lower-class Negroes can comprehend—a process of bringing mainstream culture down to a size manageable by ghettoites. The sense of inadequacy generated by failure to meet the demands of the larger culture has thus been assuaged by a sense of competence in the operation of a black counterpart. The conduct of members tends to be disciplined in order to meet efficiency requirements.

The Black Muslims started out as an Islamic religious cult, in opposition to Christianity, the religion of white Americans. Christianity, the Muslims claim, was imposed upon Negroes. God, Allah, is black not white. All white people, they insist, are devils and Allah consequently hates them. If you, a black person, are confused; if you are in jail and you have a basic hatred for the "white devil" who put you there, remember that Allah is with you. He sympathizes with what you have done. The Christian God of love is a myth. True Christianity, as you can prove from a perusal of your Bible, is a religion of hatred and violence. Separate yourself from the white man and his Christian culture and Allah, the God of black people, will give you a new life. As the sect interprets it, then, black racial antagonism

235

to whites is inseparable from Islam. According to Elijah Muhammad, "Allah hates the wicked white American. . . . He puts hate for her in the hearts of others."[24] Indeed, His hatred for whites is so complete that He would have no truck with even a white Moslem.

The Muslims' Allah is thus a black God interested primarily in the Negro problem in the United States. Preachments in the name of Allah are essentially denunciations of whites, of Negro Christian ministers, and of "educated" Negroes. In his sermons, the Messenger of Allah ordinarily made nominal reference to the "Holy Qur-An" but cited copiously from the mysteries and prophecies of the Old Testament and the Apocalypse. The Muslims have been the principal source of some of the most militant antiwhite rhetoric in the United States.

Black Muslimism is not an orthodox sect of Islam. It had a spontaneous beginning in the United States. The long time absolute leader of the movement was Robert Poole, born in Sandersville, Georgia, in 1897, the son of a Baptist minister. He was able to acquire only a fourth-grade education before moving to Detroit in 1923 with his wife and two of his children. He worked at odd jobs as an unskilled laborer. During the depression in 1930, however, he attended a house meeting led by a religious exotic, Wallace D. Fard. This contact was the initiation of his career as a Muslim. Fard, Poole later explained, took "[me] out of the gutters in the streets of Detroit and taught me knowledge of Islam."[25]

As it turned out, Fard became recognized as the incarnation of God Himself. In a statement of faith, Poole declared: "We believe that Allah, God, appeared in the Person of Master W. Fard Muhammad, in July, 1930, the long-awaited 'Messiah' of the Christians and the 'Mahdi' of the Muslims."[26] Poole claimed that he obtained his mission as the "Messenger" of Allah directly from Fard. To the whole membership of the sect, therefore, he was regarded as infallible; and, because Fard disappeared in 1934, no other could hope to acquire such a distinction.* Poole always referred to Fard worshipfully as "Allah in the Person of Master Fard Muhammad." Traditional Islam, let us note, does not believe in the incarnation of God.

---

*Robert Poole, known to the Black Muslims as Elijah Muhammad, died February 25, 1975, and was succeeded by his son, Wallace Muhammad, under whose leadership some modifications in the movement's structure and policy have been made. (Ed.)

The origins of Wallace Fard, his history and final whereabouts are still unknown. He was a house-to-house peddler of silk cloth in the Negro neighborhoods of Detroit. In the process, he related and spread occult religious ideas centering about a mystical version of American race relations. From this itinerant beginning he moved to more convenient quarters, a hall, subsequently named the Temple of Islam. It became the center of a movement he designed in all its consequential details. He provided the group's basic ideology and prescribed its puritanical observances. He explained to his mostly illiterate audiences that he was sent by Allah as a Prophet to teach Negroes, the Black Nation of Islam, their full potentialities in the face of their temporary domination by the biologically inferior, white "blue-eyed devils." He set up a school for the faithful, the "University of Islam" and, to protect the organization from physical attack, provided a corps of private guards, "The Fruit of Islam."

Then, before his disappearance in 1934, Fard appointed a minister in chief, the Minister of Islam and a corps of assistant ministers, "all of whom had been trained by the prophet." Converts were assigned their true Arabic Islamic names to replace those which "the slave masters" had given to their ancestors. This was an attempt to escape the past: the group was identified with a fictitious world and given fictitious histories, experiences, and names. The problem now was to reify these, by force if necessary, in the actual American milieu. Robert Poole was not only chosen Minister of Islam but also honored with the prestigious name, Elijah Muhammad.[27] At this time, there were about 5,000 to 8,000 followers in Detroit.

In 1932, "Temple Number Two" was established in Chicago, and this eventually became Muhammad's headquarters. By the 1960s some seventy or eighty other temples had been founded in various cities. The group also publishes a popular bi-weekly newspaper *Muhammad Speaks*. The movement would have had a history similar to that of any of the other cults that crop up among Negroes in the metropolises had it not been for two precipitating factors: the conversion of Malcolm X, and the intrusion of the movement into the expanding Negro civil rights struggle since 1954. "In fact," Essien-Udom observes, "in 1942, when Muhammad and his followers were indicted and imprisoned for violations of the Selective Service Act, the total membership of the movement came to only a few hundred.[28] It was in the late fifties that the movement made its national public appearance.

The Role of Malcolm X

Malcolm X's involvement with race relations has had its ups and downs. First, as a zealous Black Muslim, he remained fiercely opposed to the Negroes' nonviolent civil rights movement and to the very existence of white people; and secondly, as a Black Muslim outlaw, he developed an irrepressible defiance of Elijah Muhammad's authority and threatened to undermine the whole edifice of Muhammad's "religious fakery." The year between his effective expulsion from the sect and his assassination by Black Muslim gunmen (December 1963–February 1965) was spent in an attempt at personality reform, in efforts to undo the "wrongs" committed as an irresponsible Black Muslim, and in search of a convenient way to reenter a world responsive to constructive social protest. However: "Neither as a spokesman for the Black Muslims, nor later as a Black Nationalist, reputedly leaning towards the civil-rights position, did he express any new philosophy."[29]

Malcolm Little was born on May 19, 1925, in Omaha, Nebraska. His father, a Baptist minister, was "a dedicated organizer for Marcus Garvey's U.N.I.A." While still a child, his family moved to Lansing, Michigan. Their home was destroyed by fire in 1929— Malcolm believed it was arson. In 1931, his father was run over by a streetcar. The family, with great difficulty, was making its way with the help of relief when his mother became insane and was sent to the state mental hospital. The welfare agency found a home for Malcolm in Lansing where he attended high school. He remained near the top of his class.

In 1940 he went to live with his sister in Boston and soon became involved with the worst elements of the Negro slum. "The first liquor I drank, my first cigarettes, even my first reefers, I cannot specifically remember. But I know they were all mixed together with my shooting craps, playing cards, and betting my dollar a day on the numbers. . . ."[30] He moved from Boston to New York and found the situation in Harlem even more hospitable to his deviant inclinations. Here he became a "hustler" and served both white and Negro prostitutes. In his dealings with the former, however, he managed to conceive of himself as operating within the "white man's morals." "I got my first schooling about the cesspool morals of the white man from the best possible source, from his own women. And then as I got deeper into my life of evil, I saw the white man's morals with my own eyes. I even made my living helping to guide him to the sick things he wanted.''[31] Obviously, Malcolm did not have the chance to observe normal white citizens in the pursuit of their regular work.

It was in Boston, at any rate, ''that things fell apart.'' ''The cops found [our] apartment loaded with evidence—fur coats, some jewelry, other small stuff—plus the tools of our trade. A jimmy, a lockpick, glass cutters, screwdrivers, pencil-beam flashlights, flash keys . . . and a small arsenal of guns.''[32] In 1946, therefore, he was sentenced to ten years in a Massachusetts State prison. Here, in 1948, he was introduced to Allah and to the Nation of Islam through correspondence with his relatives who had already been converted. Thereafter, he studied rhetoric, enlarged his vocabulary, abandoned his impulsive habits of profanity, and became progressively involved with the substance and teachings of the Black Muslims.

Two aspects of this progress concern us: the nature of his breach with the movement, and the character of his leadership among non-Muslim Negro groups. Let us first consider the breach. To become a Black Muslim convert is to give total allegiance to the group, even at the expense of life itself, and to remove oneself from the structure of justice in the larger society. W. D. Fard had even emphasized human sacrifice. According to Beynon: ''The prophet . . . taught that Allah demands obedience unto death from his followers. No Moslem dare refuse the sacrifice of himself or of his loved ones if Allah requires it.''[33] Members submit themselves to beatings without recourse to the civil law. Their alienation and isolation from the larger society thus become institutionalized.

Disillusioned with Elijah Muhammad, Malcolm mounted the opposition. He was privy to the structural secrets of the organization and could communicate effectively with the public. He proceeded fatefully to establish a rival organization. But the mystique and the control of retributive sanctions remained with Elijah Muhammad. Malcolm charged Elijah with sexual immorality and called him a ''religious faker.''[34]

A chain of arson and violence was drawn ever tighter around Malcolm X. In response he said: ''They had to try and silence me because of what they know I know. I think that they surely know me well enough to know that they certainly can't frighten me. But when it does come to light . . . there are some things involving the Black Muslim movement which . . . will shock you.''[35] Predictably, on February 21, 1965, he was gunned down at a podium in full view of some 400 of his followers.[36]

Our second concern is the nature of Malcolm X's leadership among non-Muslim Negro groups. Although he became an outcast reprobate to the Nation of Islam, he continued to be admired by such Negro youth organizations as the restructured CORE and SNCC. A champion of Negro nationalistic and separatist groups, sections of the Negro ghetto masses responded enthusiastically to his speeches. To these groups the impressive Malcolm X was a representative and spokesman for the ideology of the Black Muslims—not the partially reformed person who lived to regret that ideology. His biographer writes:

> Recalling the incident of the young white college girl who had come to the Black Muslim restaurant and asked "What can I do?" and he told her "Nothing," and she left in tears. Malcolm X told Gordon Parks, "Well, I've lived to regret that incident. In many parts of the African continent I saw white students helping black people. Something like this kills a lot of argument. I did many things as a Muslim that I'm sorry for now. I was a zombie then—like all Muslims—I was hypnotized, pointed in a certain direction and told to march. Well, I guess a man's entitled to make a fool of himself if he is ready to pay the cost. It cost me twelve years."[37]

There are reasons why the "zombie" made a powerful impression on a variety of Negro groups. (1) He addressed white and Negro groups as a Black Muslim but they tended to regard him as just another "Negro leader" who spoke for all black people. (2) As a Black Muslim he had in effect repudiated his American citizenship. (3) His basic purpose was a separate territory and government for Negroes led by the Nation of Islam; hence the greater the alienation of Negroes in American society, the better his purpose was served. (4) To him *all* white people were evil and "devils," and he sought every opportunity to say so: his stature seemed to rise as he used the great national media of communication to return hatred for hatred. (5) He combed the history of U.S. race relations for situations and incidents of white brutality, and presented them as if they were exclusive and current. (6) Since the Civil War, he insisted, the Negro has made no progress—"not one iota of progress." (7) He argued passionately that the leaders of the NAACP and Martin Luther King, Jr., were "Uncle Toms": they want integration instead of national independence. He, on the other hand, advocated violence in retaliation for white violence, arguing that Negroes had a right to retaliate in "self-defense." During the period of their estrangement, Elijah Muhammad said of him: "Malcolm has ordered the so-called Negroes to arm themselves with shotguns and rifles to shoot when attacked (though the Messenger teaches us that Allah warned him against taking up the enemies' arms against the enemies)."[38] This, manifestly, was an attempt to alienate public sympathy from Malcolm.

To advocate "self-defense," physical retaliation by Negroes, in their mass demonstrations for civil rights is to dissipate that means and to trigger direct violence against the peace-keeping forces of the state or community. As James Farmer explains:

> The nationalists talk and harangue—their radical anger breeds radical and foolish thoughts—because they are doing nothing. They have no stake in the world, no stake in the land, and hence, little hope. This dissociated situation breeds only bravado. . . . With no real work to do in America, their advice to love blacks turns into a program to hate whites. Eager to act manfully, they can only imagine petty schemes of violence and revenge.[39]

Malcolm X was indeed a disaster to the race relations movement in the United States. His irresponsible preachments shattered and scattered it everywhere. He took the Muslim attitude toward both white and black civil rights leadership and turned the developing friendship and cooperation between white and Negro youth into anger and hatred. Yet for all his disruptiveness and distortion of the racial movement among Negroes he was "beatified" by militant nationalists. Later, when he began to see things differently, he probably would have rejected such praise, for he said of the period: "The sickness and madness of those days—I'm glad to be free from them. It's a time for martyrs now. And if I'm to be one, it will be in the cause of brotherhood."[40] The time was not vouchsafed him, however; what remained was the memory of his unqualified interracial animosity.

241

Chapter 17

The Question of Anarchy

The Problem

The anarchistic phase of Negro protest could probably best be understood by resort to the sociology of crowd behavior. More modestly, however, we shall identify it here with the action taken by some of the most thoroughly alienated Negro militants. Negro anarchism relies either on socially illogical and unattainable goals or on no goals at all, in which event the group seeks emotional catharsis from the social act itself. The ghetto uprisings of the sixties attracted much public attention. "The important thing to recognize about the new [anarchy] and the approach [it] represents," Killian observes, "is the absence of a program for societal reconstruction."[1]

Its declarations usually evince irresponsibility and dedication to violence; it takes for granted that by threats of wholesale community disruption it can coerce white America to comply with any concessions demanded *ex post facto*. Accordingly it rejects peaceful solutions to racial problems. Indeed, the use of violence itself may be regarded as psychological therapy. The anarchistic militant ordinarily refers to the plodding Negro middle class, concerned with securing civil rights and justice for the race through legislation, by such epithets as "bootlickers" and "Uncle Toms."[2] He expatiates freely upon "revolution" and the "smashing" of the native "white colonial oppressors."

Patriotism

American Negroes have on the whole, however, always considered the United States their native country and, even during slavery, overwhelmingly resisted every inducement to abandon it for some foreign land. In the face of racial discrimination, they have given of themselves loyally in all the nation's wars. Even before the Civil War, they have continually aspired to the full rights and privileges of citizenship.

It is indeed conceivable that Negroes today have a greater stake than whites in the patriotic symbols of American democracy. To venerate them is to insist upon their materialization for blacks and thus increasingly to achieve national and self-identity. To mock them is to turn one's back upon the history of the Negro struggle for freedom in the United States. Leaders such as Frederick Douglass, William Monroe Trotter, and the earlier W. E. B. DuBois would have advised only the most loyal attachment to them. In an article in *Time* magazine (Jan. 29, 1973, p. 24) entitled "Oh Say Can You See?" Stefan Kanfer said in part:

> The vast majority of Americans cannot and will not reject the flag, the anthem, or the pledge. It would be, in effect, rejecting aspects of themselves. Whatever militant blacks may feel, N.A.A.C.P. Executive Director Roy Wilkins' directive speaks with equal commitment: "There is no national anthem for Negroes. There is only one national anthem. The national anthem is for all Americans."

Since the daring public exhibition of disloyalty by a few Negro athletes at the Mexico City Olympics, there has been a tendency to associate lack of patriotism with American Negroes. There is in fact, no such uniformity of attitude.[3] As a solution to racism, we have called this negative behavior *anarchistic* because it is racially separative and leads inevitably to social dead ends.

On December 11 and 12, 1972, some of the outstanding leaders in the struggle for civil rights—among them, Lyndon B. Johnson, former Chief Justice Earl Warren, Senator Hubert Humphrey, Roy Wilkins, Clarence Mitchell—gathered in Austin, Texas, at the Lyndon Baines Johnson Library to celebrate the opening of the Johnson civil rights archives. It seemed clear that the critical problem facing the group involved President Richard Nixon's implicit determination to continue undermining the civil rights movement initiated by Franklin Roosevelt. As one reporter observed: "former Chief Justice Earl Warren obliquely but plainly warned President Nixon not to be another Rutherford Hayes and allow the country to slip back into a period of oppression and neglect where blacks are concerned."[4]

In this context, anarchistic racial behavior stemmed from the machinations of a small, anticivil rights group—reputedly led by Roy Innis, current leader of CORE—designed to disrupt the meeting. A Negro newspaper columnist, Ethel Payne, in the *New Courier* (Dec. 30, 1972), said in part:

> Here was LBJ in charge . . . when the little band of [Negro] intruders came on stage uninvited to add their own sleazy post-lude. . . . Earlier, a note was handed into the green room off stage where the participants had assembled. . . . It said that if the group representing CORE was not given time to speak, they would disrupt the session. . . . For the record, it was a shabby piece of *blackmail*. . . . An outraged Clarence Mitchell of the Washington NAACP told the watching [TV] world that if President Johnson could speak out in Texas against white demaguery, it was his duty to speak out against black demagoguery. [Italics added][5]

This kind of "blackmail" is of relatively recent date. It materialized during the sixties. We call it unpatriotic anarchy because its purpose has been to confuse, create sensation, and seize the spotlight, with nothing constructive to offer.

In the Negroes' struggle for undiluted American citizenship, this kind of anarchism has probably been the most powerful force serving to weaken and even destroy the assistance of white allies. In fact, the maneuver makes no sense. The "Negro problem" has been produced mainly by certain whites. But today many white leaders are working to solve it. Attempts by certain blacks to "drive them all out" seem tragically foolish. Anarchism will lead only to frustration.

Reparations as Protest

After the death of Martin Luther King, Jr., in 1968, the organized nonviolent protest of SNCC and CORE rapidly declined, and support, which had come largely from white religious groups in the North, dried up. The support had been voluntary. Considerable mass sympathy and self-accusation had developed among Christian and Jewish congregations.

With the withdrawal of financial assistance there yet remained a psychological soft-spot, a sense of guilt, which those Negro militants whose actions had contributed to the alienation of the whites attempted to exploit. They felt that whites should be compelled to support Negro projects. White churches, the least resistant of all organizations, became targets of their attacks. The churches, they announced, would either accede to their demands or suffer the consequences. One consequence was the forceful disruption of religious services.

Civil rights protest leaders were determined to wipe out racial discrimination. This militant, anti-Christian group demanded from whites payments for all past wrongs. We identify these various manifestations as anarchistic because there was no way to define and thus limit the charge financially. The movement reached its high point during 1969 and 1970. It became fairly common to see newspaper reports such as the following by the Associated Press (Kansas City, June 1, 1970):

> The Rev. Mr. Ralph Rolland told police the militants sat down on the platform with him and demanded that the congregation discuss their demands for reparations to blacks for white injustices. The minister said that when he refused to allow them to speak and had the microphone cut off, they called him a white racist. At that point, the Rev. Mr. Rolland said, the Negroes began ripping the American flag on the platform and several members of the congregation stepped up to stop them.

Both the approach and the reception of these militants tended to be spontaneous. A climax was reached when, on May 4, 1969, James Forman, who had been among the well-known leaders of SNCC, entered Riverside Church in New York City "to interrupt church service and proclaim a Manifesto."[6] Forman charged whites, mainly white Christians, with unlimited racial wrongdoing and "demanded five hundred million dollars [later increased to $3 billion] to be spent in various ways, including the establishment of a Southern land bank for the use of poor people; four TV networks. . . ." Forman and the groups which he represented collected hundreds of thousands of dollars in their campaign among white churches.[7] The Black Manifesto said in part: "We (the black people of this country) shall liberate all the people of the U.S. and we would be instrumental in the liberation of colored people the world around."[8]

There was, of course, no consistency of purpose or inherent logic in the anarchistic line of protest. If any logic existed in the idea of "reparations," it should obviously have been presented to legislatures, especially in the Deep South where Negro bondsmen had labored. If, moreover, demands for reparation seek to correct past injustices, they should come through the courts, especially the federal courts.

To be consistent, white workers should also demand reparations from the churches in the northeastern states where their ancestors worked as laborers and indentured servants. In order to build the phenomenal infrastructure of this nation, Negroes labored for minimal subsistance, mainly on cotton and tobacco plantations; but whites also worked in the mines and foundries for long hours at minimal wages. According to one observer: "Industrial deaths numbered tens of thousands a year. . . . Child labor, deathly long hours, filthy surroundings, brutal foremen, and other evils all added to the . . . toll."[9] If the argument for reparations were carried to its ultimate fantasy, remuneration for all past labor should be estimated and the difference between that and current standards should be paid on demand by any person or institution possessing wealth to whomever presents himself as the bona fide collector for such reparations. The element of blackmail in this form of protest, however, assured that it would be short-lived.

The Riot as a Means of Racial Visibility

The riot as a means of Negro protest is a form of social convulsion to be distinguished from insurrection or revolution because it does not contemplate a radical political change. Although race riots in general tend to arise spontaneously, they are nonetheless closely related to a given social situation. As a form of Negro protest, they are relatively recent developments, arising mostly in large cities, and tending to increase in intensity from the South to the North.

Ironically, the Negro protest riot tends to be a function of the civil rights achievements. During slavery Negroes could hardly think of "rioting," knowing full well that they would be disciplined for insubordination. After emancipation, however, when they were constitutionally endowed with a citizen's rights of self-assertion and self-defense, "real race riots" occurred in an attempt to meet white mob violence with black mass violence.

There are three general types of interracial riots: the white punitive riot, the black defensive riot, and the black protest riot. We might think of three official reports—the Congressional investigation of the 1917 East St. Louis riots, the Chicago Commission report on the 1919 race riot, and the 1968 report by the National Advisory Commission (the Kerner report)—as roughly depicting three types of race riots.[10] The white punitive riot—the riot intended as an instrument of racial repression and control—was the expected form until the onset of World War I. It was essentially a mobbing of blacks (though not a pogrom) by whites to dispel intergroup antagonisms and thus to assure the former's subordination. Furthermore, it was characterized by a lynching animus, directed against the whole Negro community, and by white mob invasions of black residential areas, intent upon beating, looting, burning, and murdering, ordinarily with white police connivance. The Memphis riot of 1865, in which forty-six Negro men, women, and children were killed and only one white was injured, was a frightful instance of this.

The Beaumont, Texas, riot of June 1943 was a relatively late eruption of this kind. "During the course of the rioting," according to one version, "most Negro citizens remained in their homes [whither] they had fled. There were no reports of organized or individual resistance. More than seventy-five Negroes were injured—two fatally. . . . Several hundred thousand dollars worth of property was destroyed or looted" by white mobs.[11] The Springfield, Illinois, riot of August 1908, which hastened stirrings for the establishment of organizations such as the NAACP, was also an anti-Negro uprising of this type.[12]

The black defensive riot involves encounters between white and Negro mobs with the latter showing a determination to retaliate. It became the common form, especially in the North, around the end of the second decade. Mass movements of Negroes from the South into many northern cities, during and after World War I, helped to produce incidents of interracial friction—on the job, in struggles for housing, and in competition for educational, recreational, and transportation facilities.

Interracial tension reached a high point in Chicago. The explosion occurred on Sunday, July 27, 1919. The consequent rioting did

not subside until the following Friday. We paraphrase here a part of
the riot report by the Chicago Commission on Race Relations.

> On Sunday afternoon hundreds of white and Negro bathers
> gathered on the lake-front beach between Twenty-sixth and
> Twenty-ninth streets, the densest area of Negro residence. An
> imaginary line in the water, generally observed by the races,
> segregated the beach. A few Negroes, however, attempted to
> cross the line, and a white-black stone-throwing fight ensued. In
> the melée a Negro youth, who had crossed the line, was struck
> and drowned. Negroes spotted the man who threw the fatal
> missile, and asked a white policeman present to arrest him. The
> officer not only refused but also found cause to arrest a Negro.
> Negroes then attacked the officer. "These two facts," says the
> Commission, "the drowning and the refusal to make the arrest
> . . . marked the beginning of the riot."[13]

Negroes then proceeded to attempt mass retaliation by render-
ing blow for blow against the white aggressors. Casualty statistics of
the consequent "reign of terror" were 38 deaths: 23 Negro and 15
white; 520 injuries: 342 Negro and 178 white; and 229 arrests: 154
Negro and 75 white. Violence flared in clashes all over the city, but
was mainly concentrated in specific areas. For example, while white
raiders in automobiles repeatedly sped through the Negro residential
community, shooting people at random, Negroes could only defend
themselves from ambush.

Although Negro leaders did not generally advocate even the
defensive riot, yet they did not condemn it out of hand. They seemed
to consider it a spontaneous answer to the white southern tradition
that Negroes could be chastised or lashed sporadically with impunity.
"There were few Americans, of whatever race or whatever persuasion as to racial policy, who could doubt that Negroes would, from
1919 on, be prepared to fight back against attack."[14] In his foreword
to the Commission's report, Frank O. Lowden, Governor of Illinois,
said appropriately: "Means must be found, therefore, whereby the
two races can live together on terms of amity."

The black protest riot is usually a confrontation with the police.[15] It may be thought of as a violent recrudescence of the nonviolent direct action confrontation as the latter emerged on the streets of
Birmingham, Alabama, and other cities of the Deep South in 1963 and
1964. The comparison, however, must end there because the means
were different; these riots were not typical of the Deep South. In-

deed, it is essentially for this reason that we define the protest riot as anarchistic. Let us illustrate. The U.S. Riot Commission wrote of the 1967 Detroit riot: "A spirit of carefree nihilism was taking hold. To riot and destroy appeared more and more to become ends in themselves. Late Sunday afternoon it appeared to one observer that the young people were 'dancing amidst the flames.'"[16]

The ideology emerging from this type of conflict, although it ordinarily remains underground, involves black nationalistic inviolability and control of the Negro community. The costly Watts riot of August 11 to 16, 1965, is a striking example. It began when a white motorcycle policeman attempted in line of duty to arrest an intoxicated Negro youth for reckless driving. "[This riot]" says the McCone Report, "was not a race riot in the usual sense. What happened was an explosion—a formless, quite senseless, and all but hopeless violent protest—engaged in by a few but bringing distress to all."[17]

In that riot the Negroes were the aggressors, and their direct opponents were mainly the police and the National Guard. "Even more dismaying," said the commission, "was the large number of brutal exhortations to violence which were uttered by some Negroes. Rather than making proposals, they laid down ultimatums with the alternative being violence."[18] Since they relied mainly on firearms, the destruction was devastating. The rioting, moreover, moved well out of the hands of "responsible" Negro citizens. Thus, in describing a critical meeting called by the Los Angeles County Human Relations Commission to "lower the emotional temperature" of the excited community, the McCone Commission explained: "It brought together every available representative of neighborhood groups and Negro leaders to discuss the problem." And then continued:

> Several community leaders asked members of the audience to use their influence to persuade area residents to stay home Thursday evening. Even Mrs. Frye [mother of the arrested inebriated driver] spoke and asked the crowd to "help me and others calm this situation down so that we will not have a riot tonight." But one Negro high school youth ran to the microphones and said the rioters would attack adjacent white areas that evening. This inflammatory remark was widely reported on television and radio. . . . Moreover, . . . the tone and conduct of the meeting shifted, as the meeting was in progress, from attempted persuasion with regard to the maintenance of law and order to a discussion of grievances felt by the Negro.[19]

The costs of the rioting, says the commission, were "staggering." There were, among them, 34 persons killed, 1,032 injured, a property loss of over $40 million, 3,438 adults arrested, 71 percent for burglary and theft, and, incidentally, 2,057 of them were born in the South. Of 514 juveniles arrested, 81 percent were charged with burglary and theft. The psychological costs of intergroup alienation and suspicion, however, were considered even more detrimental. Accordingly, the commission observed: "The first weeks after the disorders brought a floodtide of charges and recriminations. Although this has now ebbed, the feeling of fear and tension persists, largely unabated, throughout the community."[20]

Probably nothing is more conducive to residential isolation and ghettoization of Negroes than the protest riot. Lee and Humphrey observe: "Gulfs between the groups deepen, and dangers arise of intergroup conflicts on other than racial issues. Riots thus beckon demagogues to fertile soil for divisive propaganda."[21]

Negro advocates of black violence deliberately try to alienate the masses from their most effective black leaders. Martin Luther King, Jr., rebuffed in the Watts riot aftermath, sought to make this clear:

> The futility of violence in the struggle for racial justice has been tragically etched in all the *recent Negro riots*. One sees youngsters and angry adults fighting hopelessly and *aimlessly* against impossible odds. . . . Occasionally Negroes contend that the 1965 Watts riot and the other riots in various cities represented effective civil rights action. But those who express this view always end up with stumbling words when asked what concrete gains have been won as a result. At best the riots have produced a little additional anti-poverty money . . . and a few water sprinklers to cool the children of the ghettos. . . . Nowhere have the riots won any concrete improvements such as have the organized protest demonstrations.
> It is not overlooking the limitations of nonviolence and the distance we have yet to go to point out the remarkable record of achievements that have already come through nonviolent action. The 1960 sit-ins desegregated lunch counters in more than 150 cities within a year. The 1961 Freedom Rides put an end to segregation in interstate travel. The 1956 bus boycott in Montgomery, Alabama, ended segregation on the buses not only in that city but in practically every city of the South. The 1963 Birmingham movement and the climactic March on Washington won passage of the most powerful civil rights law in the century.

The 1965 Selma movement brought enactment of the Voting Rights Law. Our nonviolent marches in Chicago last summer [1966] brought about a housing agreement which, if implemented, will be the strongest step toward open housing taken in any city in the nation. Most significant is the fact that this progress occurred with minimum human sacrifice and loss of life. Fewer people have been killed in ten years of nonviolent demonstrations across the South than were killed in one night of rioting in Watts.[21a]

This list of achievements cannot be entirely attributed to the sources indicated by King; but at least they served as catalysts. Indeed, the protest riots formed part of the effluvia of the nonviolent movement. The relatively spontaneous accession to freedom generated by the movement, in addition to governmental insistence that rights guaranteed by the Fourteenth Amendment be implemented, led some Negroes to use the situation as an opportunity for license.

Because the protest riot tends increasingly to get out of hand, thus driving the races still more irrationally apart, we consider it an anarchistic, self-defeating means.

Ending the Riot

A point is finally reached when all parties desire an end of the turbulence. Riots involve socio-psychological mob traits: irrationality, hunger for excitement, the spontaneous emergence of agitators, uncritical acceptance and rapid spread of rumor, mass sanctions of violence and brutality. These traits operate differently in different types of riots; hence the disciplinary approach to rioting tends necessarily to vary.

In the punitive riot, the basis of conflict lies in the attempt by Negroes to rise above their traditional status and a determination among whites to drive them back.[22] If, then, whites could be made to accept in whole or in part the immediate aspirations of the Negroes, the riot could be ended; or it could be ended if whites become convinced that the ambitions of Negroes have been liquidated. In practice, situations vary extremely; an illustration of the process is the desegregation movement in the South.

In the Deep South the very threat of desegregating the schools became a signal for violent opposition. At Little Rock in 1957, in an atmosphere of feverish, demagogic pronouncements of approaching doom, the NAACP and the Urban League made their move to integrate Central High School. Governor Orval E. Faubus, on September

251

2, 1957, proclaimed: "I must state here in all sincerity, that it is my opinion—yes, even my conviction—that it will not be possible to restore or to maintain order and protect the lives and property of the citizens if forcible integration is carried out tomorrow in the schools of this community."[23] Besides alerting the white mob, this, no doubt, served as a warning to Negroes that they should desist. But they did not. The following, which tells part of the story of events at Central High School on September 4, 1957, indicates the essential problems involved in ending the punitive riot.

> The first Negro applicant to try to enroll at Little Rock Central High School yesterday, Elizabeth Eckford, 15, who was twice blocked from entering the grounds, walked calmly down two blocks then sat out 35 minutes of vocal abuse while waiting for a bus to go home. . . .
> The girl, silent and looking straight ahead, walked at a brisk pace down the line of troops. The crowd walked along with her and began a stream of cat-calling. A woman told her to "go back where you came from," made a lunge at the girl and was pushed back by a Guard officer. Another in the crowd said, "you've got a better school than ours so why don't you go to it?" When [Elizabeth] made an attempt in the middle of the line to cross onto the school grounds and again was stopped by Guardsmen, someone shouted "don't let her in our school—that 'nigger.'"[24]

Had a Negro man appeared on the scene to protect Elizabeth, he would probably have been beaten to death and the Negro residential community invaded. The riot was ended by the Negroes apparently giving in. The federal government, however, did not intend to allow matters to rest there. The white power structure in Arkansas had to be made to yield. Accordingly, on September 24, 1957, "President Eisenhower, informed that a mob had gathered in defiance of his 'cease and desist' proclamation, ordered Federal troops into Little Rock and federalized the Arkansas National Guard, thus removing it from Governor Faubus's command." In his address to the nation on this subject, the president declared: "Mob rule cannot be allowed to override the decisions of our courts."[25]

There were delays, circumlocution, and attempts at circumvention. In due time, however, the conquest of southern white power mitigated or quashed hundreds of potential punitive riot situations. During Reconstruction such riots ordinarily ended by the Negro's defeat.

Ending the black defensive riot calls for a different approach. The interracial fighting is best subdued by quick, powerful and unbiased action by the police and the state militia. The news media should be urged to "keep it cool." In this type of riot, if the police and troops were to show an unbiased determination to arrest white and black rioters, a large number of whites would be arrested or injured, but the riot would be shortened and the total number of casualties reduced. Moreover, a rapport of sorts would be established between the black community and the police. The aim of the "law," then, should be a nondiscriminatory separation of the rioters.

Protest rioters make demands. The alternative is guerrilla violence aimed essentially at physical subjection of the police force. To stop this type of rioting, public authorities must recognize that the driving purpose is vandalism, looting, and direct attack aimed at subduing the police. Lee and Humphrey advise as follows:

> A riot in a city is dynamite! Do not experiment with half-way measures. Do not count on the local police, but demand the state militia or army forthwith. Take immediate steps to have the riot area quarantined. In taking such a step, it is necessary to protect and provide for innocent people in the area. Through leading civic, religious, trade union, and other organizations, bring sufficient pressure to assure dissemination of accurate reports and constructive official statements.[26]

We should expect relatively more Negroes to be injured and probably killed in this type of riot; if, however, it is classified at an early stage and dealt with decisively, casualties should be fewer.

Riot in Continuity

Regular civil rights organizations—CORE, SNCC—have been infiltrated by nationalist groups and their civil rights, integrationist ideology has been dissipated. *Time* magazine, in a report on June 21, 1968 (p. 24), briefly recounted the process saying:

> Integration has been the aim of the Congress of Racial Equality since CORE was born [mainly through white leadership] in 1942. Its intramural squabbles have never been concerned with the principle of desegregation but with its pace. Two years ago, Floyd McKissick replaced Founder James Farmer because he was not moving fast enough. . . . CORE's new chief [Roy Innis], however, advocates rigid separation of the races [and retaliatory violence]. By accepting Innis' incendiary views,

> CORE alienates not only whites but black moderates as well. Thus it joins the Student Nonviolent Coordinating Committee [SNCC] . . . in a militant shift to the left.

These two organizations became casualties of the gospel of blackness, group isolation, and violence among Negroes. The career of H. Rap Brown may be taken as symbolic of the transition. He moved from adolescent criminality on the streets to apparent personal rehabilitation as a member of the earlier SNCC, to head of the later debased SNCC and spread its obscene ideology. Apprehended by the police, charged with breach of the law, he escaped into the ghetto for sanctuary and emerged with armed companions to rob Negroes in Manhattan, then to go before courts in New York. He opened his trial with a Muslim prayer; "Praise be to Allah." In this way, serious crime in the Negro community has been nationalized, justified, and merged into threats of race rioting.

The nature of the continuity of the protest riot situation in the Negro community may be further illustrated by the widely publicized sporting-goods store robbery in Brooklyn on January 19, 1973, by five armed Negro men. They behaved as if they were on a sacred, racial mission, claiming to be "Pan Suni Muslims." When arrested on January 21, "a crowd of about 200—many of them raising clenched fists in the black-power salute—greeted [them] at the precinct station." In a statement released before their capture, these burglars said in part: "We are expressing solidarity with all Muslims and oppressed peoples of the world."[27]

In view of current interracial tensions, the episode may be regarded as an attempt to initiate the race riot as blackmail. It included such critical elements as resistance to interracial communication, assumption of a universalist antiwhite posture, determination to fight it out violently with the police, robbery and looting, holding of the community both as hostage and support for criminal blacks, and resolution of the conflict in an atmosphere of mounting interracial antagonism and tension.

The basic element in this type of riot is black withdrawal of communication: conscious social severance from the larger white community. Given this condition, fighting or rioting may break out wherever Negroes gather indiscriminately. One reason for mounting tension is that Negro isolation is not equivalent to white segregation. Negro withdrawal of communication tends to become culturally costly particularly to themselves. The result, consequently, leads to further frustration, irritation, and interracial estrangement.

In a study of interracial antagonism in the armed forces for *Civil Liberties,* February 1973, David Addlestone and Susan Sherer began with the following words:

> Racial tension in the military has reached the crisis level. There is open racial warfare on the ships at sea, at bases in Europe and Asia and in bars servicing the military installations. *Self-imposed segregation,* on and off duty, is nearly as effective as official segregation was prior to 1948. [Italics added]

The novel element here is obviously not traditional white racism, which has been decreasing in America, but black "self-imposed segregation." Should interracial isolation be achieved, group differences and interracial antagonism will be accentuated.[28]

> In reaction to this racism . . . the blacks in Viet Nam segregated themselves from the other troops. Seldom were blacks and whites seen together off duty. The blacks had little real organization but referred to themselves as "The Brothers." They went even further to disassociate themselves from the system by adopting black symbols to be worn with the uniform, a black handshake—the "dap" or "power greeting" (in place of the salute?)—and an increased black vocabulary. Blacks wore power rings, large crosses around their necks, bracelets woven of shoelaces (reputedly those of dead comrades) and carried elaborately carved swagger sticks, usually with a clenched fist or extended middle finger as the head. They stretched the rules on hair length to the ultimate and often beyond, with regulation caps twisted bizarrely out of shape and perched precariously atop an Afro. . . . All of these manifestations of blackness were intended to create black solidarity. The result was solidarity—and the exclusion, annoyance, and paranoia of whites.[29]

There has thus been a studied attempt to organize black separatism and identity.

"Street corner" inhabitants of the ghetto have sought identity and respectability as Muslims and, to the extent that this situation obtains, Negroes of the community, who follow traditional assimilative social patterns, tend to become apprehensive and fearful. Some of the old criminal type assume new boldness and apparent community dominance. The police seem to be intimidated by such organizations as the "Black Liberation Army"; and incident after incident tends to keep the ghetto in a constant state of race riot emergency.

Although the street masses, the looters, may be weighted by the nonpolitical *Negro poor,* the group has been mostly led by black *nationalists* seeking to establish all black neighborhoods and community control. The "riots" in Negro colleges, and even in a majority of white institutions, are precipitated by blacks who isolate themselves in groups under some type of Malcolm X ideology. For this reason, both government and social theorists may be disappointed in their attempts to explain recent disorders as simply of *lower-class* origin and execution. Even those eruptions that followed the assassination of M. L. King, Jr., could hardly be attributed to lower-class motivation and initiation.

Chapter **18**

The Police and Alienation

Status and Role of the Police

Probably no other aspect of American race relations has so direct a bearing on interracial attitudes as police action designed for Negroes. Traditionally, the white policeman or his deputy has symbolized the immediate operational barrier between the races. As the Negro advances legally and politically, police power tends to be modified; and yet it still persists with great vigor. Recently, in a report on the murder of a Negro man in the South, the writer said: "For all the civil rights advances in the Deep South, a harsh reality remains in Mississippi courts: white men accused of violent crimes against Negroes are almost never convicted. About the only time such offenders are punished is when they are tried in federal courts. . . ."[1] The police themselves, therefore, often do not expect retribution for the use of summary and excessive force against members of the race; they respond to the racial permissiveness of the local courts and the political situation.

257

There seem to be four main reasons for the different treatment of Negroes by these upholders of law and order. First, the group has been historically subjected to a system of discriminatory public and personal rules, the basic intent of which has been to condition them to accept the idea of exploitative labor and therefore racial subordination.[2] Second, the police have been charged with direct responsibility of "keeping the Negro in his place" so that at all times the Negro will observe the "etiquette of race relations." Third, the Negro subculture, especially as it obtains among the urban lower class, is the very way of life of the group in the ghettoes. It tends to be quasi-criminal, hence a normal concern of the police. And fourth, police brutality inevitably follows as a consequence of the first three factors.

Differential Laws

We have already referred to the notorious Black Codes enacted soon after the Civil War, 1865–66. Carl Schurz, a contemporary northern journalist reporting on the spot, has this to say: "Various parish and county governments, anticipating the restoration of slavery or so much of it as might be found practicable, adopted ordinances and regulations putting the negroes under the strictest police control, stripping them almost completely of the right of free movement enjoyed by everyone else, and of the right to dispose of their persons and property."[3]

Although these laws have been declared unconstitutional, attenuated versions of them continued to influence attitudes, especially in the South. The state bestowed its official sanction upon the dual system for so prolonged a period that Negroes came to be regarded as a subrace. As Rembert Patrick puts it, the process involved "interpreting laws in one way for white people and another for Negroes, using the police power of the majority to cow the minority, and depending on juries to give more consideration to the color of skin than to evidence."[4] It is especially in a situation such as this that the police agency is expected to be not only the apprehender of persons charged with its infringement but also the racially biased "judge, juror, and sentence inflictor." For many Negroes the presence of the white policeman is regarded as symbolic of the entire racist "law" and power structure. As late as 1961, for example, a Negro youth complained to the United States Commission on Civil Rights: "The Batista police were so sadistic, once [they] put you in a scout car, you had your judge and jury, and trial and punishment before you got out."[5]

The Police and the Status Quo

On April 29, 1967, Dr. Benjamin E. Mays, President of Morehouse College, wrote in his *Pittsburgh Courier* column:

> In my childhood in South Carolina and beyond my childhood in the South, Negroes were expected and required by whites to say "yes sir" and "no sir" to them. The same politeness and more had to be shown to white women.
>
> White people in those days had to establish their superiority through force. It was a dangerous thing for any Negro, man or woman, to disregard this custom. . . . Any Negro male who didn't observe these rules of courtesy was called "uppity" and if he persisted in his "uppitiness," he had to leave town or was liquidated. It was an era when Negro adults were called "uncle," "aunt," "boy," "girl. . . ."
>
> In 1927, an officer with a gun and a club in Tampa, Florida, insisted that I say "yes sir" and "no sir" to him. . . . [He had] stopped me and in conversation I answered "yes" and "no" to his questions. He came around on the side of the car next to me and demanded that I say "yes sir. . . ." What was I to do? I said nothing. When he asked who owned the car, I replied the Tampa Urban League. . . .

Records of instances of this sort could be multiplied. They illustrate our second point, the one-sided interracial role of the police. Dr. Mays was conscious of the fact that the power of the state stood directly between him and the officer.

In situations of white mob violence, the whole Negro community may be struck by a sense of helplessness, fear, and terror. After reviewing a number of cases of white police cooperation with mobs, the United States Commission on Civil Rights said in conclusion: "In certain areas of the Deep South some policemen have recently connived in mob violence. . . . In concert with previously instilled suspicions it also has the effect of perpetuating deep fears among many Negroes that should violence strike, the police will side with the mob. No American citizen should have to live with such fears."[6]

The Police Culture

The third differentiating characteristic refers to institutionalized criminal behavior in the ghetto. In an important sense the policeman's function is here taken for granted; it is assumed to be an integral part of Negro lower-class culture. The question is hardly whether the ghetto youth knows right from wrong but rather whether the norms of middle-class society, to which the police are particularly conditioned, are effectively operative in his social milieu. Obviously he knows they are not. Let us recall Eldridge Cleaver's conception of his community: "I started out by practicing [rape] on black girls in the ghetto—in the black ghetto where dark and vicious deeds appear not as aberrations or deviations from the norm, but as part of the sufficiency of the evil of a day."[7] In his study of "street culture" in a Los Angeles ghetto, John Horton says in part:

> When I asked the question, "When a dude needs bread, how does he get it?" the universal response was "the hustle." Hustling is, of course, illegitimate from society's viewpoint. Street people know it is illegal, but they view it in no way as immoral or wrong. It is justified by the necessity of surviving. As might be expected, the unemployed admitted that they hustled and went so far as to say that a dude could make it better on the street than on the job: "There is a lot of money on the street, and there are many ways of getting it;" or simply, "This has always been my way of life."[8]

Walter B. Miller also emphasizes the point that legal norms are violated by the mere practice of following certain patterns of behavior which comprise essential elements of Negro lower-class existence. Adherence to such traits as "toughness, smartness, excitement" and thievery is structurally motivated.[9] There is thus a basic contradiction between normal rules for the urban police and behavior patterns in the ghetto. "It is regrettable, yet not surprising," says the National Commission on . . . Violence, "that particularly the tensions and frustrations of the poor and the black come to focus on the police. The antagonism is frequently mutual."[10]

In comparing their acceptance among the Negro middle class, the black policemen interviewed by Nicholas Alex "told a story of the disrepute into which they fell, the hatred, suspicion, and contempt which they sometimes aroused" among the lower class. "The basic theme that runs through their observations is that they are viewed as agents of outside white society—a repressive, discriminatory, anti-Negro society—and are constantly reminded of their Negro identities."[11]

There is here, however, a real dilemma. The Negro middle class holds a continuing grievance against white police officers, especially in the South. It cannot unreservedly take their side against the deviant behavior of elements in the black lower class. The legitimate complaints of the black middle class about the racial malpractice of the white police restrict their normal anticriminal reactions, especially in the urban North, and thus unleash criminal characters who prey upon the whole community with impunity. The hands of the Negro middle class are thus tied by white racism. Indeed a stage—not dissociated from the civil rights movement—has been reached where delinquents are able to broadcast: "We will shoot any policeman wherever we see one."[12] It is this trammeling of the black middle class by the traditional abusiveness of white policemen that produces attitudes and consequences such as the following:

> Policemen frequently take the attitude that minority groups cannot be expected to observe such standards of conduct as are expected of the rest of the community. Hence, gambling, prostitution, and other vicious activities are allowed to flourish in Negro neighborhoods although they would be sternly suppressed anywhere else. This not only exposes the children and other people in such neighborhoods to an excessive risk of vicious associations, but it supports the belief among the Negro population that the police don't care about crime as long as it affects only Negroes.[13]

The paradox, is, however, that certain upstart Negro "leaders" have been insisting that ghetto criminality is Negro culture, hence it should be accepted in the larger society as normal behavior. In other words, the new freedom which blossomed in the mid-fifties has meant, for the black "hustling group," freedom to eliminate the police from the Negro community, to take over political control of the area, and to impose street culture upon the entire ghetto.

Police Brutality

A fourth complaint against the police, peculiar to Negroes, is that of "police brutality." The particularly severe treatment inflicted upon the Negro by the police follows from the Negro's generally weak social and political position.

The history of lynching, with police connivance, provides the most overt record of this brutality. Lynching no longer makes headlines, but, as the Commission on Civil Rights reminds us, "it lives on in the memory of thousands of Negroes and reinforces the deep fear that 'lightning' may strike again. For many Negroes this raises a question of profound importance: When it strikes, will the police help me or will they help the mob?" The Commission investigated and

261

reported a number of instances of police brutality, some of them occurring after arrests and while victims were under police control.

And yet Negroes, especially those in the Deep South, are probably not so much concerned about a return of the old days as they are about undercover police connivance and official brutality. The details of the midnight shooting of the Negro civil rights workers, James Chaney and his two white companions, Andrew Goodman and Michael Schwerner, in June 1964, and their secret burial near Philadelphia, Mississippi, by Neshoba County Sheriff Lawrence Rainey, Deputy Sheriff Cecil Price, Philadelphia Policeman Richard Willis, and fourteen private citizens may better illustrate the residual temper of the police and the role they are still willing to play.

Anti-Negro violence, therefore, has been largely driven underground; it had worldwide exposure during the period of the sit-ins and marches. When the Commission on Civil Rights realized that responsible people in the South, both white and black, were afraid to give testimony on police violence in the region, they said in their report: "The very reluctance of these persons to be quoted is the clearest documentation of the climate of fear and the conspiracy of silence that exist in Birmingham." This fear has had a long period of gestation among Negroes, and its offspring has now become manifest in the metropolises of the nation. "The anger [which police abuses] instill, Paul Chevigny observed in 1969, "is part of the fuel for the violent uprisings in our cities during the past five years."[14]

In the ghetto the policeman, especially the white policeman, could now expect direct attacks from black mobs and snipers. He is sometimes prevented from making arrests. In the introduction to a recent news release on this subject, John Kifner of the *New York Times* said:

The Chicago police have become almost daily targets for bottles, bricks, and bullets from the city's ghettos. In the last month three policemen have been killed from ambush. Seven were slain last year (1969). And there have been a series of incidents in which policemen have wounded or killed blacks.

Now policemen patrolling Negro neighborhoods—particularly predominately black public housing projects—cover their rounds in constant fear of attack. For Chicago has created an underclass of angry, bitter black youths who have moved beyond a readiness for riot to what some observers consider the beginning of urban guerrilla warfare against the police."[15]

For many lower-class Negro youth, with street-gang orientation, advancement in racial status means greater personal ability to confront the police. The leaders ordinarily have a history of major criminality, and their purpose is not police reform but rather complete removal of all policemen, black as well as white, from the ghetto. This manifestly would give unbridled freedom to a street-corner society in the Negro community and perhaps throughout the city as well. Therefore, to many of the black poor—working, self-respecting, ghetto dwellers—the police remain their "only salvation." This is a unique situation in the process of assimilation experienced by other immigrant groups.

Ascendance of Lower-Cultural Stratum

The American culture is essentially middle-class: a relatively commercial, thrifty, scientific, technological, Christian, dynamic, orderly, sanitary, esthetic phenomenon. Originally contrived in medieval European cities, American whites now lead it and, on the whole, lower-class whites respect it as normal, proper, and worth striving for. It is to them, in other words, the social norm. But lower-class whites did not produce it. The continuing center of the Negro protest movement has also been middle-class oriented—a drive which postulates and accepts American middle-class values. Its recognized achievers are middle-class blacks. Frederick Douglass, Booker T. Washington, and W. E. B. DuBois advocated such values. In its struggle for social reconstruction the group has employed middle-class techniques and this has attracted to its cause an influential sector of white, middle-class liberals.

And yet, to many lower-class Negroes—perhaps to the majority—the lower-class subculture is taken as the permanent and even proper native condition.

Historically, the dangers and anxieties associated with attempts to forsake lower-class status for positions in the mainstream have been repeatedly driven home. This peculiar element of futility identified with Negro ambition is not a trait of the white lower class. We find, therefore, a remarkable inversion of American middle-class ideals among the relevant leadership of the Negro lower class; the norms and traditions of the latter have been advocated as sacred or at least socially acceptable. Middle-class Negroes are thus identified with mainstream culture, a culture which the lower class tends to distrust and fear.[16]

There remains an intriguing question regarding the wants of lower-status Negroes. Some students are quick to answer that their material wants are indistinguishable from those of the middle class, the only difference being that of economic means. And yet, realistically, wants seem to be associated with aspiration and sacrifice. In his study of ghetto behavior, John Horton says in effect: they do indeed aspire to material success but are unable to negotiate the societal pressures and norms involved in its attainment.[17]

In the ghetto, lower-class culture becomes so pervasive and stable that achievement of middle-class status may be regarded, by at least a section of the leadership, as a mark of apostasy. Indeed, the very evidences of success may be defined as symbols of "Uncle Tomism."[18] It is, no doubt, this relentless cultural drag which in part has led some sociologists to characterize Negroes as constituting a lower-status *caste*.

The lower the Negro status group, the greater its susceptibility to alienation and black nationalism. Normal preoccupation with social status mobility ordinarily leads members of the black middle class to emphasize individualism and position in the American mainstream. Negro colleges are expected to instill this basis of motivation. In concentrating upon race and nativism the lower class minimizes cultural achievement and thus acquires psychological identity with the Negro middle class. In addressing any ghetto mass, therefore, tactful spokesmen ordinarily revert to the regressive vernacular of the plantation or harp on black racial solidarity. "The lower class," observes K. B. Clark, "sets the mores and manners to which, if the Negro upper class wishes influence it must appeal; and from which the Negro middle class struggles to escape."[19]

"To Fulfill These Rights"

Recently social class contradictions came to a head in what seemed to be a revolutionary approach to race relations by the federal government. On June 4, 1965, at the Commencement ceremonies of Howard University, President Lyndon B. Johnson declared in part:

> It is not enough just to open the gates of opportunity. . . . The task is to give 20 million Negroes the same chance as every other American to learn and grow, to work and share in society, to develop their abilities . . . and to pursue their individual happiness. . . . Therefore, I want to announce tonight that this fall I intend to call a White House conference of scholars and experts

and outstanding Negro leaders—men of both races—and officials of government at every level. This White House conference's theme and title will be "To Fulfill These Rights."

In February 1966, the president appointed a council to plan and convene the first White House Conference on Civil Rights early in June 1966. His personal leadership was manifestly a decisive victory in the long struggle for civil rights. The apparent need now was for Negroes to stand solidly behind him, use his moral support everywhere in legislative and judicial appeals, and, with a sympathetic Supreme Court, attack, by nonviolent action, discrimination in employment, housing, voting and so on.

The situation, however, turned out to be not so simple. Negroes had already become fiercely divided about goals. The president's objective was that of civil rights and assimilation. He had thus automatically become an enemy of the black nationalists and their sympathizers. From this core of opposition a variety of sociological theorists pounced upon the program and criticized it as ill-conceived because it tended to place the burden of racial pathologies upon the Negro family.

We think Rainwater and Yancey, in their intensive study of developments in this conference put too little emphasis on antagonisms among Negro leaders. They conclude: "The problem . . . was one of the government asserting an 'independent' policy in the area of civil rights that would be accepted by the movement and would therefore take the lead away from the movement's leaders. How could it assert itself and co-opt the movement at the same time?"[20] Apparently what should be recognized here is that "the movement" as represented by Roy Wilkins, A. Phillip Randolph, Whitney Young, and Bayard Rustin was not the movement proclaimed by Malcolm X, CORE, SNCC, *et al.*

The civil rights movement, as represented by the first group, does not seek to take over duties of government. It fights for the right of Negroes to vote in the South, for instance, but it does not put up its own candidates for office; it struggles for equitable programs in employment, education, and welfare, but it does not seek to administer these programs. The aim of the black nationalist movement, on the other hand, is primarily separate *control* of the administration of the programs. The first group was sympathetic and willing to work with the president's council for a successful conference, while the second group flayed the proposal.

Civil rights and federal welfare programs had already become anathema to the black power, nationalistic advocates who had put faith in retributive violence and black exclusiveness among the ghetto masses. As a result, the president, his speech, and his program were denounced. On May 23, 1966, to illustrate, the reconstituted Student Nonviolent Coordinating Committee issued a statement rejecting the forthcoming White House Conference, saying in part: "We know that the executive department and the President are not serious about insuring Constitutional rights to black Americans," and concluded:

> We reaffirm our belief that people who suffer must make the decisions about how to change and direct their lives. We therefore call upon all black Americans to begin building independent political, economic, and cultural institutions that they will control and use as instruments of social change in this country.[21]

To the public this noisy negative reaction seemed to be coordinated with the current upsurge of violence and rioting in the Negro communities. As such, it was a direct challenge to the civil rights movement. In a *New York Times* news article directed to this challenge (Oct. 16, 1966), the writer observed:

> Though the slogan black power remains ill-defined and vague, for many people, it has come to mean—because of the militant and radical stance of exponents like Stokely Carmichael of the Student Nonviolent Coordinating Committee and Floyd McKissick of the Congress of Racial Equality—separatism, reverse racism, and violence. It frightened many whites, particularly when the popular definition seemed to be confirmed by the wave of ghetto riots this summer, and it has caused a decline in white support for civil rights.

Reaction

Under the heading, "Crisis and Commitment," the major Negro workers for civil rights had, earlier in the month, placed an advertisement in the same newspaper explaining their position. It was essentially an answer to the black separatists and a rededication of the group to American culture and to the realization of the Negro's right to inherit it. In a statement to the press, those who signed for their organizations said further: "we repudiate any strategies of violence, reprisal or vigilantism, and we condemn rioting and the demagoguery that feeds it. . . . We are committed to the attainment of racial justice by democratic processes . . . to integration . . . [and] to the common responsibility of all Americans, both white and black, for bringing integration to pass. . . .'' In this matrix of internal and violent interracial conflict, governmental interest in the recommendations of the White House Conference on Civil Rights, June 1 and 2, 1966, petered out.

Both SNCC and CORE, under new leadership, had finally become estranged from these middle-class methods and aspirations. They mostly adopted the antiwhite teachings of the Muslim, Malcolm X. Their methods and structure thus merged into that of the city outlaw. In the wake of community conflicts, leadership emerged spontaneously to speak violently for the race as a whole. This process may be thought of as the ascendance of elements of lower-class culture. Its institutionalization has been relatively recent; and since its methods, besides being criminal, ordinarily lead to dead ends, it may be short-lived.

Alienation as a Disposing Force

We have frequently referred to the rise of Negro alienation and its negative consequences for race relations in the United States. Our references, however, have been diffused and situationally linked. Under the present heading we propose to deal with the apparent principle which diverted the course of race relations during the sixties and intensified the problem of social control in the cities. Let us first recapitulate.

The struggle toward abatement of racial discrimination has had two principal manifestations: (a) developments in legislative enactments and in juridical mandates, and, (b) action toward substantive fulfillment of these progressive antidiscriminatory laws. Negro and white liberal assimilationist leadership has been continually concerned with strengthening the legalistic phase of race relations. Its efforts to realize the law in practice, however, have been largely circumvented, particularily in the South, either by new and more insidious laws, direct refusal to comply, or by connivance with private, white individuals or institutions to escape the sanctions: such as, for example, the white private school movement and the 1969 incident in Jackson, Mississippi, where public swimming pools were closed to forestall their integration but the local YMCA managed to keep its pool open for whites only.

The 1954 U.S. Supreme Court desegregation mandate was decisive in that it obligated the district courts to oversee directly the dismantlement of the structure of the public, dual school system. The government thus entered the action phase of the abolishment of racial discrimination. Negroes were thenceforth implicitly challenged to assert their civil rights not only in education but also in every other public situation. Ultimately—as Little Rock demonstrated—the U.S. army stood ready to guarantee their legitimate claims.

It was in this atmosphere of encouragement that many individuals and organized groups decided to exercise their rights as American citizens in the face of ruling-class white opposition. The nonviolent direct action movement dramatized race relations and brought down many a structure of racial discrimination even in the Deep South.

The actionists were mainly middle-class youth supported by such organizations as the NAACP and the American Civil Liberties Union. Their outstanding leader was Martin Luther King, Jr., who enunciated the historic ideology of racial assimiliation through abolishment of segregation and discrimination but now by civil disobedience and other nonviolent approaches. Such groups as SNCC and CORE accepted and advocated this program. Even before King's death, however, black nationalism had wormed its way into the direct action movement, contravened its ideology, and dissipated its forces. Thus racial hatred, violence, and separatism superseded goodwill, nonviolence, and interracial cooperation.

Contributing Factors

We have concluded that the critical attitude, which underlies separatism and which tends to find spontaneous acceptance mainly among lower-class Negro youth, is racial alienation. Racial alienation, perennially latent in the group, crystalized with the nationalistic preachments of the unreformed Muslim, Malcolm X. It constituted the essential element at the ideological base of a number of nationalistic groups which mushroomed *pari pasu* with the decline of assimilationist action groups. It strives to cultivate spontaneous black rejection of the larger American society. As we should expect, then, Negro racial alienation has had its current incitement in the leadership of the Nation of Islam.

The same force which contributed enormously to the development of the civil rights movement in the late fifties and sixties also put the leading anticivil rights advocates upon the map, and thus gave them legitimacy and prestige in the unwary Negro community. The mass media played up black nationalism led by Malcolm X with probably as much fervor as they did the efforts of civil rights organizations. They presented it essentially as an alternative means toward the same ends as those sought by the NAACP and King. The process, however, gave direction and support to a division of leadership among Negroes and to an antimiddle-class attitude.

Malcolm X was not simply a nationalist in the sense that Garvey was—that is, dedicated to putting Africa on the same road to ascendancy as that followed by Great Britain or the United States. He represented rather a distinct culture, a sort of Arabic utopia. There was, accordingly, no ground for compromise between his idea of interracial struggle and that of the established Negro leadership. The means relied upon were essentially those which he had found to be serviceable during his days of delinquency in the ghetto, hence the success of his appeal to splinter groups of young Negro militants calling for violent action in the Negro community.

It could probably be said, moreover, that white liberals in control of mass media, especially in the North, helped significantly (though apparently unintentionally) to disrupt the civil rights movement by emphasizing, as representative of the Negro people, the spurious, alienated ideology expounded by Malcolm X and the groups which he inspired. Let us now consider the nature of this alienation.

We use the concept alienation here in a nonpsychiatric, non-Hegelian-Marxian sense. The Negro as a freeman becomes racially alienated not because of the objectivity of the capitalistic market, the boredom or ennui of routinized work, or the process of accumulating private capital, but rather because of his economic and social limitations within the society plus his resolution to accept social isolation and to deal with mainstream culture from that position.[22]

The alienated express a consummate disdain for American culture. They frequently plan to migrate to some exclusive territory abroad or within the United States, but failing that, to establish independent, antiwhite governments for control of metropolitan, ghetto communities—always with an eye on public subsidy.

They do not identify themselves with the social status structure of the United States; they tend thus to be immune to the discipline of upward mobility in the larger society. And they consistently denigrate any movement or event leading to Negro identification with that society.

They do not value their American nationality and may even declare openly that they are not citizens of the United States; therefore they reject as counterproductive any overtures made by white political leaders to further racial inclusion and reconciliation. Such a political stance leaves room for considerable race relations racketeering. The alienated rely on a religious mystique of "brotherhood" among all Negroes, domestic as well as foreign, a sort of black ethnocentrism.

They may show their antagonism toward whites by expressed or implicit black racism. They ennunciate a philosophy of talion, "an eye for an eye" or that Negroes should take the initiative to settle accounts because of past injustices against the race. Since 1960, alienated Negroes have been trigger-happy and have responded with violence to racial situations. Frequently the Negroes themselves have suffered some of the unfortunate consequences of these actions.

There may be other traits characteristic of the socially alienated Negro; and those mentioned may not always apply to every individual. But the depiction probably identifies the group. It shows, at least, the limiting social incidence of alienation. Behavior consistent with racial alienation enlarges the scope of social frustration which further induces and perpetuates resentment. It automatically constricts the individual's usefulness in improving interracial understanding. In effect, the alienated tend to assure their own social isolation and rejection.

The particular tragedy of the alienated Negro in race relations—especially of those who claim leadership status—is that they lack courage; they give up, are not willing to confront real issues, take what they can get from the system, seek cover under some exotic name or dress, and withdraw into the shadows of the ghetto.

Constructive Negro leadership has repeatedly sought to circumvent the rise of alienation within the group. As we have seen, Frederick Douglass, among others, had to deal with it even before the Civil War; and W. E. B. DuBois valiantly fought it after World War I. The present misfortune is that is has arrived again, wreaking its disruption and stultification upon the Negro community itself.

An Alternative

What, then, might we say of the long run? One way in which Negroes might develop practicable motivation is through purposeful

American identification. American citizenship, it seems, should be claimed with pride and as an unabridged right. Negroes must consciously seek to enjoy the values of their great cultural heritage, which includes organization for social change.

In July 1969, at the annual meeting of the NAACP in Jackson, Mississippi, Clarence Mitchell, director of the Washington Office, explained a conference slogan to reporters, saying it means "continued faith in integration, rejection of black for black's sake: 'I make no claim to importance merely because I share common ancestry with the people of Africa. I am a part of the people who mingled our share of toil with the labors of immigrants from Europe. This is my country; it is the land I love.'"[23]

271

Chapter **19**

The Road Ahead

The Place of Economics

If our study and analysis of race relations are valid, the on-going, day-to-day social process should be consistent with them. The student does not create social situations; he seeks rather to arrive at verifiable explanations of them. Different investigators of this subject have chosen different points of reference: moral, psychological, political, religious, economic, "cultural," and so on; or a combination of these with similar emphases. We have chosen the socio-economic approach and attempted to arrive at a specific meaning of the term "economic."

The term economic is, *per se,* indefinite, and thus likely to be misleading. The concept, in its present usage, is necessarily always modified by the relevant social system. It is in context, therefore, that we employ it. The economics of the mercantile-industrial city, for example, is by no means identical with the economics of the feudal manor, of the Hindu village, or of the tribal village of Africa. Histori-

272

cally, convergence of these systems has resulted in revolutionary clashes.

As race relations increasingly become the direct concern of the American government, we should normally expect socially therapeutic measures to be mainly economically structured. Let us then observe the place given to economics. We start with a current view. On June 6, 1965, a *New York Times* editorial on a speech, "To Fulfill These Rights," by President L. B. Johnson, emphasizing the crucial place of family welfare in the Negro problem, concluded:

> The cures for the social afflictions that hold the Negro in thrall lie in public and private programs that make the present war on poverty and all its related undertakings for expanded education, urban renewal and improved welfare services seem incredibly puny. In the absence of much more massive action to engender full employment, clear the slums and make more schooling available to more people, the chief effect of these programs may be to confront the United States with problems not unlike those of the "revolutions of rising expectations" in Africa and Asia.

At the head of the list of remedies suggested here is full employment. This is assumed to be the critical means by which the Negro might enter the mainstream. The "job gap" showing an unemployment rate consistently twice that of whites must be closed, an undertaking calling for a faster rate of economic advancement for Negroes than for whites. As Vivian Henderson puts it:

> Basically, the question facing the nation, the South, and Negroes today is whether Negroes are narrowing the gaps in their economic status. The issue is not whether Negroes have been making progress, but whether it has been rapid enough to enable them to adjust to an economy whose rate of change is cumulative and intense. The issue is whether the momentum of change is great enough, to generate an economic base among Negroes which will guarantee their continued movement up the economic ladder.[1]

We have taken employment, then, as a primary concern of Negroes and of those engaged with programs for their social adjustment. Incidentally, Frederick Douglass recalled an experience of his which suggests the engrossing place of employment in the Negro's conception of himself. He refers to Negro clerks working in the Freedmen's Bank in Washington, D.C., during the Reconstruction period.

The magnificent dimensions of the building bore testimony to its flourishing condition. In passing it on the street I often peeped into its spacious windows and looked down the row of its gentlemanly and elegantly dressed colored clerks, with their pens behind their ears and button-hole bouquets in their coat-fronts, and felt my very eyes enriched. It was a sight I had never expected to see. I was amazed by the facility with which they counted the money; they threw off the thousands with dexterity, if not the accuracy, of old and experienced clerks. The whole thing was beautiful.[2]

This reaction might have been expected; a man tends to be what he does; and unemployment, of course, means that he does nothing. Incidentally, the record of even such a small movement in economic status among Negroes should put militants on guard with respect to assertions that there has been no consequential change in the social and economic status of Negroes since 1860.

The Mainstream

We have used the "mainstream" view to define the traditional tendency among Negro Americans. There have been, however, persistent nationalist episodes all through the history of race relations. Sometimes, as in the pre-Civil War era, they have been fostered directly by whites as panaceas for the racial situation. Nationalism, as an intermittent movement, has been led by militant Negroes frequently supported by conservative whites. It has been characterized by black nativism, separatism, and racism. It tends to have greater mass appeal among Negroes than assimilationism. The chances, however, of a black nation arising within the larger American society seem illogical and unrealistic.

If we rule out utopias, we may assume, on reliable grounds, that there are only two types of viable societies presently available to mankind: capitalism and socialism. Modern socialism is a direct outgrowth of capitalism, and the process of its evolution continues universally with increasing determination. This development does not apply to Negroes as a group in the United States any more than to, say, American Indians. And yet, unlike the future of the peoples of the "Third World" the future of Negroes is inevitably involved in the change.

Some years ago there was a popular school of race relations which defined blacks and whites in the United States as constituting two castes. The groups thus conceived were compared in detail and identified with relationships among Hindu castes. There is currently an opposite, rapidly developing tendency to regard American race relations as essentially a form of colonialism. Negroes, it is said, are colonials seeking "liberation." This, obviously, provides a theoretical base for the advocacy of "guerrilla warfare" which in reality constitutes a diversionary, dead-end recourse. Frantz Fanon, who lived during the depths of the Algerian revolution and wrote about the colonized people under fire as *les damnés de la terre,* has been generally regarded by Negro militants as the chief ideologist of this conception.

Between 1950 and 1960 a real difference in the racial significance of the ballot developed among the people of the South. That development cannot be characterized as progress toward liberation of "the black colony" in the area. But it was a major step in the political inclusion of the group. Arguments based on colonial assumptions often lead to preposterous conclusions and merely serve to justify socially erratic behavior among American Negroes.

Solution to the Problem

To some students of race relations there can be no solution to the race problem in the United States. To them analytical answers are but evidence of desperation and escapism. According to Lewis M. Killian, for instance, "there may be social ills for which there is no cure. . . . Reluctantly the author must state his honest conclusion: there is no way out." In support of this decision he cites what seems to be the irreducible obstacle: "Above all [the Negro] is still visibly a Negro, and he can change that identity only if he is able to 'pass.' The United States is ceasing to be a Protestant, rural nation, but it still remains a white man's country."[3] Impeccable though this reasoning may seem, it is nevertheless illusory.

In the study of race relations the critical data are not to be sought in the biological stability of color but rather in its changing cultural definition. Between 1860 and 1870, for example, there was a radical shift in the significance of color without, of course, any modification of complexion itself and, since then, there has been a consistent trend that changes the meaning of color, in spite of the fact that, in the foreseeable future, the United States will remain demographically a "white man's country."

National political power will theoretically remain in the hands of whites. And yet the circumstances of the Civil War should disabuse us of any notion that, in American race relations, whites are always solidly arrayed on one side and blacks on the other. The ecology of the races, moreover, significantly contradicts the assertion. This society, therefore, is inevitably also a "black man's country."

Indeed, the nation is *inherently* "color-blind." If it were not, there could be no logic in the insistence that it demonstrate this trait. Actual power increasingly becomes an attribute of citizens regardless of race. And yet, at this stage, color remains an empirical fact. As Chief Justice Warren Burger declared in a leading case: "Just as [against the background of segregation] the race of the students must be considered in determining whether a constitutional violation has occurred, so also must race be considered in formulating a remedy."[4] The color of the different peoples of the world has remained stable since about 1500 A.D., but its relative political and social significance has been changing continuously. Sociologically, the biological fact in itself is meaningless.

In a sense, there is no alternative to the integration of the American Negro population. The very cultural forces have absorbed millions of white immigrants, abolished slavery, produced the Thirteenth, Fourteenth and Fifteenth Amendments to the constitution, endured Reconstruction, brought pressure on the courts to concretize those amendments, and have recently motivated Congress and the chief executive to act positively. As one federal agency puts it, "since 1957 [Congress] has passed five civil rights laws, including the landmark Civil Rights Act of 1964, the Voting Rights Act of 1965, and the Federal Fair Housing Act of 1968." Furthermore this source continues:

> The various laws, Executive orders, and judicial decisions constitute a formidable array of civil rights guarantees providing broad protections against discrimination in virtually every aspect of life—in education, employment, housing, voting, administration of justice, access to places of public accommodation, and participation in the benefits of federally assisted programs.[5]

Thus the direction of the major effort in race relations has been staked out. Immediate problems arise from questions of enforcement, and from the willingness or ability of Negroes to accept existing opportunities. But the road to integration now seems clearly indicated, and the federal government has recognized its obligation to keep it open.

For Negroes, then, the very process of living in America as citizens implicates them in an interminable struggle for social equality. The major civil rights organizations—the NAACP, the Urban League—are working

with the government for the realization of such available values. The immediate source of Negro inequality has been private and governmental discrimination especially in economic life. Equality—freedom of access to mainstream culture—is thus being approached at different rates in different areas of life. Our preoccupation has not been with the question of whether there is a solution to the race problem, but rather with the process by which it is being and must inevitably be resolved.

The Problem as White Nationalism

In spite of all we have said, the primary instrument in American race relations might still seem to be obscured. Even though it remains brutal, violent, and fiercely intimidating, the driving force of race relations seems to remain hidden. Lower-class Negroes especially seem to think that every white person is capable only of self-interest. This self-interest was emotionally solidified in the white southern nation as that country prepared for civil war. It has never been completely vanquished.

The South is still at war—implicitly at least—over its position regarding the place of blacks in the United States. The Confederate flag, Confederate songs and hymns, are still flaunted in the face of Negroes as warnings lest they forget their subordination and humiliation. It is this threat of oppression which, when tapped by counternationalistic Negro orators, can provoke Negro crowds to mass hysteria.

It has taken actual armed force by the federal government to confront elements of the white ruling class in attempts to secure the increments of citizenship rights for blacks in specific situations. At the end of every military engagement, some leaders of the white ruling class have pulled away, regrouped, and taken another life-or-death stand on racial subordination.

To some Negroes, therefore, white nationalism and racism represent the source of a problem that the achievement of civil rights has not solved. Society, they feel, ought to devise means of attacking this attitude directly as well as the acts which it generates. Racism, in other words, should be labeled as morally wrong and thus opposed independently by the northern liberal government. In a "free society" it is difficult to legalize this attitude. And yet, historically, the government has moved from congressional Reconstruction to a hands-off policy, to its present tentative actions to further racial equality. The political structure is thus by no means helpless.

Place of Negroes in the City

In the foreseeable future, Negro Americans will continue to concentrate in the central cities and whites will gravitate toward the suburbs. Conceivably, great cities like Newark and Detroit may become 100 percent black by the year 2000. And yet the city cannot be essentially abandoned by mainstream society; whites cannot forsake it altogether. Negroes, moreover, cannot take it over completely. Capitalist enterprise produced the modern city as its indispensable milieu; and its survival apparently will be critically affected by the fate of its metropolises. We may be sure that the city will not be allowed to wither away without a frantic struggle to maintain it; and in the process the concept of the Negro will be changed.

The city, in other words, is the locus of capitalist entrepreneurial production; it did not evolve as a vehicle of endogenous consumer demand. The tendency to identify mere numbers of Negroes in the city with the extent of their contribution to the city's wealth and with its productive characteristics has been grossly misleading. Left to Negroes alone, the city would probably crumble and vanish; indeed, left to white labor alone, the city would also quickly perish. There is, however, a peculiar functional continuum between white labor and white entrepreneurship in the city, a phenomenon still largely missing in the Negro relationship. The distorted, temporary reaction to this limitation has been ghettoization, or development of a black community on the periphery of mainstream culture.[6] The ghetto is anything but self-sufficient.

Ghettoization polarizes whites and blacks in the central cities. As the weight of numbers increasingly emphasizes the presence of blacks, city government tends to become their responsibility. The city is thus faced with the paradox of having a possibly alienated group in control of its political destiny. One perceptive journalist suggests the outlook for the rest of metropolitan America as follows:

> There is a white-dominated, business-oriented Newark, and there are the densely populated sections where blacks and

Puerto Ricans live. Business Newark looks almost as prosperous as ever. . . . But out of the west and south, in the Central and the South wards is a different story. "It is a jungle," says one cab driver, and another adds: "This city is dead." The juxtaposition of white authority and the jungle strikes one with forcible impact. . . . Shattered, gaping, sightless windows stare out at the county buildings, and only a short jog away . . . one comes upon still ghastly rubble of a war-ravaged [riot] Newark.[7]

This state of cultural incongruity cannot be resolved merely by improving employment conditions among blacks. The problem is not essentially a moral one. To enter the mainstream of urban life, Negroes would have to become in practice and in attitude, part of the imperialistic tradition of American capitalism. Jews, for example, have always participated in it. The Negroes' solidarity could be creatively centered in the characteristic patriotism derived from competition and conflict with other nations for the resources and markets of the globe. That is the psychological matrix in which the great cities have arisen and prospered.

What then? Are Negroes to be forever excluded from the core of American patriotism? Three considerations seem to modify the negative implications of this question: (1) Negroes are not currently being deprived of market positions previously held by them—these positions are indeed recognizably improving; (2) the center of creativity in the system seems to be moving gradually from rampant competitiveness for economic dominance abroad toward reliance on technological progress and efficiency in domestic production; and (3) all signs seem to indicate that social inclusion will be increasingly a matter of education and absence of racial discrimination in the distribution of jobs. These trends are not entirely new; they may be considered projections on an upward turning curve.

Although better education and greater access to jobs would not provide all the ultimate answers, they would provide escape from the depressing conceptions Negroes have of themselves as "the unwanted." Fortunately, the capacity of society itself to include Negroes has been expanding.

The Negro as a Problem to Negroes

There has hardly ever been a period when Negroes have been completely in agreement on a course of action in dealing with whites and the dominant culture. Indeed they became functionally split even during the seventeenth and eighteenth centuries when some West

African tribesmen made good livings by rounding up other natives for sale on the Guinea Coast. Since then there have been continual differences over racial policy.

The various Negro movements tended to evolve within the ineluctable cultural process of the larger global society. Overseas, peoples of color became acculturated, nationalistic, and independent. In the United States, Negroes became more educated, more clearly identified with the culture, and politically more responsible. A social watershed materialized when, in 1954, the U.S. Supreme Court decided, in effect, to condemn any curtailment of the Negroes' civil rights.

Paradoxically, however, opposition developed among Negroes themselves. With the federal courts assuming leadership in the struggle for civil rights, the trend toward Negro assimilation was not only expedited but also, for the first time, societally confirmed. The group now possessed their citizenship status not on sufferance but by inherent right. Activist Negroes and white sympathizers thus sought confrontation after confrontation and repeatedly forced conservative whites to retreat.

The internal problem for Negroes arose mainly from the basic position of the Black Muslims. The Negro middle class was disparaged and denounced for its identification with mainstream culture, and the life of the lower class was, willy-nilly, extolled. Values of the ghetto, almost without lower limits, now attained prestige even among some of the Negro middle class. The whole attack was couched in the fiery emotions of black nationalism. The mainstream middle class seemed to be cornered and intimidated.

This anticultural tendency wormed its way among militants of various stripes; and some whites seemed to condone it. The hearing accorded it in the mass media proved to be an invaluable stimulus. For example, in his study of the change in attitude among white liberals, Gene Roberts of the *New York Times* observed: "A growing number are saying that integration is impossible for the foreseeable future, that the nation should concentrate instead on building up Negro institutions, and that only then—perhaps in a generation or two—can it talk about integration."[8] The separatist philosophy tended to converge with the attitude of extreme white racists.

Nothing seems more elusive than the recurrent belief that Negroes in the central cities of the metropolitan areas live by some unitary culture comparable and equivalent to that of the larger society; and that it may be stabilized for future parallel growth with the culture of the dominant society. This messianic version, no doubt, has been mainly responsible for widespread personal frustrations and destructive behavior.

Normally, mainstream culture resists the typical Negro way of life. Where Negroes hold numerical majorities as, for example, in college dormitories on black campuses—not to mention places of amusement in the ghettoes—whites tend to be repulsed. It is a tendency toward stabilization of this self-isolating subculture that separatism inevitably imposes. Its elements are almost totally lower class, and must, therefore, be abandoned through reeducation. That indeed was precisely what slave masters attempted to do for those Negroes who, in the mid-nineteenth century, faced independence through emigration.

There should be no hesitancy or doubt in the minds of social scientists about the nature of cultural maturity in the modern world. There is no harking back nor lateral approaches to cultural advancement. Everywhere in the modern world social maturity inevitably means mastery of Western culture. Socialism seeks essentially to modify and render capitalist culture more effective in the service of its people.

The Negroes' cultural problem is not similar to that of religious groups such as the Jews.[9] It is, rather, inevitably a dependent offshoot of the larger culture. *Development* can thus have no other realistic meaning than incremental inclusion of the group with its generative society. Essentially, the effective Negroes' social posture entails in-fighting—not separatism.

Education

Since abolition, and indeed even during slavery, the question of education for Negroes has been at the very forefront in considerations of their status. In order to repress the race, its education had to be limited and controlled. Even in the North, the education of Negroes was restricted and sometimes barred altogether. Improvement in the social status of Negroes, therefore, has been marked by their enlarging educational opportunities.

The decisions of the Supreme Court in the fifties revolutionized the nation's attitude toward education for blacks. The Court declared, in effect, that education is a civil right which should not be racially restricted by law. Of particular significance for an understanding of the future of race relations is that this doctrine fell upon relatively fallow ground. Not even the white conservatives of the Deep South have been able fully to withstand it.

The vicissitudes normally associated with its realization and the schemes devised to escape its effects have indeed been staggering. But the country as a whole has apparently become reconciled. This, no doubt, is the stand from which the future of Negro education may be judged.

Since the drive for equality in education is consistent with larger social trends, we should expect such contrary forces as resegregation in the metropolises, black-studies campaigns,[10] the politics of devotion to neighborhood schools, the white private school movement, the self-serving aversion to busing of school children, to take only temporary root. A luminous straw in the wind, arising from efforts to deal with the obstinate facts of school segregation in northern cities, was U.S. District Court Judge Stephen J. Roth's dictum on the question of *de jure* or *de facto* segregation in the public schools of Detroit. In September 1971 he explained:

> It is unfortunate that we cannot deal with public school segregation on a no-fault basis; for if racial segregation in our public schools is an evil, then it should make no difference whether we classify it *de jure* or *de facto*. Our objective, legally, should be to remedy a condition which we believe needs correction.[11]

Freedom of education for Negroes will probably produce a new breed of people. We should expect no significant regression of the group.

New Dependence on Politics

The politics of race relations in the cities tends to be its own realistic confirmation of the social processes discussed above. It also embodies its own extremes in social paradoxes. Population movements in the metropolitan areas are entrusting political leadership, in an ever larger number of central cities, to the hands of blacks. A sobering datum, frequently cited, it the estimate of the National Advisory Commission on Civil Disorders that, by 1984, thirteen central cities including Chicago, St. Louis, Philadelphia, Los Angeles, Detroit, Atlanta, and Baltimore will be over 50 percent Negro. The U.S. Census shows that:

> Among the 30 places in the Nation with the highest proportion of Negroes in 1970, there has been a dramatic increase since

1960 in the number that have at least as many Negroes as whites. The count is now 16, compared to 3 in 1960.[12]

In 1970, to illustrate at random, Gary, Indiana was included among the thirty *places* in the nation with highest proportion of Negroes. In 1960 about 39 percent of Gary's population were Negro; but, in 1970, 53 percent were Negro. That city is therefore one of the sixteen places referred to that have at least as many Negroes as whites. The trend is upward. Negroes, moreover, may become mayors of important cities before their black population reaches 50 percent.

Sometimes the mayoralty and membership in city councils have been regarded merely as economic plums to be exploited by victors at the polls. The cities, however, are the fundamental loci of capitalist organization. They embody the ultimate in the cultural achievements of the system: the perfection of its economic institutions, its art and architecture, its societal order, its science and education, and the nuclei of its global communications. It is ironic that Negroes, who have been traditionally regarded as subcitizens incapable of comprehending this complex cultural matrix, are now likely to find themselves in positions of political authority calling for initiative in its development and guidance.

The central city, manifestly, cannot be suburbanized. Unless our basic political structure is radically to be transformed, we should expect the nation's future sense of responsibility for the Negro's education and cultural participation to be given new self-interested consideration. In any event, black leadership in these strategic urban positions will, no doubt, have very much to learn. The obligations of this function should give Negroes a greater sense of identification with their country and its prevailing culture. There is apparently no alternative; the Rubicon has been crossed.

Although the Negro executive might have won the highest political office in the state or the city because of the size of the Negro vote, he cannot logically regard that office as an institution primarily in the service of the special interests of Negroes. At most he has gained only a means of enlarging opportunities for blacks without killing the goose in the process. This theory has not always been accepted, however. For instance, in a closely reasoned essay, Edward Greer says:

> I believe that until new concepts are worked out, the best way of understanding this process [of a Negro's winning the mayoralty

of an American city] is by analogy with certain national liberation movements in colonial or neocolonial countries. Of course, the participants . . . are Americans, and they aren't calling for a UN plebiscite. But they were clearly conscious of themselves as using elections as a tool, as a step toward a much larger ultimate goal—a goal whose key elements of economic change, political power . . . defense of a ''new'' culture and so forth are very close to those of colonial people. . . . [His] campaign can be thought of as part of a nationalist process that has a trajectory quite similar to that of anticolonial liberation movements.[13]

We think on the contrary that the success of the city under white leadership depends upon its economic prosperity. That indeed is the source of attraction of both Negro and white migrants. Under a black governor or mayor, economic prosperity must continue to be the primary concern. The black urban executive is structurally in competition with leaders of other cities for all legitimate business. Manifestly, then, he must make his city as attractive as possible to businessmen.

It is indeed through devotion to the welfare of the state or city that he, like the white executive, can most effectively show his devotion to the citizens, black or white. If he reveals himself, to the black people who mainly elected him, as hostile to and alienated from the fundamental political structure and major economic processes of the city, he will fail in his task.

It was the operation of mainstream politics, in Gary, Indiana, which Edward Greer saw as socially unfortunate. As he put it:

Richard G. Hatcher's insurgency was contained within the existing national political system. Or, to express it somewhat differently, the attempt by black forces to use the electoral process to further their national liberation was aborted by a countervailing process of neocolonialism carried out by the federal government. Bluntly speaking, the piecemeal achievement of power through parliamentary means is a fraud—at least as far as black Americans are concerned.[14]

The situation in Gary illustrates two aspects of the political situation with which the Negro who attains the mayoralty becomes involved: severe white opposition, and temptation of black ideologists to convert the city into a black nation. Let us observe the Gary model briefly. Mayor Hatcher became involved with both these forces in his campaign for office in January 1968.

Hatcher did what he could to resist fraud and corruption by local Democratic and Republican factions, equalize economic and welfare opportunities for Negroes, and counter the overwhelming control by the great corporations in the city. When, in May 1973, Thomas Bradley was made mayor of Los Angeles, a city of only about 16 percent black voters, he was the first Negro to hold that position. He "promised to make the city safe from violence, build a rapid transit system, trim waste in government, and cut taxes from those most heavily burdened."[15] Other black mayors: Kenneth Gibson of Newark, Carl Stokes of Cleveland, Charles Evers of Fayette, Mississippi, faced their problems in a similar way.

Hatcher, on the contrary, engaged in a bold attempt to lead an "independent" black political movement. In March 1972, he delivered the keynote address at a three-day convention (March 10–12) assembled in Gary for this purpose. He declared before the National Black Political Convention: "We must emerge from this convention with an independent national black political agenda: a dynamic program for black liberation that, in the process, will liberate all America from its current decadence." And the mayor issued the following challenge:

> Democrats or Republicans . . . how much difference has it really made to black people? . . . Hereafter, we shall rely on the power of our own black unity. . . . Every political party must make up its mind. It cannot represent both the corporations and the people. . . . The 70's will be the decade of an independent black political thrust.[16]

The convention was constituted by Negro representatives from all over the United States; present, besides Hatcher, were Congressman Charles C. Diggs, Jr., Roy Innis, and Imamu Baraka (the former LeRoi Jones). The National Black Political Agenda which emerged was amended and eventually published on May 6, 1972. This agenda, a fifty-five-page program, is even more explicit:

> [The agenda] . . . is an attempt to define essential changes which must take place in this land as we move to self-determination and true independence. . . . A new Black Politics must come to birth . . . the Black Politics of Gary must accept major responsibility for creating both the atmosphere and program for fundamental, far-reaching change in America. . . . The society we seek cannot come unless Black people organize to advance its

285

coming. . . . So, Brothers and Sisters of our developing Black nation, we now stand at Gary as people whose time has come. . . . We begin here and now in Gary . . . an independent Black political movement . . . an independent Black spirit. . . . An incalculable social indebtedness has been generated, a debt owed to Black people by the general American society. So we must not rest until American society has recognized our . . . right to reparations, to a massive claim on the financial assets of the American economy.[17]

This then is the nature of the black separatism with which the mayor of a great American city identified himself. It is obviously elusive but it returns like a refrain, interspersed with demands for something for practically every Negro group. It is consistent with the vaguely expressed moral philosophy at the base of Negro criminality in the cities. And indeed Gary has become known as one of the worst such spots. For example the mayor seems to be perplexed by the following report:

An apparent gang war for control of drug traffic here that has left 17 [black] bodies dumped in alleys, streets, and parked cars has prompted an intensive effort by local and Federal officials to stem the Gary area's heroin supply. . . . Mayor Richard G. Hatcher was so concerned . . . that he flew to Washington . . . to stress the situation's gravity to Senator George McGovern, the Democratic Presidential nominee. . . . Mr. Hatcher said that the initial attitude . . . was to ''let the pushers kill each other off.'' But then you realize innocent by-standers are caught in the crossfire. And if a gang can organize to take over drug traffic, what's to stop them from taking over businesses in the same fashion?[18]

Perhaps a different attitude among the political leaders might have brought about different results. Negroes could have been given a sense of belonging—a sense of being Americans. Without taking our point of view, Edward Greer recognized ''the erosion of popular support after the successful mobilization of energies involved in the campaign. . . . [Moreover, the black people's] political experiences are not enlarged, their understanding of the larger society and how it functions has not improved, and they are not being trained to better organize for their own interests. . . . After the inauguration, old supporters found themselves on the outside looking in.''[19]

The immediate difficulty here, of course, resides in the irreconcilability of black nationalism and Americanism. On this point delegates to the Gary Convention were split—some walked out. The NAACP did not attend at all; nor did Congresswoman Shirley Chisholm. However, influential politicians like Congressman Charles Diggs, Jr., and indeed Mayor Hatcher himself were manipulated by such seasoned nationalists as Imamu Baraka and Roy Innis.

It was mainly the artful influence of the latter group which led many to characterize the proceedings as "irresponsible and separatist."[20] It should be said that the Negro politician who attains a position of power and responsibility through the operation of the American political system and then uses the opportunity to serve the purposes of black nationalists inevitably betrays the Negro people.

We may consider the following as characterizations and projections of the Negro's political position in the United States:

(1) Negroes now vote all over the United States as normal citizens. The federal government stands ready to assume responsibility for removal of sporadic racial limitations.

(2) Currently, it is expected that Negroes will vote solidly as a group for black candidates and thus automatically against white opposing contestants.

(3) The deeper South the political contest, the more racial considerations tend to determine the ballot count.

(4) In the North and West particularly, Negro politicians may win office in places with smaller percentages of black voters than white politicians with higher percentages of white voters.

(5) Negro candidates have a better chance to win office in areas of less than 50 percent black voters than white candidates backed by white voters.

(6) Ordinarily, in the larger cities, Negro politicians may count on votes from the solid Negro bloc, the habitual white Democrats, and the freewheeling white voters attracted to the black candidate because of his personality or his position on issues.

(7) The winning of office by Senator Edward Brooke of Massachusetts and Thomas Bradley of Los Angeles suggests that in the long run we may expect Negroes to run for office more and more because of their qualifications and less and less because of their race.

(8) When white candidates running for elective office win in black majority communities over black candidates for reasons of merit, then the race issue will have become an inconsequential factor in American politics.

Chapter 20

The Final Logic of Race Relations

The Outcome

Although in this study of race relations we cannot write a conclusion, in the ordinary sense of the term, a few ideas seem appropriate. Programs for the inclusion of Negroes as full citizens in American society will increase in number and intensity. The more numerous and practicable the remedies devised to alleviate the Negro's debasement, the greater will be his deterimination and capacity to resist discrimination. In the thick of the interracial conflict of the sixties a popular periodical expressed this idea:

> The U.S. has certainly come an incredibly long way since Abraham Lincoln, shortly before the end of the Civil War, asked his logistics experts to determine whether the U.S. could muster enough transportation to export the Negroes—only to be told that Negro babies were being born faster than all the nation's ships could carry them from the country.
> The Negro has been a permanent part of America ever since

288

then, and perhaps the greatest advance of recent years is the realization by white people that his problems cannot be ignored. The Negro's recent progress, far from making him content, has greatly intensified his aspirations. The job of helping him to meet his legitimate needs may well continue to be the nation's most urgent piece of domestic business for decades to come.[1]

To attempt to project beyond the foreseeable future is likely to become mystically speculative. But just as certain predictable transitional points have been reached in the developing struggle—the Civil War and its related constitutional amendments, and the slow but irrepressible rise toward social integration and justice—further progress will certainly facilitate the Negroes' capacity to defend themselves in dealing with racial discrimination.

If whites and blacks, regardless of sex, are free to associate with one another as friends in the streets of the South, if they will accept the Negro's authority according to his ability or seniority, the further resolution of the problem may be left to interpersonal relations and adjustments. In this connection, we find Everett C. Hughes's concept of conditions for ultimate peace between the races too static and perfectionist. He writes:

> Even if many whites and Negroes were drawn into such common social nuclei, there would remain the problem of the great hangover from centuries of discrimination. And even if all discriminatory practices based on race alone were to disappear, their accumulated effects would remain. How long would it be before Negroes would have, in the same proportion as other Americans, the characteristics which would allow them to move freely in our society and economy; how long before they would be distributed in the same proportions as others among occupations, and would be like them in income, consumption habits, education, and in all respects but race itself? It would certainly take a long, long time. Many other social events and currents, could change the direction and rates of change in the Negro's condition—and that of others—in the interim.[2]

To some of these queries it would be reasonable to answer, never. An imperishable ecological fact of race relations is that the Negro population will remain approximately one-tenth of the total. Moreover there has been nothing to suggest that the group will ever become culturally superior. American culture will proceed to develop mainly in the hands of whites. And yet it seems obvious that interracial peace will be achieved only when Negro citizens are not excluded from participating in productive situations according to their abilities. In reality, this is the most to which any citizen can aspire. It is the ultimate meaning of assimilation in American society.

We may be fairly certain also that Negroes will not be "distributed in the same proportion as all others among occupations" any more than, for example, Jews or Italians are. It seems doubtful also whether the income gap between Negroes and whites will be completely closed in the foreseeable future. The vitalizing force will remain a constant competitive movement toward a closing of the gap. The disparity will probably lose its racial significance when Negroes are no longer confronted by governmentally supported racial barriers to their occupational and other ambitions. They will not have to concentrate on "sports" if other fields are similarly open to them.

But we think Hughes overlooks another critical point. The constricting fact about the Negro's situation in the United States has been the popular conception of his group as an unalterably inferior entity. The social variables determining Negro isolation today will not only be of different significance in the long run but also applicable to a culturally different social group. It is not inconceivable that some of these variables may have a reverse moral effect. The mainstream is a cultural phenomenon in constant transition.

"Yes! But How Long?"

In dealing with the future of race relations, I have found a number of Negroes—by no means the majority, however—who seem to be grieviously perturbed about the absence of a satisfactory answer to the question: "Must we wait for generations until one by one, we catch up culturally with whites?"[3] Indeed, the awful, silent barrier of big business operations may seem to quash all faith in the promises of the system. Sometimes, without making it explicit, this skeptical group seems to be affected primarily by the prospects of universal social change. Let us illustrate.

In the spring of 1971, a young man came to my apartment, without invitation, introduced himself, and—knowing that I had given thought to the subject—said he was interested in clarifying some of his own ideas. It gradually transpired that he was a dissident labor organizer in the automobile industry and that he had intentions far beyond the routine program of unionism. His organization, thus far limited to Michigan, but well-known in Detroit, had been attempting to organize separately all blacks in the industry, to initiate through them a general strike, leading to the "overthrow" of the state government and eventually that of the "racist" American nation as well.

At this stage his group did not include whites, but it was not a direct offshoot of the Black Panthers or any other established organization. His sincerity and determination left me with the feeling that I was observing children playing with dynamite in the bedroom of the household. I made no detailed study of this "revolutionary" group—it meets regularly in the city, has a newspaper and office. (The name of the organization is not of consequence here. There is a profusion of such nationalistic, political class groups in the United States.)[4] My guest impressed me as a ghetto high school dropout. I was surprised, at the termination of our conversation, when he asked whether I could suggest literary sources for a study of "dialectics." He was obviously being self-educated. Among some of the material he carried was Amilcar Cabral's *Revolution in [Portuguese] Guinea: An African People's Struggle* (London, 1969). I looked it through. The chapter most heavily marked by previous readers was titled: "The Weapon of Theory." All of the following passage, from this section of the work on guerrilla warfare and social ideology, was underlined:

> the reality of our times, allows us to state that the history of one human group, or of humanity, goes through at least *three stages*. The *first* is characterized by a low level of productive forces—of man's domination over nature; the mode of production is of a rudimentary character, private appropriation of the means of production does not yet exist, there are no classes, nor, consequently is there any class struggle. In the *second stage*, the increased level of productive forces leads to private appropriation of the means of production, progressively complicates the mode of production, provokes conflicts of interests within the socio-economic whole in movement, and makes possible the appearance of the phenomenon "class" and hence class struggle, the social expression of the contradiction in the economic field between the mode of production and private appropriation of the means of production. In the *third stage*, once a certain level of productive forces is reached, the elimination of private appropriation in the means of production is made possible, and is carried out, together with the elimination of the phenomenon "class," and hence the class struggle; new and hitherto unknown forces in the historical process of the economic whole are then unleashed. [P. 78]

291

This illustrates the mystical interpretation of social change which is likely to fascinate some Negroes looking for instant solutions to the problem of race relations in the United States. I have cited the incident because I think it is an important straw in the wind. There are few if any contemporary sociologists or economists who deal realistically with this problem. Marxists are already convinced, and traditionalists tend to disregard the question altogether. A few words of clarification seem, therefore, in order.

Two clamorous social facts presently obtain: the transition of capitalism to socialism, and universal indecision as to what constitutes socialism. This lack of knowledge is not total, but it is sufficient to affect our understanding of the process of transition. Inevitably, the doctrines of Marx are involved not so much because of the validity of his philosophy and classical economics but rather because of the consummate use which he made of his intellectual powers to explain why capitalism is a "transient" form of social organization. Today, it is difficult to see how this fundamental preoccupation could be gainsaid.

And yet, acceptance of his essentially erroneous analysis of the nature of capitalism and the process of its transition has been costly both materially and psychically to many of those caught in the currents of revolutionary situations. Of primary significance, we think, are his assumptions concerning social change based upon the concept of "dialectical materialism." Modern sociology has been properly skeptical about any variation of the Hegelian thesis-antithesis-synthesis philosophy of societal change and development.[5] Another elemental assumption stems from Marx's labor theory of value, surplus value, and the formation and accumulation of capital. This whole truistic system of thought identifies Marx as a classical social theorist deriving his modified ideas about the place of labor in the capitalist system mainly from Adam Smith, David Ricardo, and others of that period. The critical illusion here does not involve questions about consistency of its detailed logic but rather about the larger conceptualization of the capitalist system itself. The Marxist orientation follows the original diversion of Adam Smith and the classical economists in the domestication of the capitalist system—an internalized reciprocation of capital and labor.

I have attempted to show that capitalism, as a form of social organization, defines the economic significance of labor and that an essential part of this organization includes its foreign relations.[6] It is of primary consequence, therefore, to recognize that the dynamics of capitalism does not rest essentially upon a domestic interplay between surplus value and labor as the postulated basis of capital accumulation.

An important corollary of the labor theory of value is that capitalist production alienates labor. It is here, perhaps, that Marx has his clearest opportunity not only to express his humanitarianism but also his condemnation of capitalism. "We started with an economic fact," he hypothesizes, "the separation of the worker from the means of production. From this fact flows our concept of alienated or estranged labor. . . . *Private property* results from the phenomenon of alienated labor."[7] We must be brief about this very large but pertinent subject involving psychology and philosophy.[8] Basically, all labor is alienating—indeed Genesis conceives of it as a curse of God. Hardly anyone likes work for its own sake.

We may take for granted also that human beings in all societies must work and that labor will be structured differentially according to the social status system. Alienation thus implies alternative opportunities for employment. It is not that work in capitalist society produces capital—the means by which, according to Marx, the worker is progressively rejected—nor that it disassociates the worker from "control" of the product of his labor; but rather that under capitalism, the worker becomes *free* to consider alternative occupational possibilities. Indeed for the first time he is able to conceive of an alternative of no work at all.

Professor Walter Kaufmann addresses himself to this point: "There is a widespread tendency to assume that in preindustrial society men were much less alienated—perhaps not at all—and that they were not only happier and more intimate with nature but also more humane. Those who take this for granted should come to grips with the abundant evidence to the contrary. . . ."[9] It is not, moreover, that work becomes *creative* and thus attractive under such systems as feudalism, Hinduism, or tribalism, but rather that workers in such forms of social organization are not societally free to become alienated. One suspects that current emphasis upon transformed "human nature", which some writers foresee as arising under socialism and thus eliminating the prospects of alienation, may be due mainly to a loss of capitalist freedom to harbor alienated attitudes. It was, let us recall, especially the freedom to escape undesirable labor which attracted the run-away feudal serf to the medieval capitalist city.

293

The indications seem to be that alienation will be an even more serious problem under "socialism" than under capitalism. The uneven cultural development in different countries of a socialist world may produce the basis of psychological estrangement. The use of capital goods in production will undoubtedly be maximized and consequently both division of labor and remoteness from final consumption will be increased. "Can we," to quote Kaufmann again, "eliminate boring jobs? So far, no society, socialist or capitalist, has solved this problem; and the solution does not seem to depend on who owns the means of production. It depends on technical developments—specifically, on the future of automation."[10] Apparently, factors to be considered are the stage of technological development of the country and the education and personality of given individuals.

What then are the relevant processes of contemporary societal change? We should recognize that there is a critical distinction between the history of the origin of capitalism and that of socialism. Capitalism did not evolve from any other social system—decidedly not from European feudalism. I have called its emergence a unique cultural invention, a chance occurrence. The arrival of socialism, on the other hand, is so closely dependent upon capitalist preconditions that it may be thought of as a normal historical transition of the latter system. In other words, progressive socialism as a type of social organization could not come into being in the absence of a developed capitalism *as a system*. One of the great problems of the socialist theory of change inheres in the question of just how much of capitalist culture should be preserved and perfected under socialism.

There seem to be, however, but two essential preconditions for the establishment of a successful socialist state: organized central planning of production instead of private enterprise; and effective exploitation of science and technology in production.[11] As the mercantilists never ceased to emphasize, the welfare of the capitalist nation depends upon the success of its business enterprises—the most powerful and consequential sector of which has been engaged in foreign commerce. But the welfare of the socialist state necessitates increasing productivity through rationalized technology. There are physical conditions, of course, which affect the development of technology.

The decline of capitalism has been due to two principal causes: the impossibility for backward countries to develop along the historic lines of the leading capitalist nations; and the withdrawal of colonial countries from the system. This, let us note, is not a Marxian premise. For Marx, the principal "grave-diggers" are the revolutionary proletariat in the leading capitalist nations. We need no abstruse theory to demonstrate that the revolutionary change is being fought out internationally mainly in the backward countries supported by Russia and China—two previously backward countries—and opposed directly by the United States. To lose this critical international struggle is to seal the transition of the capitalist system.

There seems to be, moreover, every indication that the movement cannot be reversed. Great Britain, for example, cannot return to her Victorian security and international ascendancy. Moreover, the defense of capitalism in Viet Nam, for instance, exposed the appalling costs awaiting the United States as protector of the status quo. It may be easier, however, to win socialist revolutions than to run socialist states. For one thing, the atomistic coercions of capitalist competition will be largely removed, and ideas about the best way to conduct the society—from a conviction that *work* ought to be abolished to the doctrine that he who malingers on his assigned job or does shoddy work ought to be legally punished—will proliferate.

Insofar as initiation of the system is concerned, there is primarily the problem of optimum size—the size below which no country can hope to "take off" and develop independently. A country must be able to reach the point of self-initiating technological and scientific growth or it will remain perpetually a satellite of some larger industrial socialist state. That is currently the situation of Cuba, Guinea and the East European communist countries. Potential satellites—such as all the West Indies and most of the African and South American countries—will no doubt eventually merge with larger neighboring states to constitute viable socialist communities.

The present movement toward consolidation of western European countries seems to be an implicit answer to requirements of a practicable base for the organization of a socialist state. None of the African nations, except perhaps Zaire (the Congo), and none of the South American countries, except perhaps Brazil, could separately establish a socialist state capable of continuous development. A socialist country may use the international market for its own purpose but it cannot be dependent on the system of foreign exchange in the way that small nations in the capitalist system can. The underdeveloped country, whether socialist or capitalist, that perpetually imports its industrial production machinery must expect increasing unemployment.

Socialism has not yet solved its problem of leadership—charisma still plays a much more crucial role there than in the capitalist system. Errors in planning and in social programs are thus likely to be more protracted and severe than under capitalism. The place of *doctrine* will, most likely, also be more determinative of social behavior. The dynamics of socialist development will, therefore, necessarily depend upon the inherent characteristics of science, technology and correlative thinking—which sprang from the capitalist need for efficiency—to expand at an increasing rate. In order to achieve the desiderata of economic growth, the basis of social welfare, the state must obviously give primacy to the exploitation of science and technology.

There Must be Some Other Way Out

Socialism, then, visionary or otherwise, has become an exceedingly attractive "way out" for some Negroes. Since labor is their special contribution, this attitude is understandable. They seem fascinated by the idea of a "take-over by workers." Apparently, however, they do not realize that a "labor" revolution could mean economic disaster for a people. There are, for example, many Negro-controlled countries in the West Indies and in Africa which could easily declare themselves "socialist," but they do not. The experiment by President Julius Nyerere in Tanzania of "African socialism," seems to be based upon the idea of the determinative potency of labor in economic development. Hard, unified labor can build a nation of happy, contented people. Nothing seems more certain, however, than that "Ujamaa" will fail. No doubt, many reasons other than manifest utopian planning will be summoned to explain this failure which can be predicted if attempted according to the announced plans.[12]

The American Negro's place in this universal transition is necessarily limited. As a social ideologist, he would be welcomed neither by Africa nor the West Indies. Moreover, the progress of Africa toward socialist organization has no lesson of direct interest for him. The most salutary strategy of the West Indies is to remain within the capitalist orbit until some future time when they may become absorbed by larger socialist blocks on this continent. Africa will be glad to have, forthwith, such American Negro experts as theoretical scientists, technicians, engineers, physicians, mathematicians, agronomists and so on, but unfortunately there is not only a deficiency of these skills for export but also an abnormal scarcity of them at home.

The "black studies," black power preoccupations have not stimulated interest in technical fields—fields that are emphasized in all socialist states. Africa, moreover, seems to have little if any interest in "black science."

Conscious of the fact that when he attempted to say the same thing in an address in 1969 at a Harlem library, the late Tom Mboya was pelted with eggs and shouted down by black separatists, he put his point, as gently as possible in writing:

> I consider the call for mass movement to Africa an academic argument since . . . in today's world and conditions such movement is not practical. . . . Those who wish to come and make a home in Africa should be free to do so. There are many opportunities in the new nations especially for trained and skilled persons. . . . The African of today is a modern man. He has the right to benefit by the developments of technology and science. . . . Too often white people confuse the symptoms of our poverty with African culture. I hope our élite [blacks] will not make the same mistake. We walk barefoot, we live in mud and wattle huts, we buy and wear cheap Hong Kong fabrics— not because it is part of our culture, but because of our state of poverty.[13]

On the other hand, David Edeani, a Nigerian journalist in the United States, surveyed current movements among Negroes for emigration to Africa and enumerated the benefits to be derived by individuals, the race as a whole, and the American society. His advocacy of such a program depends finally, however, upon financial subsidy, mainly by the United States. To the "black bourgeoisie" and the U.S. government, one important recompense for financial assistance would be the country's riddance of unruly black militants. "In this way, much frustration and its attendant disorders will be averted, and some of the energies and time that black leaders would expend in absorbing the shock waves of such disorders . . . would be released for more fruitful tasks."[14]

Edeani's argument in favor of back-to-Africa movements is not essentially different from that of Garvey and others of his persuasion. It is just as naive in its appeal for subsidy from the United States and, indeed, just as contradictory. Thus, he explains: "The majority of those who will opt to emigrate are definitely going to be those who will need more financial assistance. . . . [but] Africa will benefit economically, culturally, and politically. Apart from the American culture which the Afro-American would be taking with him, there is the middle-level, or even high-level, technical skills he would . . . be transferring to the African economy."[15]

I think it should be recognized that concern about Negro emigration is basically a trivial preoccupation in race relations. It involves no urgent problem. Even before emancipation Negroes had the right and freedom to go. From my personal experience in Africa and in the West Indies, it seems possible to conclude that if the movement of black people were reciprocally free, we should expect that for every black American who voluntarily leaves the United States for Africa, in order to find opportunities for community service and self-improvement, there will be scores of Africans ready and happy to move permanently in the opposite direction into the United States. The pull is still far greater than the push. The Negro who alienates himself psychologically from the United States is most likely to remain stranded, a man without a country.[16]

New Theories and Agendas

Eventually, racial theories call for societal support and realization. Basically—to illustrate—Garveyism found societal support neither in Africa, the West Indies, nor the United States; in a 1961 contest with the NAACP over the principle of talion as racial policy, Robert Williams said he found himself uncomfortable in other parts of the world, including Cuba and China, returning thereafter to his country enlightened and chastened; Malcolm X, master preacher of interracial hatred, employed his last days mainly in confessions of grievous ideological sins committed while he had admittedly lost control of his faculties as a Black Muslim nationalist. In his attempt to rehabilitate himself, he was murdered by his erstwhile Muslim brothers (using methods which he, himself, had taught them). Leading young converts to his brand of black nationalism, such as Stokely Carmichael, worked themselves into places like Guinea where they sought to achieve recognition as teachers of elementary Western culture and leisure to acquire knowledge of the nature of modern social change and its frustrations; and some, like H. Rap Brown, cornered by the larger society, returned to the street culture of their adolescence to make their living by violence; others, like the nationalistic communists, Huey Newton and Eldridge Cleaver, split on Black Panther politics: Newton to live off the fat of the land, as head of a racial blackmail enterprise, a "black Mafia," in Oakland, California, and Cleaver

298

to contemplate his status as a Panther outcast in Algeria and elsewhere.

Perhaps the most lamentable of these seekers after some compatible societal harbinger of their doctrines was the great W. E. B. DuBois himself. Mboya could have told him that Ghana had no place for his type of personality or his ideology—that he would merely be a guest of Kwame Nkrumah. His death (1963), before the banishment of Nkrumah (1966), probably spared him some of the bitterest frustrations of his long productive life. This is by no means a complete listing of the course of all the spurious racial theories and their programs. Recently they have mushroomed all over the community, and they range from the highly ridiculous to the reasonably plausible. We cite them as illustrations of dead ends in the quest for leadership among Negroes.

The action phase of the civil rights movement has been largely disoriented and squelched through infiltration of anticivil rights, black racist elements. A major loss has been the disappearance of its nonviolent, civil disobedience ideological basis. We tend to forget that the power and universal appeal of the Negro protest activities of the early sixties emanated from its character of "passive resistance." It was the early Congress of Racial Equality, supported mainly by whites, which, with relatively little publicity, gradually spread the doctrines of the Sermon on the Mount, Henry David Thoreau, Leo Tolstoy, M. K. Gandhi, and others in their persistent attacks upon the fortress of American racial discrimination.

The following is part of King's story of disagreement during the James Meredith, Mississippi march in June 1966. After visiting Meredith in a Memphis hospital, King, Floyd McKissick (then National Director of CORE), and Stokely Carmichael (the reoriented chairman of SNCC) decided to continue the Mississippi Freedom March:

As we walked down [Highway 51 where Meredith had been shot], there was much talk and many questions raised.

"I'm not for that nonviolence stuff anymore," shouted one of the younger activists.

"If one of these damn white Mississippi crackers touches me, I'm gonna knock the hell out of him," shouted another.

Later on a discussion of the composition of the march came up.

"This should be an all-black march," said one marcher. "We

299

don't need any more white phonies and liberals invading our movement. This is our march.''

Once during the afternoon we stopped to sing "We Shall Overcome." The voices rang out with all the traditional fervor, the glad thunder and gentle strength that had always characterized the singing of this noble song. But when we came to the stanza which speaks of "black and white together," the voices of a few of the marchers were muted. I asked them later why they refused to sing that verse. The retort was:

"This is a new day; we don't sing those words any more. In fact the song should be discarded. Not 'We Shall Overcome,' but 'We Shall Overrun.'''

As I listened to these comments, the words fell on my ears *like strange music from a foreign land.* My hearing was not attuned to the sound of such bitterness. . . .

The discussion continued at [a] motel. I decided that I would plead patiently with my brothers to remain true to the time-honored principles of our movement. I began with a plea for nonviolence. This immediately aroused some of our friends from the Deacons for Defense, who contended that self-defense was essential and that therefore nonviolence should not be a prerequisite for participation in a march. They were joined in this view by some of the activists from CORE and SNCC.

I tried to make it clear that *besides opposing violence on principle,* I could imagine nothing more impractical and disastrous than for any of us, through misguided judgment, to precipitate a violent confrontation in Mississippi. We had neither the resources nor the techniques to win. Furthermore, I asserted, many Mississippi whites, from government on down, would enjoy nothing more than for us to turn to violence in order to use this as an excuse to wipe out scores of Negroes in and out of the march. Finally, I contended that the debate over the question of self-defense was unnecessary since few people suggested that Negroes should not defend themselves as individuals when attacked. The question was . . . whether it was tactically wise to use a gun while participating in an organized demonstration. If they lowered the banner of nonviolence, I said, Mississippi injustice would not be exposed and moral issues would be obscured.

Next the question of the participation of whites was raised. Stokely Carmichael contended that the inclusion of whites in the march should be de-emphasized and that the dominant appeal should be made for black participation. Others in the room agreed. As I listened to Stokely, I thought about the years that we had worked together in communities all across the South, and how joyously we had then welcomed and accepted white allies in the movement. What accounted for this reversal in Stokely's philosophy? . . .

300

I implored everyone in the room to see the morality of making the march completely interracial. Consciences must be enlisted in our movement, I said, not merely racial groups. I reminded them of the dedicated whites who had suffered, bled, and died in the cause of racial justice, and suggested that to reject white participation now would be a shameful repudiation of all for which they had sacrificed.

Finally, I said that the formidable foe we now faced demanded more unity than ever before and that I would stretch every point to maintain this unity, but that I could not in good conscience agree to continue my personal involvement and that of SCLC in the march if it were not publicly affirmed that it was based on nonviolence and the participation of both black and white. After a few minutes of discussion, Floyd and Stokely agreed that we could unite around these principles *as far as the march was concerned.* The next morning we had a joint press conference affirming that the march was nonviolent and that whites were welcomed.[17]

This, then, may be taken as the point at which interracial action against discrimination lost its coherence. The "strange music" which King now recognized in the advocacy of Carmichael, McKissick and others was, in fact, the voice of alienation, and their new champions were Malcolm X and Frantz Fanon. The inspiration, dedication, and interracial attraction of the original CORE was gone, and King left no successor able to express without reservation the cogency of "Christian love" in direct action against racism. Racial hatred, the cult of violence, and a view of the black community as a plum to be exploited by blacks, grew apace.

In the United States, it seems clear, Negroes may participate to advantage in the larger movement for social change but they cannot realistically hope to lead it. No one, apparently, can predict with any degree of certainty how and when the transition will take place. To this Marx does not supply a reliable guide. It may arrive peaceably.

One conclusion is evident: acts of violence and destruction of property by organized Negro groups, with the intention of subverting society as a whole, must expect retaliation from the state that would make previous treatment of ghetto rioters seem mere pampering. There is manifestly no escape from the need for interracial identification and continued movement, in spite of discouraging incidents, into the arcanum of American society. Optimists tend to be supported by a conviction that this solution involves cultural, not biological, change.

Since the early sixteenth century, under the powerful and irreversible pressures of capitalist culture, the whole world entered a process of unification and assimilation. The emergent cultural standard of this assimilation has been first that of Great Britain and then the United States. There seems to be every indication that the trend will continue. In the interest of efficiency and growth, national barriers will lose significance. Demographic and ecological imperatives would increasingly force the total population to deal with the resources of the planet as a whole.

NOTES

For complete citations see Bibliography

Introduction
1. Brimmer, 1968–69, 642.
2. Durkheim, 1915, 94.

Chapter 1
1. Foner, 1947, I, 250ff.
2. Tannenbaum, 1947, 108.
3. Boeke, 1953, 209.
4. Cox, 1964, 210ff.
5. Reuter, 1939, 54.
6. Raleigh, VIII, 353.
7. Child, 1751, 42–43; also Tucker, 1753.
8. de Klerck, I, 326.
9. Cox, 1948, 353ff.
10. I consider a simple culture or society one without some form of written language, i.e., preliterate societies.
11. Cf. Turnbull, 1972, 228–34.
12. Cf. Handlin, 1950, 214.
13. Miller, 1958, 26–27.
14. Regarding the impact of colonialism, Furnivall, 1956, 306.
15. For an earlier discussion of "Situations of Race Relations," see Cox, 1948, 353–91; also Hunter, 1965, 240, 256–61; van den Berghe, 1967, 25ff.
16. Cox, 1959, 405–83.
17. Bacon, Aphorism 129.
18. Hazlitt, 1900, II, 653.
19. Hunter, 1965, 4.

20. Blumer, 1965, 253.
21. Blumer, 1965, 241.
22. Blumer, 1965, 245, 251.
23. Blumer, 1965, 227, 233, 251, 252.
24. Jackson, 1913, 23–24.
25. Harmon, Lindsay, Woodson, 1929, 3.
26. Harmon, Lindsay, Woodson, 1929, 4–6, 41ff.
27. Pierce, 1947, 7ff; Harris, 1936, 5–24; Kinzer and Sagarin, 1950, 35–7.
28. Grady, 1890, 239, 244, 245, 249, 251.
29. Washington, 1901, 217.
30. Washington, 1901, 221.
31. Brimmer, 1966, 291.
32. Pierce, 1947, 14–5.
33. Harmon, Lindsay, Woodson, 1929, 39–40.
34. Pierce, 1947, 31–2.

Chapter 2

1. See Nehru, 1946, 293–94, on situational evidences of racial prejudice.
2. Franklin, 1947, 427.
3. Rose, 1950, 407.
4. Although Skolnick and his associates did not take this approach in their study of race prejudice, they concluded that ". . . a campaign to reduce prejudice should be applied to the motivational bases of prejudice." Skolnick, 1969, 196.
5. Cox, 1948, 347.
6. Blumer, 1958, 3–7.
7. Blumer, 1958, 4, 5.
8. Sheatsley, 1966, 323; Allport, 1958, 204–5 *passim.*
9. Hall, 1971, 151.
10. Katz and Gurin, 1969, 368ff.
11. Gossett, 1963, 3–12; Sherwin-White, 1967, 1, 101; Cox, 1948, 477ff; Fredrickson, 1971.
12. For Merton's prejudice-discrimination syndrome, see his "Discrimination and the American Creed." In *Discrimination and National Welfare,* edited by R. M. MacIver, 99–126.
13. MacNutt, 1909, 288; cf. Snyder, 1939, 315.
14. Puzzo, 1964, 579–86.
15. Puzzo, 1964, 29.
16. Hitler, 1930, 994. For the "doctrine of pan-Nordicism" as advocated by the Third Reich, Snyder, 1939, 192–8.
17. Feldstein, 1972, 79.
18. Gossett, 1963, 69; Benedict, 1947, 22–39; Ashley Montagu, 1942, 30.
19. Gossett, 1963, 123–4.
20. For "Teutonic Origins Theory," Gossett, 1963, chap. 5.
21. de Gobineau, 1915; Chamberlain, 1968; analysis of de Gobineau's work, see Biddiss, 1966, 255–70.

22. de Gobineau, 1915, xiv–xv.

23. de Gobineau, 1915, 93, 209, 212. For a repetition of his argument, Chamberlain, 1968, I, 542.

24. de Gobineau, 1915, 181, 205.

25. de Gobineau, 1915, 206–7.

26. de Gobineau, 1915, 207, 208. Italics added. See also Grant, 1916; Stoddard, 1920; McDougall, 1921; Montagu, 1965, 32–3.

27. Chamberlain, 1968, xiv, 432, 577–8; also Gossett, 1963, 351, on Wilhelm II's use of the book.

28. Hitler, 1930, 398–9.

29. Hitler, 1930, 518.

30. Elkins, 1959, 130–1. For slavery as it existed in comparatively mild form among African tribes, Tuden, 1970, 47–58; Wolff, 1972, 443–62, for slavery controlled mainly by Arabs until the end of the 19th-century.

31. Elkins, 1959, 97–8; similar reference in Herskovits, 1938, I, 29ff.

32. Elkins, 1959, 81.

33. Elkins, 1959, 42, 49, 50, 87.

34. Elkins, 1959, 104.

35. For a discussion characterizing plantation society according to availability and status of labor in the capitalist market, Mandle, 1972, 49–62.

36. See Vallières, 1971.

37. The planter found it convenient to regard the normal personality of the slave as that of a child. For such pre-Civil War views toward the Negro slave, Fishel and Quarles, 1970, 91–95.

38. Elkins, 1959, 230.

39. Miller, 1959, 189; Lane, 1971.

40. Park, 1950, 149.

41. Park and Burgess, 1924, 734.

42. Brown, 1934, 47, italics added. For an analysis of the concept as theory, Lyman, 1968, 16–22.

43. Brown, 1934, 42–3.

44. See Hertzler, 1942, 84–5, 98.

45. Brown, 1934, 46. For a different interpretation of Brown, see Berry, 1958, 154–6.

46. Berry, 1958, 158. Also Liberson, 1961, 902–10.

Chapter 3

1. Elkins, 1959, 141; Genovese, 1965, 19ff.; and chap. 7.

2. Douglass, 1941, 416; Miller, 1958, 229.

3. Myrdal, 1944, I, 223; Raper, 1936, 97.

4. Cf. Bryce-LaPorte, 1971, 281.

5. Beale, 1966, 162; Vance, 1932, 187.

6. Raper, 1936, 150.

7. Davis, Gardner, and Gardner, 1941, 403–5.

8. Beale, 1966, 162.

9. Raper, 1936, ix; Shay, 1938, 70 *passim*.

10. Woofter, 1936, 1; Thompson, 1935, 314.

11. For sources of plantation data, *U.S. Census of Agriculture,* 1959, 2: 1007.

12. Bureau of the Census, 1935, 568–9.

13. *U.S. Census of Agriculture,* 1959, 2: 1029, and 1964, 2, chap. 8: 760.

14. Holley, Winston, and Woofter, 1940, 15.

15. The 1964 *Census of Agriculture* defines types of tenancy as:
    Full owners—operate only the land they own.
    Part owners—operate land they own and also land rented from others.
    Managers—operate land for others for wage, salary and/or commission.
    Tenants—rent from others, or work on shares for others.
        cash tenants—pay cash rent.
        share-cash tenants—pay part of rent in cash and part in share of the crops or livestock.
        crop-share tenants—pay share of the crops but not livestock.
        livestock-share tenants—pay share of livestock; may/may not pay a share of the crops.
        cropper—furnishes only labor and receives share of crops.
    See, Holley, Winston, and Woofter, 1940, 7.

16. Beale, 1966, 175. On elimination of hand labor through mechanization in cotton production, Day, 1967, 427–9.

17. Holley, Winston, and Woofter, 1940, xvi.

18. *U.S. Census of Agriculture,* 1959, 2: 1025.

19. Davis, Gardner, and Gardner, 1941, 413.

20. Holley, Winston, and Woofter, 1940, xx; for an intimate discussion of the problems of Negro tenancy, Woodson, 1930, 45–66.

21. Raper, 1936, 87.

22. Raper, 1936, 148.

23. Holley, Winston, and Woofter, 1940, xix.

24. Davis, Gardner, and Gardner, 1941, 403.

25. Woofter, 1936, 9–10.

26. Raper, 1936, 107–8.

27. Davie, 1949, 60.

28. *U.S. Census of Agriculture,* 1959, 2: 1029.

29. *U.S. Census of Agriculture,* 1959, 2: 1029–30.

30. Raper, 1936, 22.

31. Vance, 1939, 106.

32. Vance, 1939, 110.

33. Beale, 1966, 196.

Chapter 4

1. Holley, Winston, and Woofter, 1940, xxiii.

2. Brooks, 1914.

3. Holley, Winston, and Woofter, 1940, xviii; also, Brandfon, 1967, 135 *passim.*

4. Raper, 1936, 98.

5. Patrick, 1964, 113–4.

6. Raper, 1936, 22–3.

7. Wesley, 1927, 286.

8. Holley, Winston, and Woofter, 1940, 11.

9. Holley, Winston, and Woofter, 1940, xxvii–xxviii, for description of the habitat of the tenant.

10. In 1911 the U.S. Supreme Court declared peonage unconstitutional: *Bailey* v. *Alabama,* 219 U.S. 242; the tradition, however, tended to persist.

11. Myrdal, 1944, I, 247–8.

12. Davis, Gardner, and Gardner, 1941, 395.

13. Davis, Gardner, and Gardner, 1941, 400. Also, Cox, 1945, 576–88.

14. Raper, 1936, 171.

15. Myrdal, 1944, I, 240; Woodson, 1931, 433.

16. Cf. Hughes, 1966, 826–49; Dollard, 1957, chap. 12; McCarthy and Yancey, 1971, 648–72; Boskin, 1970, 165–85.

17. Cf. Vance, 1945, 247.

18. For the invasion of the beetle and the effects of its ravages on the lives of Negroes, Beale, 1966, 164.

19. Beale, 1966, 166.

20. Raper, 1936, 6.

21. Beale, 1966, 202.

22. Kennedy, 1930, 40.

Chapter 5

1. In Heistand, 1964, xiv.

2. Blalock, 1967, 37ff.

3. Franklin, 1947, 189.

4. Spero and Harris, 1931, 11–4. Also, Greene and Woodson, 1930, 11–8; DuBois, 1902, 14–20; Logan, 1954, 117ff.

5. U.S. Congress, Senate, Subcommittee on Employment and Manpower of the Committee on Labor and Public Welfare. *Equal Employment Opportunities.* 88th Cong., 1st sess., Jul.-Aug. 1963, 157.

6. Wesley, 1927, 121.

7. Stampp, 1965, 129.

8. Ross, 1967, 575.

9. *Equal Employment Opportunities,* 397, italics added. See also, *Report* on a national survey in *U.S. News and World Report,* June 24, 1963; Ross, 1967, 578; U.S. Commission on Civil Rights, *Civil Rights '63* (Washington, D.C.), 154–5.

10. *Civil Rights '63,* 197.

11. *Civil Rights '63,* 292.

12. "Symposium," 1970, 355.

13. "Symposium," 1970, 280, 392, and testimony of Walter W. Wheeler, Jr., 211.

14. "Symposium," 99.

15. Eckstein, 1968, 17.

16. *Equal Employment Opportunities,* 177.

17. Beard and Beard, II, 116–7; for the role of the businessmen, especially northern businessmen, Stampp, 1965, 130–1, 206–8.

18. National Alliance of Businessmen, *JOBS,* a pamphlet (Washington, D.C., 1969).

19. *Equal Employment Opportunities,* 117.

20. Maddox, 1967, 148.

21. See *Economic Report of the President* (Jan., 1966), 110.

22. Spaulding, 1961, 161.

23. Ginzberg and Eichner, 1964, 300.

24. Hoffman, 1966, 412.

25. Moynihan, 1964, 79.

26. Pettigrew, 1964, 55.

27. Hentoff, 1964, 240–1.

28. The Committee for Economic Development, *Training and Jobs for the Urban Poor,* 1970, 12. For the history and functions of the MDTA, see U.S. Department of Labor, *Manpower Report of the President* (Jan., 1969), 3ff.

29. "Businessmen Urged to Join Job Drive," *St. Louis Post-Dispatch,* Jan. 27, 1968.

30. U.S. Department of Labor, *The JOBS Program,* a pamphlet (Washington, D.C., 1969).

31. For the interplay of party politics, the self-interestedness of business, and the failure of the JOBS program, see Blaustein and Faux, 1972, 88ff.

32. At least eight federal agencies have some sort of manpower development program: the Departments of Labor, of Health, Education, and Welfare, of Housing and Urban Development, of Agriculture, of Commerce, of the Interior, the Office of Economic Opportunity, and the U.S. Civil Service Commission.

33. National Alliance of Businessmen, *JOBS,* a pamphlet (Washington, D.C., 1969). For an estimate of achievement by JOBS, Blaustein and Faux, 1972, 97.

34. Urban Coalition, *Forming Urban Coalitions,* a pamphlet (Washington, D.C., 1967).

35. Cf. *Industrial Relations,* "A Symposium: Equal Employment Opportunity: Comparative Community Experience," Reports on Chicago, New York, Boston, Memphis, and Los Angeles (May, 1970), 277–355.

36. *Newsweek,* Nov. 20, 1967, 24.

37. Silberman, 1964, 241. See also, on traditional "preferential treatment" of whites, Fein, 1965, 842.

38. U.S. Congress, House of Representatives, Committee on Labor, *Prohibition against Discrimination in Employment: Hearings on H.R. 3986, H.R. 4004, and H.R. 4005,* 78 Cong. 2nd Sess., 155.

39. Roy Reed, "Top Businessmen Join U.S. Effort to Find More Jobs," *New York Times,* Feb. 25, 1968.

40. Peter B. Doeringer and Michael J. Piore, "Equal Employment Opportunity in Boston," *Industrial Relations* (May, 1970), 339, italics added.

41. "Federal versus State-Local Government Responsibility," in Committee for Economic Development, *Training and Jobs for the Urban Poor,* 1970, 13.

Chapter 6

1. Even before 1860 some Negro leaders were conscious of it. See Delany, 1852, 195, 203–5; Bracey, 1970, 235ff.

2. *Viz.* Richard M. Nixon, "Bridges to Human Dignity," an address on the CBS Radio Network, Apr. 25, 1968. The future President delivered two speeches on this subject (Apr. 25 and May 2) but used the term "black capitalism" only in the first. On these speeches, McClaughry, 1969, 39–40.

3. Cf. Comptroller General of the United States, *Limited Success of Federally Financed Minority Businesses* (Nov. 8, 1973), 2, 79 *passim.*

4. Editorial, *St. Louis Post-Dispatch*, Jan. 31, 1970. The point was made on the same page in an article by Andrew F. Bremmer and Henry S. Terrell, "Black Capitalism: Is It a Realistic Goal?"

5. J. B. Blayton quoted in Pierce, 1947, 24.

6. Henry A. Hill, in *Negro in the Field of Business*, Report of the National Conference on Small Business, ed. by H. N. Fitzhugh (U.S. Dept. of Commerce, 1962), 51–2. For biographical discussions of leading Negro businessmen, Seder and Burrell, 1971.

7. Why have Negroes, compared to Japanese and Chinese in the United States, owned so small a number of neighborhood businesses? See Light, 1972, 10–8, 21.

8. Andreason, 1971, 196.

9. Cf. Stafford, 1968, 619–30, for discussion of differences in product preference by Negroes and whites.

10. Adams, 1970, 43; Clark, 1965, 27.

11. The problem of residence is real; there is in it, however, an element of social class behaviour regardless of color. See Andreasen, 1971, 201.

12. Berman, 1970, 7.

13. Samuels, 1969, 60.

14. Rosenbloom and Shanks, 1970, 95.

15. See Samuels, 1969, 2.

16. Both this point of view and the opposite are analyzed in Brown and Lusterman, 1971, 2 *passim*.

17. Pierce, 1947, 157.

18. Ofari, 1970, 122–3.

19. Andreasen, 1971, 199.

20. Harmon, Lindsay, and Woodson, 1929, 3–4; Pierce, 1947, 8ff; U.S. Bureau of the Census, *Minority-Owned Businesses: 1969* (Washington, 1971), 3.

21. *Minority-Owned Businesses: 1969*, 4; for a descriptive census of the "Nation's 100 Top Black Businesses," see *Black Enterprise*, June, 1973, 29ff.

22. *Minority-Owned Businesses: 1969*, Table 9.

23. Harmon, Lindsay, and Woodson, 1929, 32; cf. Seldin and Sumichrast, 1969, 9–12; Brown and Lusterman, 1971, 3–4.

24. *Minority-Owned Businesses: 1969*, Table 1, pt. B.

25. *Minority-Owned Businesses: 1969*, Table 1, pt. B.

26. Brimmer, 1966, 316.

27. Franklin, 1947, 399–400, for a brief statement on the rise of Negro insurance from self-help benefit associations and fraternal orders.

28. Pierce, 1947, 113; Brimmer, 1966, 316.

29. In a lateral reference to the problems of mismanagement and fraud which he encountered as President of the Freedman's Bank in 1874, Douglass, 1941, 444–5.

30. W. R. Pettiford, "Report on the 14th Annual Convention of the National Negro Business League," (Washington, 1913), 219.

31. Kinzer and Sagarin, 1950, 169, italics added.

32. See, for example: "The Birth Pangs of Black Capitalism," *Time*, Oct. 18, 1968, 98ff; "416 Businessmen Take Strides to Build Economic Power in Nation's Black Communities," *Crusader*, Oct. 5, 1968; J. H. Fenton, "More Boston Negroes Enter Business," *New York Times*, Mar. 9, 1969; "Giants of Black Capitalism," *Ebony*, May, 1969, 164ff; Marilyn Bender, "For Blacks, Corporate Door is Ajar, but is It

Closing?" *New York Times,* June 27, 1972. For the rise of a black millionaire through skillful cultivation of the black cosmetics market *pari passu* with the "black-is-beautiful" movement, see *Time,* Dec. 7, 1970, 87–8.

33. Seldin and Sumichrast, 1969, 12.

34. Cf. Brimmer, 1962, 48; Schuster, 1961, 78.

35. Brown and Lusterman, 1971, 4; Blaustein and Faux, 1972, 13–29.

36. Eckstein, 1969, 243; for a more extensive listing, see, Puryear, 1973, 425–35.

37. Puryear and West, 1973, 37.

38. For development and operation of OMBE, see, Comptroller General, *Minority Business,* 3 *passim.*

39. The federal Small Business Administration (SBA) with lending power not to exceed $150,000 became law in 1953, and represents the government's concern for the general American small businessman. The MESBIC took notice of further limitations peculiar to minority entrepreneurs.

40. Rosenbloom and Shank, 1970, 92.

41. Rosenbloom and Shank, 1970, 97. For an example of debt financing see Berman, 1970, 5ff. Also Blaustein and Faux, 1972, 147–78.

42. Rosenbloom and Shank, 1970, 92.

43. Comptroller General, *Minority Business,* 14.

44. Quoted in "What Ever Happened to Black Capitalism?" *Finance,* Sept. 1970, 28. See also Blaustein and Faux, 1972, 254–5.

45. See, Jack Lefler, "Corporate Giants Striving to Make Headway in Solving Ghetto Problems," *St. Louis Post-Dispatch,* Sept. 16, 1968.

46. William F. Vogler, "Black Capitalist Project," *St. Louis Post-Dispatch,* Sept. 11, 1968.

47. Vogler, "Black Capitalist Project." For further details, Skala, 1969, 151–71.

48. Allen, 1969.

49. *New Crusader,* Nov. 2, 1968.

50. See Alex Poinsett, "The Economics of Liberation," *Ebony,* Aug. 1969, 150–4; Henderson and Ledebur, 1970, 337–51.

51. Foley, 1966, 428.

52. Blaustein and Faux, 1972, 261–2.

53. *New Courier,* Feb. 22, 1969.

54. Bell, 1970, 228.

55. *Inner City Business,* 206.

56. That available opportunities in the Negro market are worth some $27 billion in buying power annually, Connor, 1966, iv. Since 1961, at least, eleven interracially managed banks have been established. See Emmer Lancaster, *1964 Annual Report of Banking Institutions Owned and Operated by Negroes,* issued by the National Bankers Association (Washington, D.C.), 4.

57. Bell, 1970, 229; Haddad and Pugh, 1964, 2–3.

58. It has been appropriately argued that "gilding" the ghetto does not solve the social problems generated by the ghetto. See Kain and Persky, 1969, 183–4.

59. Brimmer, 1956, 323, 329.

60. Pierce, 1947, 25ff.; also Cross, 1970, 138–9, 207.

Chapter 7

1. Fein, 1966, 827–8. Cf. Silberman, 1970, 74ff.

2. U.S. Dept. of Labor, *Manpower Report*, 1971, Table A-14.

3. U.S. Dept. of Commerce, *Social and Economic Status*, 1970, Table 44.

4. Senate Subcommittee on Employment and Manpower, *Equal Employment Opportunities* (June 1–16, 1944), 95, italics added.

5. Batchelder, 1965, 535.

6. U.S. Bureau of Labor Statistics, *Occupational*, 1966.

7. Jaffe and Gordon, 1966, 1–4; Campbell and Belcher, 1967, 325–7.

8. U.S. Dept. Commerce, *Social and Economic Status*, 1970, 671.

9. U.S. Dept. of Labor, *Social and Economic Conditions*, 1967, 111.

10. U.S. Dept. of Commerce, *Social and Economic Status*, 1970, Table 42.

11. Cox, 1940, 157–65; Cox, 1941, 39–42.

12. Cox, 1941, 162.

13. Modifications and variations of this point are brought out for the situation of the Negro physician by Reitzes, 1958.

14. Fall, 1963, 16–7.

15. Bond, 1966, 580ff.

Chapter 8

1. Herskovits, 1942, for opposite position; also, Frazier, 1957, chap. 1. For an introduction to African slave trade and west African origin of American Negroes, Davie, 1949, chaps. 1, 2; Elkins, 1959, 89–98.

2. Essien-Udom, 1964, 104.

3. For stock-in-trade approach throughout the 18th and 19th centuries, Roche-Tilhac, I, 6.

4. Stampp, 1965, 120–1; Woodward, 1965.

5. Cf. Patrick, 1964, 117–8, for status differentiation among slave Negroes.

6. Douglass, 1881, 419–20.

7. Parsons, 1966, xxii. The definitive work on this question is Frazier, *Black Bourgeoisie*, 1957; also Hare, 1965.

8. U.S. Dept. of Labor, *The Negroes*, 1966, 1–3.

9. U.S. Bureau of Labor, *Social and Economic Conditions*, 1967, 12. For a segregation index to show the extent to which residential areas in different cities tend to be racially exclusive, Taeuber, 1965, 12–9; Taeuber and Taeuber, 1965, 12–9; Bell and Willis, 1957, 59–75.

10. Data: Bureau of the Census. Also, Current Population Reports, Series P-23, table 8, p. 18.

11. U.S. Bureau of Labor, *The Negroes*, 1966, 75.

12. Taeuber and Taeuber, 1966, 129.

13. U.S. Dept. of Commerce, *Social and Economic Status*, 1970, 17.

14. U.S. Dept. of Health, Educ., and Welfare, *Vital Statistics*, 1970, 2.

15. Projections of nonwhite fertility rates: U.S. Dept. of Commerce, *Projections*, 1967, 34–35.

16. U.S. Dept. of Commerce, *Social and Economic Status*, 1970, 20.

17. U.S. Bureau of Labor Statistics, *The Negroes*, 1966, 72.

18. "Report on the National Advisory Commission on Civil Disorders," *New York Times,* Mar. 1968, 392.

19. U.S. Bureau of the Census, *Projections,* 1967, 14–5, 60–3.

20. U.S. Bureau of Labor Statistics, *The Negroes,* 1966, 221.

21. In 1967 about seven in every ten homicides and aggravated assaults were against Negro victims by Negro assailants. Cf. U.S. Dept. of Commerce, *The Social and Economic Status,* 1970, Table 84.

22. Hodge and Hauser, 1968, 51–3.

23. Table 21.

24. *Report of the National Advisory Commission on Civil Disorders,* New York, 1968, 391.

Chapter 9

1. For the 15th-century origin of the term "ghetto," Cox, 1959, 97 *passim.*

2. U.S. Bureau of Labor Statistics, *The Negroes,* 1966, 3 and 15. Also McEntire, 1960, chap. 5; *Report of National Advisory Commission on Civil Disorders* (New York, 1968), 473.

3. U.S. Bureau of Labor Statistics, *The Negroes,* 1966, 3.

4. U.S. Bureau of Labor Statistics, *Social and Economic Conditions,* 1967, 12. For essentially the same changes in Negro-white population growth for Detroit, Mayer and Hoult, 1971, 3–17.

5. U.S. Bureau of Labor Statistics, *Social and Economic Conditions,* 1967, 54.

6. *Report of the National Advisory Commission on Civil Disorders* (New York, 1968), 470.

7. *Report of the National Advisory Commission on Civil Disorders* (New York, 1968), 471.

8. U.S. Dept. of Labor Statistics, *Social and Economic Conditions,* 1967, 58.

9. Abrams, 1955, 153 *passim.*

10. McEntire, 1960, 248–50.

11. Cf. Commission on Race and Housing, *Where Shall We Live?* (Berkeley, 1958), 28.

12. Long and Johnson, 1947, 68–9.

13. In *Shelley* v. *Kraemer,* 334 U.S. 1 (May 3, 1948), the court denied action against Negroes who did not sign the covenant; then, in *Burrows* v. *Jackson,* 346 U.S. 249 (1953), it declared that damages could not be recovered even from a cosigner for breach of such an agreement.

14. Long and Johnson, 1947, 67.

15. Abrams, 1955, 156.

16. Quoted from a propaganda sheet of the Jefferson City, Mo., Board of Realtors, Sept. 1966. See McEntire, 1960, 248; Pearl and Turner, 1965, 156; Sauer, 1964, 544ff.

17. The act defines the term "slum" as "any area where dwellings predominate which, by reason of dilapidation, overcrowding, faulty arrangement or design, lack of ventilation, light or sanitation facilities, or any combination of these factors, are detrimental to safety, health or morals"; and "slum clearance" refers to the demolition and removal of buildings from any slum area.

18. The Federal National Mortgage Association (FNMA) is largely a secondary financial agency providing a market for the orderly liquidation of the portfolio of FHA-insured and VA-guaranteed mortgages.

19. U.S. Housing and Home Finance Agency, *Capital Funds for Housing in the United States* (Washington, 1960), 32.

20. *Burrows* v. *Jackson* 346 U.S. 249 (1953).

21. Federal Housing Administration Underwriting Manual (1938), secs. 933–7, italics added.

22. Abrams, 1955, 229–30, 236.

23. Federal Housing Administration Underwriting Manual (1952), sec. 242—rev. 1949.

24. U.S. Commission on Civil Rights, *Housing, Washington, D.C.* (1962), 33.

25. McEntire, 1960, 316–7.

26. McEntire, 1960, 315.

27. Weaver, 1948, 74.

28. Abrams, 1955, 306.

29. Abrams, 1955, 310–1; McEntire, 1960, 329; Kirkhorn, 109–10.

30. McEntire, 1960, 329.

31. Abrams, 1955, 248.

32. U.S. Commission on Civil Rights, *Housing* (Washington, D.C., 1962), 32.

33. Sherrill, 1971, 397–402.

34. U.S. Commission on Civil Rights, *Summary, The Federal Civil Rights Enforcement Effort* (Washington, D.C., 1971), 12–3.

Chapter 10

1. Foner, 1952, III, 410–1.

2. Douglass, 1881, 389, italics added.

3. Patrick, 1964, 126–7.

4. *The Washington Post,* June 28, 1968.

5. Douglass, 1952, III, 392. Franklin, 1943, 192–221, examines various aspects.

6. *New York Times,* May 12, 1956.

7. *New York Times,* Mar. 2, 1956, Apr. 1, 1956, Feb. 11, 1963.

8. Grodzins, 1962, 99.

9. Cf. Myrdal, II, 968ff.

10. Mrydal, II, 267–8.

11. Myrdal, II, 267.

12. *Report,* National Advisory Commission on Civil Disorders, 268.

13. The lower class can be divided into categories called "church centered," "respectable," "underworld," and "shady," groups: Drake and Cayton, II, 523–5; cf. Hannerz, I, 34–58.

14. Hunter, 1964, 10.

15. *Report,* National Advisory Commission on Civil Disorders, 273.

16. *Report,* National Advisory Commission on Civil Disorders, 262.

Chapter 11

1. Myrdal, I, 589–90.

2. Ballagh, 1902, 46.

3. Ballagh, 1902, 46.

4. Bickell, 1925, 120.

5. Ballagh, 1902, 46–7.

6. Ballagh, 1902, 48.
7. Ballagh, 1902, 48.
8. Godwyn, 1685.
9. Douglass, 1881, 390.
10. Mather in Osofsky, 1967, 38–9.
11. Tannenbaum, 1947, 77.
12. *Frazier* v. *Spear,* Kentucky, 1811, in Catterall, 1926, I, 287.
13. *Brewer* v. *Harris,* Virginia, 1846, in Catterall, 1926, I, 216.
14. *Armstrong* v. *Hodges,* Kentucky, 1841, in Catterall, 1926, I, 357.
15. Stroud, quoted in Tannenbaum, 1947, 67.
16. Quoted in Turner, 1911, 30n.
17. See Reuter, 1928, 175–6.
18. Ballagh, 1902, 75.
19. Ballagh, 1902, 58.
20. Ballagh, 1902, 59.
21. Tannenbaum, 1947, 64, also 88—9; and Pierson, 1942, 143.
22. de Tocqueville, 1960, I, 359.
23. DuBois, 1935, 707.
24. From Franklin, 1947, 203.
25. Carter, 1968, 347–80.
26. Cf. Winberger, 1967, 68–71.
27. James C. Millstone, "Suit Attacks Laws Against Marriages of Different Races," *St. Louis Post-Dispatch,* April 16, 1967.
28. "A Marriage of Enlightment," *Time,* Sept. 29, 1967, 29.
29. 106 U.S. 583 (1883).
30. *Loving* v. *Virginia,* 395 U.S. Supreme Court, June 12, 1967.
31. "Court Ruling Removing Bars to Interracial Marriages Has Little Impact," *New York Times,* July 28, 1968.

Chapter 12

1. The position taken here deviates from that taken in *The Negro Family,* Office of Policy Planning and Research, U.S. Dept. of Labor (Mar. 1965). For discussion of this study, Rainwater and Yancy, 1967.
2. Burgess and Locke, 1945, 18. Cf. Billingsley, 1968, 191 *passim.*
3. Burgess and Locke, 1945, 29 *passim.*
4. Rainwater, 1966, 200.
5. Cf. B. Brown, 1971, 871–985.
6. Scanzoni, 1971, 324.
7. de Tocqueville, I, 332.
8. Donald, 1952, 12.
9. Donald, 1952, 57.
10. Cf. Stephenson, 1910, 67–8.
11. See 1866 address by Clinton B. Fisk reproduced in Osofsky, 1967, 154–5.
12. Davis, Gardner, and Gardner, 1941, 327–8.
13. Osofsky, 1967, 15ff.

14. Donald, 1952, 58ff.
15. Donald, 1952, 65.
16. Clark, 1967, 143.
17. Donald, 1952, 70.
18. Donald, 1952, 69.
19. Donald, 1952, 66.
20. Cox, 1938, 76–8.
21. U.S. Dept. of Commerce, *Social and Economic Status,* 1970, table 29, p. 38.
22. Cf. Bernard, 1966, 388, for "marriage trajectory."
23. U.S. Dept. of Commerce, *Social and Economic Status,* 1970, 131.
24. U.S. Dept. of Labor, *Negro Family,* 1965, table 13, p. 69.
25. U.S. Dept. of Labor, *Negro Family,* 1965, 21.
26. U.S. Dept. of Commerce, *Social and Economic Status,* 1970, 110.
27. U.S. Dept. of Commerce, *Social and Economic Status,* 1970, table 90, p. 111.
28. U.S. Dept. of Labor, *Negro Family,* 1965, 47.

Chapter 13

1. For official publication, Landers, 1966.
2. For the proposition in Detroit, Grant, 1971, 62–79.
3. Maynard, 1970, 102.
4. Decter, 1964, 25–34; Rogres, 1968, 21ff.
5. Cf. Surkin, 1971.
6. See Fein, 1970, 85.
7. Bundy, 1967, italics added.
8. See Bender, 1969, 184.
9. Mayer, "Story of Ocean Hill," *New York Times Magazine,* Feb. 2, 1969, 19.
10. Bundy, 1967.
11. Galamison, 1968, 313.
12. Weisbord and Stein, 1970, esp. 161–205; Karp and Shapiro, 1969, 129–41.
12a. Galamison, 1968, 313.
13. The lengths to which this idea of the peculiar "needs" of Negro pupils has been carried is illustrated by the movement to use "black English" as a more effective vehicle in teaching them. See Jerry M. Flint, "Black Students at Former White Schools in Detroit Learn Racial Pride," *The New York Times,* May 16, 1971.
14. Maynard, 1970, 109.
15. Gordon, 1971, 9.
16. Van den Berghe, 1971, 430, 433.
17. *St. Louis Post-Dispatch,* July 18, 1969.
18. *St. Louis Post-Dispatch,* July 18, 1969.
19. Coleman, 1966, 22.
20. *United States* v. *Jefferson County Board of Education,* 380 F. 2d. 385 (5th Cir., Mar. 29, 1967).

Chapter 14

1. Donnan, 1930, I, 1. Cf. Osofsky, 1967, 6–23.
2. de Tocqueville, 1960, I, 335.

3. Aptheker, 1963.

4. Aptheker, 1966, 130, 131.

5. Douglass, 1865, 36–9.

6. Miller, 1917, 4.

7. de Tocqueville, II, 256.

8. The question has been repeatedly raised. See Frazier's debate with Herskovits in Frazier, 1957, 3–21.

9. Elkins, 1959, 101–2.

10. Woodward, 1965, 146.

11. Harrington, 1967, 239.

12. Drake and Cayton, 1945, II, 602.

13. R. Brown, 1969, 53.

14. Larry Bryant, "Black English: a Separate Language," *St. Louis Post-Dispatch,* Nov. 7, 1969.

15. Bryant, "Black English. . . ."

16. Hughes, 1966, 873.

17. Hughes, 1966, 873. For further discussion of the work of the Center for Applied Linguistics see "Culture," *Time,* May 9, 1969; also Dillard, 1972.

18. Tom Mboya, "The American Negro Cannot Look to Africa for Escape," *New York Times Magazine,* July 13, 1969, 30ff.

19. For discussion of the distinction between integration and assimilation, W. D. Borrie, *The Cultural Integration of Immigrants* (UNESCO, 1959), 89ff.

20. From Cox, unpublished ms. on the Chicago boycott movement.

21. King, 1958, 45; on E. D. Nixon's role, Reddick, 1959, 124–6 *passim.*

22. King, 1959, 214–23.

23. Meier and Rudwick, 1969, 213–22; also Meier and Rudwick, 1973.

24. Miller, 1917, 16.

25. *New York Times,* Mar. 14, 1965.

26. Anthony Lewis, "Civil Rights: Decade of Progress," *New York Times,* Dec. 20, 1964.

27. *Washington Post,* June 25, 1968.

Chapter 15

1. Two ideas, *colonizationism* and *colonialism,* are apparently involved here. Colonization may refer to the ideology and tactics involved in the emigration movements of American Negroes, which reached a high point between 1815 and 1860. Colonialism may be thought of as a modern postcolonial theory which holds that the racial situation of American Negroes and that of other peoples of color in "independent" nations is in fact colonial.

2. Fanon, 1968, 216.

3. Sellers, 1973, 266.

4. Furnivall, 1941, 76–7.

5. For an extreme case of an ideology harking back to African communal, tribal organization for principles of socialism, see Nyerere, 1968; Legum, 1962, 127–9.

6. Newton, 1970, 69, 71.

7. Cf. J. Kirk Sales, "Wasema Kiswahili, Bwana?" *New York Times Magazine,* Feb. 4, 1968, 28–9.

8. Lloyd Garrison, "Debate on 'Negritude' Splits Festival in Dakar," *New York Times,* Apr. 24, 1966.

9. Reuter, 1918, 388–9; also Woodson, 1931, 607–19.

10. For "back to Africa" movements since 1714: Lewis, 1966, 38–43; Aptheker, 1956, 104–11; Redkey, 1969.

11. Franklin, 1947, 277.

12. Dvorin, 1952.

13. Galamison, 1964, 196.

14. R. S. Brown, "The Case for Two Americas—One Black One White," *New York Times Magazine,* Aug. 11, 1968, 12ff.

15. From an address by W. Arthur Lewis, in "Why Black Separatism Won't Work," *St. Louis Post-Dispatch,* Apr. 15, 1969.

16. B. E. Mays, "Where are the Answers?" *Pittsburgh Courier,* Dec. 14, 1968.

17. "Negro Economic Gains—Impressive but Precarious," *Fortune,* July, 1970, 127.

18. K. Prager, "Right on Toward a New Black Pluralism," *Time,* Feb. 22, 1971, 14.

19. Cox, 1950, 265.

20. Nolan, 1951, 45–71.

21. Stone, 1968, 238.

22. Cronon, 1955, 124ff.

23. Carmichael, 1969, 40–1.

24. See DuBois, *Current History,* 1935, 265–70.

25. Roy Reed, "Julian Bond Emerges as Symbol of Black America's Problems and Promise," *New York Times,* Jan. 4, 1970.

26. Frazier, 1951, 334–5.

27. I am not referring here to derogatory slave names of the "Sambo-Rastus" genre but rather to societal versus antisocietal names. The substitution of Muslim Arabic names for normal American names is part of the process of alienation from the society in which the individual must inescapably live. See Osofsky, 1967, 32–4; Boskin, 1970, 179–80.

28. King, 1967, *passim.*

29. Massimo, 1969, 16–19, 100—2.

30. Jacques-Garvey, 1923, 22.

31. Scott and Brockriede, 1969, 133.

32. Scott and Brockriede, 1969, 41.

33. Wilkins, 1966, 353–4; also Hastie, 1971, 243.

34. Carmichael, 1969, 41.

Chapter 16

1. Cf. Rainwater and Yancy, 1967, 293.

2. Cox, 1950, 270ff.

3. Johnson, 1934, 17–8.

4. See Killian, 1968, 126.

5. Owens, 1964, 56.

6. Cf. Franklin, 1947, 158; Hill and Kilson, 1969.

7. King, 1967, 74.

8. Gossett, 1963, 459.

9. Garvey, 1923, intro.

10. Jacques-Garvey, 1923, I, 52–3.

11. Jacques-Garvey, 1923, I, 261.

12. Jacques-Garvey, 1923, II, 71.

13. Owens, 1964, 52.

14. Jacques-Garvey, 1923, II, 82, italics added.

15. Owens, 1964, 54.

16. Tom Mboya, "The American Negro Cannot Look to Africa for Escape," *New York Times Magazine,* July 13, 1969, 30ff.

17. Fauset, 1944, 48.

18. Elijah Muhammad, "What the Muslims Want," *New Crusader,* Apr. 15, 1967.

19. Elijah Muhammad, "So-Called Negroes Love White Americans, Their Open Enemies," *New Crusader,* May 2, 1964.

20. Elijah Muhammad, "What the Muslims Want," *New Crusader,* Apr. 15, 1967.

21. Elijah Muhammad, "Lazarus Lying at the Rich Man's Gate," *New Crusader,* May 11, 1968.

22. Elijah Muhammad, "Black Man Must Unite with his God and People, *New Crusader,* Sept. 14, 1968.

23. "Muslims in Alabama," *Time,* Feb. 2, 1970, 12–3.

24. Elijah Muhammad, "The Fall of America and the Problem of the So-Called Negroes," *New Crusader,* Jan. 16, 1965. On Hatred see Lincoln, 1961, 67 and *passim.*

25. Lomax, 1963, 52.

26. Elijah Muhammad, "What the Muslims Want," *New Crusader,* Oct. 15, 1964.

27. See Lincoln, 1961, 15.

28. Essiem-Udom, 1962, 4; Breitman, 1967, 12–3.

29. "The Enigma of Malcolm X," *Crisis,* Apr. 1965, 226.

30. Malcolm X, 1965, 52.

31. Malcolm X, 1965, 92.

32. Malcolm X, 1965, 150.

33. Beynon, 1937–38, 903.

34. Cf. M. S. Handler, "Malcolm Claims New Muslim Role," *New York Times,* Oct. 11, 1964; M. S. Handler, "Malcolm's Plans Irk Muslims," *New York Times,* Nov. 8, 1964.

35. Breitman, 1965, 176–7.

36. For the persecution and murder of Malcolm X, see Goldman, 1973, 191–204, 262–78.

37. Malcolm X, 1965, 429.

38. Elijah Muhammad, *New Crusader,* Mar. 28, 1964.

39. Farmer, 1965, 106.

40. Malcolm X, 1965, 429.

Chapter 17

1. Killian, 1968, 172.

2. Martin Kilson, "Militant Rhetoric and the Bourgeoisie," *New York Times Book Review,* Feb. 21, 1971, 2ff., 28–9.

3. For survey among outstanding athletes regarding the flag and national anthem at athletic events, Neil Amdur, "Reforms Sought to Reduce Nationalism at the

Olympics," and Dave Anderson, "The Star-Spangled Habit," *New York Times,* Jan. 21, 1973; Gaston, 1971, 5–20.

4. "Civil Rights," *New York Times,* Dec. 17, 1972.

5. Reported in "Johnson Mediates a Rights Dispute," *New York Times,* Dec. 13, 1972.

6. Forman, 1972, 545.

7. Forman, 1972, 547–8.

8. Fishel and Quarles, 1970, 568.

9. Miller, 1958, 304.

10. Johnson, 1971, 60–82; The Chicago Commission, 1922; Kerner, 1968.

11. Guzman, 1947, 234.

12. See William Walling's description, reprinted in Fishel and Quarles, 1970, 376–8.

13. The Chicago Commission, 1922, 596–8.

14. Waskow, 1967, 208.

15. McCone, 1965, 28; for the Detroit riot of July, 1967, Widick, 1972, 166–85.

16. *Report of the National Advisory Commission on Civil Disorders* (New York, 1968), 91.

17. McCone, 1965, 4–5.

18. McCone, 1965, 7.

19. McCone, 1965, 13.

20. McCone, 1965, 25; King, 1968, 24–5.

21. Lee and Humphrey, 1943, 13. For the riots of the sixties considered as a boost to Negro business, "The Nation's 100 Top Black Businesses," *Black Enterprise,* June, 1973, 33.

21a. King, 1968, 66–7, italics added.

22. For a different classification race riots, Janowitz, 1968, 10ff.

23. Cf. Record and Record, 1960, 37.

24. Record and Record, 1960, 40–1.

25. Quoted in Record and Record, 1960, 64, 65.

26. Lee and Humphrey, 1943, 137–8.

27. United Press International, New York, Jan. 21, 1973.

28. Boesel, 1971, 77–8.

29. Addlestone and Sherer, 1973. For a perspective study of this type of racial discrimination, Grady, 1973, 233–6.

Chapter 18

1. *Time,* Nov. 22, 1968, 41.

2. See Cox, 1945, 576–88; Teachout, 1963, 78–9.

3. Ginzberg and Eichner, 1964, 144–5, italics added.

4. Patrick, 1964, 128.

5. 1961 U.S. Comm. on Civil Rights Report, Book 5, *Justice,* 12.

6. 1961 U.S. Comm. on Civil Rights Report, Book 5, *Justice,* 44.

7. Cleaver, 1968.

8. Horton, 1967, 6.

9. W. B. Miller, 1958, 5–19.

10. National Commission, 1969, 4.

11. Alex, 1969, 144.

12. See almost any newspaper of the Black Panthers. An editorial titled "Stop the Cop Killers," in *Crisis,* Apr. 1972, 114, illustrates this social-class ambivalence toward the police.

13. McEntire and Weckler, 1962, 483.

14. Chevigny, 1969, 283.

15. John Kilner, "In the Ghettos of Chicago, Policemen are Targets," *New York Times,* Aug. 9, 1970.

16. Kilson, 1972, 105.

17. Horton, 1967, 12.

18. Frazier, *Black Bourgeoisie,* 1957; Frazier, 1949, 680.

19. Clark, 1965, 21.

20. In the definitive study of the conference, Rainwater and Yancy, 1967, 274.

21. *National Guardian,* May 28, 1966.

22. See Lystad, 1971, 90–113.

23. See "Races," *Time,* July 11, 1969.

Chapter 19

1. Vivian W. Henderson, *The Economic Status of Negroes,* Southern Regional Council pamphlet (1965), 5.

2. Douglass, 1881, 409–10.

3. Killian, 1968, xv, 25.

4. See *North Carolina State Board of Education, et al.* v. *James E. Swann,* U.S. Supreme Court (Apr. 20, 1971), 39 *Law Week* 4449.

5. U.S. Comm. on Civil Rights, 1970, 2.

6. Simons and Simons, 1969, 616.

7. F. J. Cook, "Mayor Kenneth Gibson says: 'Wherever the Central Cities Are Going, Newark is Going to Get There First.'" *New York Times Magazine,* July 25, 1971, 7ff.

8. "A White Liberal Shift on Integration," *New York Times,* Dec. 17, 1967.

9. For distinction of the social position of Jews and Negroes, Glazer, 1970, 545–6.

10. For a review of the rise and progress of black studies, Draper, 1970, chap. 10.

11. *Time,* Oct. 11, 1971, 23–4.

12. U.S. Dept. of Commerce, *Social and Economic Status,* 1970, table 13, p. 19.

13. Greer, 1973, 500.

14. Greer, 1973, 501.

15. *Detroit News,* May 30, 1973.

16. *New Courier,* Mar. 25, 1972.

17. National Black Political Convention, 1972.

18. A. H. Malcolm, "17 Slayings Spur a Drive on Heroin Traffic in Gary," *New York Times,* Aug. 13, 1972.

19. Greer, 1973, 499.

20. *Detroit News,* Mar. 13, 1972.

Chapter 20

1. *Time,* Oct. 28, 1966, 33.

2. Hughes, 1965, 1145.

3. For example, Nathan Hare, Jr., "Black Power, Its Goals and Methods," *U.S. News and World Report,* May 22, 1967, 64–8.

4. For the thinking of these groups, see for example DRUM Constitution reproduced in Bracey, Meier, and Rudwick, *Black Nationalism in America* (Indianapolis, 1970), 551–5.

5. For the use of dialectics in historical interpretations: Boulding, 1970, 37ff.

6. Cf. Cox, 1959.

7. Marx, 1962, 101–3.

8. For the "sociological literature" on alienation, Schacht, 1970, 153–96.

9. Tawney, 1937, 30–1.

10. Kaufmann, 1970, xlii.

11. Cf. Paul M. Sweezy, "Toward a Program of Studies of the Transition to Socialism," *Monthly Review* 23 (1972), 1–13.

12. Nyerere, 1968, 1–12.

13. Mboya, 1970, 104–5.

14. D. O. Edeani, "Realities of Migration to Africa," *Crisis,* Feb. 1972, 45.

15. Edeani, 1972, 45.

16. Cf. Davidson, 1966, 229.

17. King, 1967, 29–33, *passim,* italics added.

BIBLIOGRAPHY

Abrams, Charles. *Forbidden Neighbors*. New York, 1955.

Adams, E. Sherman. "Coping with Ghetto Employment." *Conference Board Record,* May 1970.

Alex, Nicholas. *Black in Blue: a Study of the Negro Policeman*. New York, 1969.

Allen, Louis L. "Making Capitalism Work in the Ghettos." *Harvard Business Review,* May-June 1969.

Allport, Gordon W. *The Nature of Prejudice*. New York, 1958.

Andreason, Alan. *Inner City Business*. New York, 1971.

Aptheker, Herbert. *Toward Negro Freedom*. New York, 1956.

———*American Negro Slave Revolts*. New York, 1963.

———*Nat Turner's Slave Rebellion*. New York, 1966.

Bacon, Francis. *Novum Organum*.

Ballagh, James C. *A History of Slavery in Virginia*. Baltimore, 1902.

Batchelder, Alan. "Poverty: The Special Case of the Negro." *American Economic Review* 55 (1965).

Beale, Calvin L. "The Negro in American Agriculture." In *The American Negro Reference Book,* ed. by John P. Davis. Englewood Cliffs, 1966.

Beard, Charles A. and Mary R. *The Rise of American Civilization*. 2 vols. New York, 1930.

Bell, Carolyn S. *The Economics of the Ghetto*. New York, 1970.

Bell, Wendell, and Willis, Ernest M. "The Segregation of Negroes in American Cities." *Social and Economic Studies* 6 (1957).

Bender, Robert. *The Politics of Schools*. New York, 1969.

Benedict, Ruth. *Race: Science and Politics*. New York, 1947.

Berman, Jeffrey A. "The Birth of a Black Business." *Harvard Business Review,* Sept.-Oct. 1970.

Bernard, Jessie. *Marriage and Family Among Negroes.* Englewood Cliffs, 1966.

Berry, Brewton. *Race and Ethnic Relations.* Boston, 1958.

Beynon, Erdman D. "The Voodoo Cult Among Negro Migrants in Detroit." *American Journal of Sociology* 43 (1937–38).

Bickell, R. *The West Indies as They Are.* London, 1825.

Biddiss, Michael D. "Gobineau and the Origins of European Racism." *Race* 7 (1966).

Billingsley, Andrew. *Black Families in White America.* Englewood Cliffs, 1968.

Blalock, Hubert M. *Toward a Theory of Minority-Group Relations.* New York, 1967.

Blaustein, Arthur I., and Faux, Geoffrey. *The Star-Spangled Hustle.* New York, 1972.

Blumer, Herbert. "Race Prejudice as a Sense of Group Position." *Pacific Sociological Review* 1 (1958).

————"Industrialization and Race Relations." In *Industrialization and Race Relations,* ed. by G. Hunter. New York, 1965.

Boeke, Julius H. *Economics and Economic Policies of Dual Societies.* New York, 1953.

Boesel, David, *et al.* "Rebellion in Plainfield." In *Cities Under Siege,* ed. by D. Boesel and P. H. Rossi. New York, 1971.

Bond, Horace M. "The Negro Scholar and Professional in America." In *The American Negro Reference Book,* ed. by J. P. Davis. Englewood Cliffs, 1966.

Boskin, Joseph. "Sambo, the National Jester in the Popular Culture." In *The Great Fear,* ed. by G. B. Nash and R. Weiss. New York, 1970.

Boulding, Kenneth E. *A Primer on Social Dynamics.* New York, 1970.

Bracey, Jr., J. H. ed. *Black Nationalism in America.* New York, 1970.

Brandfon, Robert L. *Cotton Kingdom of the New South.* Cambridge, Mass., 1967.

Breitman, George. *The Last Years of Malcolm X.* New York, 1967.

Brimmer, Andrew F. "The Negro in the National Economy." In *The American Negro Reference Book,* ed. by John P. Davis. Englewood Cliffs, 1966.

————"The Black Revolution and the Economic Future of Negroes in the United States." *American Scholar* 38 (1968–69).

Brooks, Robert P. "The Agrarian Revolution in Georgia 1856–1912." *Bulletin of the University of Wisconsin* 639 (1914).

Brown, Barbara, *et al.* "The Equal Rights Amendment." *Yale Law Journal* 80 (1971).

Brown, James K., and Lusterman, S. *Business and the Development of Ghetto Enterprise.* New York, 1971.

Brown, Rap. *Die Nigger Die!* New York, 1969.

Brown, W. O. "Culture Contact and Race Conflict." In *Race and Culture Contacts,* ed. by E. B. Reuter. New York, 1934.

Browne, Robert S. "Black Businesses and the U.S. Economy." *Black Enterprise,* June 1973.

Bryce-LaPorte, R. S. "The Slave Plantation." In *Race, Change and Urban Society,* ed. by P. Orleans and W. Ellis, Jr. Beverly Hills, 1971.

Bundy, McGeorge. Mayor's Advisory Panel on Decentralization of the New York City Schools, "Reconnection for Learning: A Community School System for New York," Nov. 9, 1967.

Bureau of the Census. *Negroes in the United States, 1920–32.* Washington, 1935.

Bibliography

Burgess, E. W., and Locke, H. J. *The Family*. New York, 1945.

Campbell, Joel T., and Belcher, Leon H. "Changes in Nonwhite Employment, 1960–1966." *Phylon* 27 (1967).

Carmichael, Stokely. "Pan-Africanism—Land and Power." *Black Scholar,* Nov. 1969.

Carter, Lewis F. "Racial—Caste Hypogamy: a Social Myth?" *Phylon* 28 (1968).

Catterall, Helen T. *Judicial Cases Concerning American Slavery and the Negro*. 5 vols. Washington, 1926.

Chamberlain, H. S. *Foundations of the Nineteenth Century*. Trans. by J. Lee. 2 vols. New York, 1968.

Chevigny, Paul. *Police Power*. New York, 1969.

Chicago Commission on Race Relations. *The Negro in Chicago*. Chicago, 1922.

Child, Josiah. *A New Discourse on Trade*. 5th ed. Glasgow, 1751.

Clark, Kenneth B. *Dark Ghetto*. New York, 1965.

————"Sex, Status, and Underemployment of the Negro Male." In *Employment, Race, and Poverty,* ed. by A. M. Ross and H. Hill. New York, 1967.

Cleaver, Eldridge. *Soul on Ice*. New York, 1968.

Coleman, James, *et al. Equality of Educational Opportunity*. U.S., H.E.W. Washington, 1966.

Cox, Oliver Cromwell. "Factors Affecting Marital Status of Negroes in the United States." Ph.D. dissertation, University of Chicago, 1938.

————"Marital Status and Employment of Women." *Sociology and Social Research* 25 (1940).

————"Employment, Education, and Marriage of Young Negro Adults." *Journal of Negro Education* 10 (1941).

————"Lynching and the Status Quo." *Journal of Negro Education* 14 (1945).

————*Caste, Class and Race*. New York, 1948.

————"Leadership Among Negroes in the United States." In *Studies in Leadership,* ed. by A. W. Gouldner. New York, 1950.

————*Foundations of Capitalism*. New York, 1959.

————*Capitalism as a System*. New York, 1964.

Cronon, Edmund D. *Black Moses*. Madison, 1955.

Cross, Thodor L. *Black Capitalism: Strategy for Business in the Ghetto*. New York, 1970.

Current Population Reports. Series P-23, no. 42. *The Social and Economic Status of the Black Population in the United States* (1971).

Davidson, Basil. *A History of West Africa*. New York, 1966.

Davie, Maurite. *Negroes in American Society*. New York, 1949.

Davis, Allison; Gardner, Burleigh B.; and Gardner, Mary R. *Deep South*. Chicago, 1941.

Day, Richard H. "The Economics of Technological Change and the Demise of the Sharecropper." *American Economic Review,* June 1967.

Decter, Midge. "The Negro and the New York School." *Commentary,* Sept. 1964.

Delany, Martin R. *The Condition, Elevation, Emigration, and Destiny of the Colored People of the United States*. Philadelphia, 1852.

Dillard, J. L. *Black English*. New York, 1972.

Dollard, John. *Caste and Class in a Southern Town*. New York, 1957.

Donald, Henderson H. *The Negro Freedman*. New York, 1952.

Donnan, Elizabeth. *Documents Illustrative of the History of the Slave Trade to America*. 2 vols. Washington, 1930.

Douglass, Frederick. *The Equality of All Men Before the Law Claimed and Defended*. Boston, 1865.

——*Life and Times of Frederick Douglass*. Hartford, 1881.

——*Life and Times of Frederick Douglass Written by Himself*. New York, 1941.

Drake, St. Clair, and Cayton, Horace R. *Black Metropolis: a Study of Negro Life in a Northern City*. 2 vols. New York, 1962.

Draper, Theodore. *The Rediscovery of Black Nationalism*. New York, 1970.

Du Bois, W. E. D. *The Negro Artisan*. Atlanta, 1902.

——"A Negro Nation Within a Nation." *Current History,* June 1935.

——*Black Reconstruction*. New York, 1935.

Durkheim, Emile. *The Elementary Forms of the Religious Life*. Trans. by J. W. Swain. New York, 1915.

Dvorin, Eugene P. *Racial Separation in South Africa*. New York, 1947.

Eckstein, George. "Black Business—Bleak Business." *Nation,* Sept. 15, 1969.

Eckstein, Otto. *Education, Employment, and Equality*. Washington, 1968.

Edeani, David O. "Realities of Migration to Africa." *Crisis,* Feb. 1972.

Elkins, Stanley M. *Slavery*. Chicago, 1959.

Essien-Udom, E. V. *Black Nationalism*. Chicago, 1962.

——"The Nationalist Movements of Harlem." In *Harlem: a Community in Transition,* ed. by J. H. Clarke. New York, 1964.

Fall, A. G. "The Search for Negro Medical Students." *Integrated Education,* June 1963.

Farmer, James. *Freedom—When?* New York, 1965.

Fanon, Frantz. *The Wretched of the Earth*. New York, 1968.

Fauset, Arthur H. *Black Gods of the Metropolis*. Philadelphia, 1944.

Fein, Leonard J. "Community Schools and Social Theory." In *Community Control of Schools,* ed. by H. M. Levin. Washington, 1970.

Fein, Rashi. "An Economic and Social Profile of the Negro American." *Daedalus* 94 (1965).

——*An Economic and Social Profile of the Negro American*. Washington, 1966.

Feldstein, Stanley, ed. *The Poisoned Tongue*. New York, 1972.

Fishel, L. H., and B. Quarles. *The Black American: a Documentary History*. Glenview, 1970.

Foley, Eugene. "Transcript of the American Academy Conference on the Negro American." *Daedalus* 95 (1966).

Foner, Philip S. *History of the Labor Movement in the United States*. 4 vols. New York, 1947.

——*The Life and Writings of Frederick Douglass*. New York, 1952.

Forman, James. *The Making of Black Revolutionaries*. New York, 1972.

Franklin, John H. *The Free Negro in North Carolina*. Chapel Hill, 1943.

Bibliography

——*From Slavery to Freedom.* New York, 1947.

Frazier, E. Franklin. "Human, All Too Human." Reprinted in *Race Prejudice and Discrimination,* ed. by A. M. Rose. New York, 1951.

——*The Negro in the United States.* New York, 1957.

——*Black Bourgeoisie.* Glencoe, 1957.

Fredrickson, George M. *The Black Image in the White Mind.* New York, 1971.

Furnivall, J. S. *Progress and Welfare in Southeast Asia.* New York, 1941.

——*Colonial Policy and Practice.* New York, 1956.

Galamison, Milton A. "Bedford-Stuyvesant—Land of Superlatives." In *Harlem: a Community in Transition,* ed. by J. H. Clarke. New York, 1964.

——"Educational Values and Community Power." *Freedomways,* Fall 1968.

Garvey, Marcus. *An Appeal to the Soul of White America.* New York, 1923.

Gaston, Paul M. "The Region in Perspective." In *The South and her Children, School Desegregation 1970–1971.* Atlanta, 1971.

Genovese, Eugene D. *The Political Economy of Slavery.* New York, 1965.

Ginzberg, Eli, ed. *The Negro Challenge to the Business Community.* New York, 1964.

Ginzberg, Eli, and Eichner, Alfred S. *The Troublesome Presence: American Democracy and the Negro.* New York, 1964.

Glazer, Nathan. "Race Relation: New York in 1969." In *Agenda for a City,* ed. by L. C. Fitch and A. H. Walsh. Beverly Hills, 1970.

de Gobineau, Arthur. *The Inequality of Human Races.* Trans. by A. Collins. New York, 1915.

Godwyn, Morgan. *Trade Preferr'd Before Religion.* . . . London, 1685.

Goldman, Peter. *The Death and Life of Malcolm X.* New York, 1973.

Goode, Kenneth G. "Query: Can the Afro-American be an Effective Executive?" *California Management Review,* Fall 1970.

Gordon, David C. *Self-Determination and History in the Third World.* New Jersey, 1971.

Gossett, Thomas F. *Race: the History of an Idea in America.* Dallas, 1963.

Grady, Henry W. *The New South.* New York, 1890.

Grady, John. "Administrative Discharges: the Less than Honorable Solution." *Nation,* Feb. 19, 1973.

Grant, Madison. *The Passing of the Great Race.* New York, 1916.

Grant, William R. "Community Control vs. School Integration." *The Public Interest* 24 (1971).

Greene, Lorenzo J., and Woodson, Carter G. *The Negro Wage Earner.* New York, 1930.

Greer, Edward. "The 'Liberation' of Gary, Indiana." In *Cities in Change,* ed. by J. Walton and D. E. Carns. Boston, 1973.

Grodzins, Morton. "The Metropolitan Area as a Racial Problem." In *American Race Relations Today,* ed. by E. Rabb. New York, 1962.

Guzman, Jessie P., ed. *Negro Year Book, 1941–1946.* Tuskegee Inst., 1947.

Hall, Gwendolyn. *Social Control in Slave Plantation Societies.* Baltimore, 1971.

Handlin, Oscar and Mary. "Origins of the Southern Labor System." *William and Mary Quarterly* 7 (1950).

Hannerz, Ulf. *Soulside*. 2 vols. New York, 1969.

Hare, Nathan. *The Black Anglo-Saxons*. New York, 1965.

Harmon, John H.; Lindsay, A. G.; and Woodson, Carter G. *The Negro as Business Man*. Washington, 1929.

Harrington, Michael. "The Economics of Protest." In *Employment, Race and Poverty*, ed. by A. M. Ross and H. Hill. New York, 1967.

Harris, Abram L. *The Negro as Capitalist*. Philadelphia, 1936.

Hastie, William H. "The Black Mystique Pitfall." *Crisis*, Oct. 1971.

Hazlitt, William C. *The Venetian Republic*. London, 1900.

Henderson, Vivian W. *The Economic Status of Negroes*. Southern Regional Council Pamphlet (1965).

Henderson, W. L., and Ledebur, L. C. "Programs for the Economic Development of the American Negro Community." *American Journal of Economics and Sociology*, Oct. 1970.

Hentoff, Nat. *The New Equality*. New York, 1964.

Herskovits, Melville J. *Dahomey*. 2 vols. New York, 1938.

——*The Myth of the Negro Past*. New York, 1942.

——*The Negro in the United States*. New York, 1957.

Hertzler, J. O. "The Sociology of Anti-Semitism." In *Jews in a Gentile World*, ed. by I. Graeber and S. H. Britt. New York, 1942.

Hiestand, Dale L. *Economic Growth and Employment Opportunities for Minorities*. New York, 1964.

Hill, A. C., and Kilson, M. *Apropos of Africa*. London, 1969.

Hitler, Adolf. *Mein Kampf*. Boston, 1930.

Hodge, Patricia, and Hauser, Philip. *The Challenge of America's Metropolitan Population Outlook, 1960 to 1985*. Washington, 1968.

Hoffman, Marvin. "The New Plantation." *Nation*, Oct. 1966.

Holley, William C.; Winston, Ellen; and Woofter, T. J. *The Plantation South 1934–37*. Washington, 1940.

Horton, John. "Time and Cool People." *Trans-Action Magazine* 4 and 5 (April 1967).

Hughes, Everett C. "Anomalies and Projections." *Daedalus* 94 (1965).

Hughes, Langston. "The Negro and American Entertainment." *The American Negro Reference Book*, ed. by John P. Davis. Englewood Cliffs, 1966.

Hunter, David R. *The Slums*. New York, 1964.

Hunter, Guy, ed. *Industrialization and Race Relations*. New York, 1965.

Jackson, Algernon B. "Report of the 14th Annual Convention of the National Negro Business League." Washington, D.C., 1913.

Jacques-Garvey, Amy, ed. *Philosophy and Opinion of Marcus Garvey*. New York, 1923.

Jaffe, A. J., and Gordon, J. B. "A Note on Occupational Mobility for White and Nonwhite Males, 1950–1965." *New York Statistician* 18 (1966).

Janowitz, Morris. *Social Control of Escalated Riots*. Chicago, 1968.

Johnson, Ben, *et al.* "Report on the Special Committee Authorized by Congress to Investigate the East St. Louis Riots." In *The Politics of Riot Commissions 1917–1970*, ed. by A. Platt. New York, 1971.

327

Johnson, James W. *Negro Americans, What Now?* New York, 1934.

Kain, John, and Persky, Joseph. "Alternatives to the Gilded Ghetto." In *Race and Poverty,* ed. by J. Kain. Englewood Cliffs, 1969.

Karp, Walter, and Shapiro. H. R. "Exploding the Myth of Black Anti-Semitism." In *Black Anti-Semitism and Jewish Racism,* ed. by N. Hentoff. New York, 1969.

Karuna-Karan, Arthur, and Smith, Earl R. "A Constructive Look at Mesbics." *Calif090fornia Management Review,* Spring 1972.

Katz, Irwin, and Gurin, Patricia. "Race Relations and the Social Sciences." In *Race and Social Sciences,* ed. by Katz and Gurin. New York, 1969.

Kaufmann, Walter. "Introduction" to Schacht, R. *Alienation.* New York, 1970.

Kennedy, Louise Venable. *The Negro Peasant Turns Civilized.* New York, 1930.

Kerner, Otto. *Report of the National Advisory Commission.* New York, 1968.

Killian, Lewis M. The Impossible Revolution. New York, 1968.

Kilson, Martin. "Dynamics of Nationalism and Political Militancy Among Negro Americans." In *Racial Tensions and National Identity,* ed. by E. Q. Campbell. Nashville, 1972.

King, Jr., Martin Luther. *Stride Toward Freedom.* New York, 1958.

——*Where Do We Go from Here?* New York, 1967.

Kinzer, Robert H., and Sagarin, Edward. *The Negro in American Business.* New York, 1950.

Kirkhorn, Michael. "Oak Park Toes the Color Line." *Nation,* Jan. 26, 1974.

deKlerck, Edward S. *History of the Netherlands East Indies.* 2 vols. Rotterdam, 1938.

Kovarsky, Irving, and Albrecht, W. *Black Employment.* Ames, 1970.

Landers, Jacob. *Improving Ethnic Distribution of New York City Pupils.* New York Board of Educ., 1965.

Lane, Ann J., ed. *The Debate over Slavery.* Urbana, 1971.

Lee, Alfred, and Humphrey, Norman. *Race Riot.* New York, 1943.

Legum, Colin. *Pan-Africanism.* New York, 1962.

Lewis, M. Reginald. "Back to Africa: 1850–1880." *Journal of the Association of Social Science Teachers,* Dec. 1966.

Liberson, Stanley. "A Societal Theory of Race and Ethnic Relations." *American Sociological Review* 26 (1961).

Light, Ivan. *Ethnic Enterprise in America.* Los Angeles, 1972.

Lincoln, C. Eric. *The Black Muslims in America.* Boston, 1961.

Logan, Rayford W. *The Negro in American Life and Thought.* New York, 1954.

Lomax, Louis E. *When the Word is Given.* New York, 1963.

Long, Herman H., and Johnson, Charles S. *People vs. Property.* Nashville, 1947.

Lyman, Stanford M. "Race Relations Cycle of Robert E. Park." *Pacific Sociological Review* 11 (1968).

Lystad, Mary H. "Social Alienation: a Review of Current Literature." *Sociological Quarterly* 13 (1971).

MacNutt, Francis A. *Bartholomew de las Casas.* Cleveland, 1909.

Maddox, James G., *et al. The Advancing South.* New York, 1967.

Malcolm X. *The Autobiography of Malcolm X.* New York, 1965.

Mandles, Jay R. "The Plantation Economy." *Science and Society* 36 (1972).

Marx, Karl. "Alienated Labor." In *Man Alone,* ed. by E. and M. Josephson. New York, 1962.

Massimo, Teodori. *The New Left.* New York, 1969.

Mayer, A. J., and Hoult, T. F. "Race and Residence in Detroit." In *A City in Racial Crisis,* ed. by Leonard Gordon. Detroit, 1971.

Maynard, Robert C. "Black Nationalism and Community Schools." In *Community Control of Schools,* ed. by H. M. Levin. Washington, 1970.

Mboya, Tom. "Rebuttal." In *The Black Revolution,* ed. by J. H. Johnson. Chicago, 1970.

McCarthy, John D., and Yancey, William L. "Uncle Tom and Mr. Charlie." *American Sociological Review* 76 (1971).

McClaughry, John. "Black Ownership and National Politics." In *Black Economic Development,* ed. by W. F. Haddad and G. D. Pugh. Englewood Cliffs, 1969.

McCone, John A., chairman. *Violence in the City.* Governor's Commission on the Los Angeles Riots. 1965.

McDougall, William. *Is America Safe for Democracy?* New York, 1921.

McEntire, Davis. *Race and Residence.* Berkeley, 1960.

McEntire, Davis, and Weckler, Joseph E. "The Role of the Police." In *American Minorities,* ed. by M. L. Barron. New York, 1962.

Meier, A., and Rudwick, Elliott. "The First Freedom Ride." *Phylon* 30 (1969).

————*Core: a Study in the Civil Rights Movement, 1942–1968.* New York, 1973.

Miller, Kelly. *The Disgrace of Democracy.* Washington, 1917.

Miller, Walter B. "Lower Class Culture as a Generating Milieu of Gang Delinquency." *Journal of Social Issues* 14 (1958).

Miller, William. *A New History of the United States.* New York, 1958.

Montagu, M. F. Ashley. *Man's Most Dangerous Myth: the Fallacy of Race.* 4th ed. New York, 1942.

Moynihan, Daniel P. "Political Perspectives." In *Challenge to the Business Community,* ed. by Eli Ginzberg. New York, 1964.

Myrdal, Gunnar, *et al. An American Dilemma.* 2 vols. New York, 1944.

National Black Political Convention, Inc. *The National Black Political Agenda.* Washington, 1972.

National Commission on the Causes and Prevention of Violence. *Violence and Law Enforcement* (Oct. 1969).

Nehru, Jawaharlal. *Discovery of India.* New York, 1946.

Newton, Huey. "Message on the Peace Movement." In *The Black Panthers Speak,* ed. by P. Foner. New York, 1970.

Nolan, William A. *Communism versus the Negro.* Chicago, 1951.

Nyerere, Julius K. *Ujamaa: Essays on Socialism.* Tanzania, 1968.

Ofari, Earl. *The Myth of Black Capitalism.* New York, 1970.

Osofsky, Gilbert, ed. *The Burden of Race.* New York, 1967.

Owens, Chandler. "Black Nationalism: the Early Debate." *Studies on the Left.* Summer 1964.

Park, R. E. *Race and Culture.* New York, 1950.

Bibliography

Park, R. E. and Burgess, E. W. *Introduction to the Science of Sociology*. Chicago, 1924.

Parsons, Talcott. "Why 'Freedom Now,' Not Yesterday?" In *The Negro American,* ed. by T. Parsons and K. B. Clark. Boston, 1966.

Patrick, Rembert W. "The Deep South, Past and Present." In *The Deep South in Transformation,* ed. by Robert B. Highsaw. Tuscaloosa, 1964.

Pearl, Lawrence D., and Turner, Benjamin B. "Fair Housing Laws: Halfway Mark." *Georgetown Law Journal* 54 (1965).

Pettigrew, Thomas. "White Negro Confrontation." In *The Challenge to the Business Community,* ed. by Eli Ginzberg. New York, 1964.

Pierce, Joseph A. *Negro Business and Business Education*. New York, 1947.

Pierson, Donald. *Negroes in Brazil*. Chicago, 1942.

Puryear, Alvin, and West, Charles. *Black Enterprise, Inc*. New York, 1973.

Puzzo, Dante A. "Racism and the Western Tradition." *Journal of the History of Ideas* 25 (1964).

Rainwater, Lee. "Crucible of Identity: the Negro Lower-Class Family." *Daedalus* 95 (1966).

Rainwater, Lee, and Yancey, William L., eds. *The Moynihan Report*. Cambridge, Mass., 1967.

Raleigh, Walter. *The Works of Sir Walter Raleigh*. Oxford, Ohio, 1829.

Raper, Arthur F. *Preface to Peasantry*. Chapel Hill, 1936.

Record, Wilson and Jane. *Little Rock, U.S.A.* San Francisco, 1960.

Redkey, Edwin S. *Black Exodus*. New Haven, 1969.

Reitzes, Dietrich C. *Negro and Medicine*. Cambridge, Mass., 1958.

Reuter, Edward B. *The Mulatto in the United States*. Boston, 1918.

———"Competition and Racial Division of Labor." In *Race Relations and Race Problems,* ed. by E. T. Thompson. Durham, 1939.

de la Roche-Tilhac, Jean Charles. *Tableau du Commerce*. 2 vols. Paris, 1783.

Rogres, David. *110 Livingston Street*. New York, 1968.

Rose, Arnold M. "The Causes of Prejudice." In *Social Problems,* ed. by F. E. Merrill. New York, 1950.

Rosenbloom, Richard S., and Shank, John K. "Let's Write Off MESBICs." *Harvard Business Review,* Sept.–Oct. 1970.

Ross, Arthur M. "Will the Negro Succeed?" In *Employment, Race and Poverty,* ed. by A. M. Ross and H. Hill. New York, 1967.

Rustin, Bayard. "The Failure of Black Separatism." *Harper's,* Jan. 1970.

Samuels, Howard J. "Black Capitalism in the Ghetto." *Employment Service Review,* Oct.–Nov. 1968.

———"Compensatory Capitalism." In *Black Economic Development,* ed. by W. F. Haddad and G. D. Pugh. Englewood Cliffs, 1969.

Sauer, Robert A. "Free Choice in Housing." *New York Law Forum* 10 (1964).

Scanzoni, J. H. *The Black in Modern Society*. Boston, 1971.

Schacht, Richard. *Alienation*. New York, 1970.

Schuster, Louis H. "Business Enterprises of Negroes in Tennessee." *SMBA* (Washington, 1961).

Scott, Robert L., and Brockriede, Wayne. *The Rhetoric of Black Power*. New York, 1969.

Seder, J., and Burrell, B. *Getting It Together: Black Businessmen in America*. New York, 1971.

Seldin, Maury, and Sumichrast, Michael. "Negro Entrepreneurship in the District of Columbia." *SBA Economic Review* 2 (1969).

Sellers, Cleveland. *The River of No Return*. New York, 1973.

Shay, Frank. *Judge Lynch*. New York, 1938.

Sheatsley, Paul. "White Attitudes Toward the Negro." In *The Negro American,* ed. by T. Parsons and K. B. Clark. Boston, 1966.

Sherrill, Robert. "The Black Humor of Housing." *Nation,* Mar. 29, 1971.

Sherwin-White, A. N. *Racial Prejudice in Imperial Rome*. London, 1967.

Silberman, Charles E. *Crisis in Black and White*. New York, 1964.

Simons, H. J. and R. E. *Class and Colour in South Africa*. Baltimoe, 1969.

Skolnick, Jerome H. *The Politics of Protest*. New York, 1969.

Snyder, Louis L. *Race*. New York, 1939.

Spaulding, C. B. *Industrial Sociology*. San Francisco, 1961.

Spero, Sterling, and Harris, Abraham L. *The Black Worker*. New York, 1931.

Stafford, James, *et al.* "Some Consumptive Pattern Differences Between Urban Whites and Negroes." *Social Science Quarterly* 49 (1968).

Stampp, Kenneth M. *The Era of Reconstruction*. New York, 1965.

Stephenson, Gilbert T. *Race Distinction in American Law*. New York, 1910.

Stoddard, Lothrop. *The Rising Tide of Color*. New York, 1920.

Stone, Chuck, *Black Political Power in America*. New York, 1968.

Stroud, George M. *A Sketch of the Laws Relating to Slavery of the Several States of the United States of America*. 2nd ed. Philadelphia, 1856.

Surkin, Marvin. "The Myth of Community Control." In *Race Change and Urban Society,* ed. by P. Orleans and W. Ellis, Jr. Beverly Hills, 1971.

Sweezy, Paul M. "Toward a Program of Studies of the Transition to Socialism." *Monthly Review* 23 (1972).

"Symposium: Equal Employment Opportunity." *Journal of Industrial Relations* 9 (1970).

Taeuber, Karl. "Residential Segregation." *Scientific American,* Aug. 1965.

Taeuber, Karl and Alma. *Negroes in Cities*. Chicago, 1965.

————"The Negro Population of the United States." In *The American Negro Reference Book,* ed. by J. P. Davis. Englewood Cliffs, 1966.

Tannenbaum, Frank. *Slave and Citizen*. New York, 1947.

Tawney, R. H. *Religion and the Rise of Capitalism*. New York, 1937.

Teachout, Peter R. "Louisiana Underlaw." In *Southern Justice,* ed. by L. Friedman. New York, 1963.

Thompson, Edgar T. "Population Expansion and the Plantation System." *American Journal of Sociology* 41 (1935).

de Tocqueville, Alexis. *Democracy in America*. 2 vols. New York, 1960.

Tucker, Josiah. *A Brief Essay on the Advantages which Respectively attend France and Great Britain, with Regard to Trade*. London, 1753.

Bibliography

Tuden, Arthur. "Slavery and Stratification among the Ila of Central Africa." In *Social Stratification in Africa,* ed. by A. Tuden and L. Plotnicov. New York, 1970.

Turnbull, Clive. "Tasmania: the Ultimate Solution." In *Racism: the Australian Experience,* ed. by F. S. Stevens. New York, 1972.

Turner, Edward R. *The Negro in Pennsylvania, 1639–1861.* Washington, 1911.

U.S. Commission on Civil Rights. *Civil Rights '63* (1963).

———*The Federal Civil Rights Enforcement Effort* (1970).

U.S. Department of Commerce. Bureau of the Census. *Projections of the Population of the United States, by Age, Sex, and Color to 1990* (Dec. 1967).

———*The Social and Economic Status of Negroes in the United States* (1970).

U.S. Department of Health, Education, and Welfare. *Vital Statistics Report: Final Natality Statistics, 1968* (1970).

U.S. Department of Labor. *The Negro Family* (1965).

———*Manpower Report to the President* (1971).

———Bureau of Labor Statistics. *The Negroes in the United States* Bulletin no. 1511 (1966).

———*Occupational Outlook Quarterly,* Dec. 1966.

———*Social and Economic Conditions of Negroes in the United States* (1967).

Vallières, Pierre. *White Niggers of America.* New York, 1971.

Vance, Rupert B. *Human Geography of the South.* Chapel Hill, 1932.

——— "Racial Competition for the Land." In *Race Relations and Race Problems,* ed. by Edgar Thompson. Durham, 1939.

———*All These People.* Chapel Hill, 1945.

Van den Berghe, Pierre L. *Race and Racism.* New York, 1967.

———"Pluralism at a Nigerian University." *Race,* April 1971.

Washington, Booker T. *Up from Slavery.* New York, 1901.

Waskow, Arthur I. *From Race Riot to Sit-in.* New York, 1967.

Weaver, Robert C. *The Negro Ghetto.* New York, 1948.

Weisbord, R. G. and Stein, A. *Bittersweet Encounter: the Afro-American and the American Jew.* Westport, 1970.

Wesley, Charles. *Negro Labor in the U.S., 1850–1925.* New York, 1927.

Widick, B. J. *Detroit.* Chicago, 1972.

Wilkins, Roy. "Whither 'Black Power'?" *Crisis,* Aug.–Sept. 1966.

Winberger, Andrew D. "Interracial Marriage in the United States." *Crisis,* Mar. 1967.

Wolff, Richard D. "British Imperialism and the East African Slave Trade." *Science and Society* 36 (1972).

Woodson, Carter G. *The Rural Negro.* Washington, 1930.

———*The Negro in Our History.* Washington, 1931.

Woodward, C. Vann. "Flight from History: the Heritage of the Negro." *Nation,* Sept. 1965.

Woofter, T. J. *Landlord and Tenant on the Cotton Plantation.* Washington, 1936.

INDEX

Oliver C. Cox was for many years a member of the sociology department of Lincoln University in Missouri and later taught at Wayne State University. His many books and articles written during his long and productive academic career won him a nationwide reputation as a social scientist.

Following his retirement, he continued to engage actively in research and writing and continued to contribute to leading academic journals until his death in 1974.

The manuscript was edited by Elaine P. Halperin. The book was designed by Don Ross. The typeface for the text is Times Roman, designed under the supervision of Stanley Morison about 1932; and the display face is Prisma, which is an inline version of Rudolf Koch's Cable.

The text is printed on S. D. Warren's Olde Style paper and the book is bound in Columbia Mills' Bayside Vellum over binders boards. Manufactured in the United States of America.